Salvation Goods a

Salvation Goods and Religious Markets

Theory and Applications

Jörg Stolz (Ed.)

PETER LANG

Bern · Berlin · Bruxelles · Frankfurt am Main · New York · Oxford · Wien

Bibliographic information published by Die Deutsche Bibliothek
Die Deutsche Bibliothek lists this publication in the Deutsche Nationalbibliografie;
detailed bibliographic data is available on the Internet at ‹http://dnb.ddb.de›.

British Library and Library of Congress Cataloguing-in-Publication Data:
A catalogue record for this book is available from The British Library, Great Britain.

Library of Congress Cataloging-in-Publication Data

Salvation goods and religious markets : theory and applications / Jörg Stolz (ed.).
p. cm.
Includes index.
ISBN-13: 978-3-03-911211-1 (alk. paper) 1. Religious pluralism. 2. Religion–
Economic aspects. 3. Religion and sociology. I. Stolz, Jörg.

BL85.S33 2008

306.6–dc22

2007045685

The publication of this book has been made possible through financial aid by
the 450ème Fund, the Section des Sciences des Religions and the Interfacultary
Department of the Study of Religions (all University of Lausanne).

Cover design: Thomas Jaberg, Peter Lang AG

ISBN 978-3-03911-211-1

© Peter Lang AG, International Academic Publishers, Bern 2008
Hochfeldstrasse 32, Postfach 746, CH-3000 Bern 9, Switzerland
info@peterlang.com, www.peterlang.com, www.peterlang.net

Printed in Germany

Table of Contents

Part 2
Applications

Jörg STOLZ

Introduction: A New Look at the Question of Salvation Goods and Religious Markets

In a widely cited article in the *American Journal of Sociology*, Stephen Warner (1993) argues that sociology of religion has moved to a new "paradigm": rational choice. Since former approaches – Warner tells us – could not explain social and religious reality in a satisfactory manner, the work of scholars like Rodney Stark, William S. Bainbridge, Roger Finke, Laurence R. Iannaccone and others has imposed itself. By depicting churches and sects as "religious firms" that produce "religious goods" in a "religious market", these authors claim to be able to explain many phenomena that have remained mysterious anomalies in former theories. In a seemingly elegant way, the new paradigm makes us understand why religion is so important in the USA, why many religious groups prescribe seemingly irrational behavior, why "strict churches" are stronger than laxist ones, etc. While not everyone accepts the validity of these explanations, it is nevertheless safe to say that the new paradigm has made a major impact on the entire field of sociology of religion. It has become fashionable to talk about the "religious market", "selling god", and the like, even for those who do not consider themselves rational choice adherents at all. However, this very success of the market model also tends to provoke skepticism. Are we facing a scientific model or simply a metaphor? Are there clear limits to, and conditions for, the applicability of the model? What exactly are the "goods" that are assumedly "exchanged"? Are predictions of the theory really borne out by the data? Finally, is the current US-American way of discussing religious goods and markets the only existing possibility? An interesting debate has emerged around all of these questions.

1. Goals of the book

The main reason for this book is the insight that the current discussion on salvation goods and religious markets lacks a certain depth regarding two specific domains. First, it is astounding that the works of Max Weber (1978(1920), 1988(1920)) and Pierre Bourdieu (1971a, b, 1987), which are central to the question of "religious goods", has not yet been really received in this respect in the literature. Second, contributions to the discussion about religious markets often take the applicability of the model for granted or else refute it from the start. Rare are the texts by scholars from the sociology and study of religion that ask whether and how the model is applicable to their specific field of expertise. Because of these shortcomings, certain questions have not yet been answered satisfactorily. What is the nature of "salvation goods"; what types of salvation goods can we distinguish; and how do individuals or communities produce and/or use them? What are the strengths and limits of the concept of the "religious market", and what are the alternatives to the market concept? In what social structures are "salvation goods" "produced", "exchanged" or "used"? When drawing on Weberian and Bourdieusian theoretical resources, and when applying these notions to religious phenomena not normally focused on within the rational choice debate, we may expect unusual insights and results. This is why we invited scholars from various backgrounds who were experts on either the social theory or a specific religious area to a conference on "salvation goods and religious markets" in Lausanne.[1] We asked them either to write a theoretical contribution

---

[1]   The international conference organized by the Observatory of Religions in Switzerland (ORS) on "Salvation Goods and Religious Markets: Theoretical Perspectives and Applications in Sociology and Sciences of Religions" took place on 14-15 April, 2005, in Lausanne. All but two of the contributions of this book have been presented at the conference in 2005. Six of the contributions have appeared in Social Compass (2006) 53: 1, three in French (Bruce, Bastian, Mayer) three in English (Stolz, Pace, Burger). We thank Sage for permission to include these articles in this volume.

concerning Weber, Bourdieu or rational choice, or to contribute an "application" of either "salvation goods" or "religious markets" (or both). All authors have taken this task very seriously. Additionally, a great deal of work has been put into criticism and rewriting in order to make the book as focused as possible.[2] In short, the purpose of this book is to add to the existing literature by treating the question of salvation goods and religious markets in a different way than other contributions[3] have done, by widening the theoretical horizon that authors draw on Weberian, Bourdieusian and rational choice theories, and by applying the models in new ways.

2. Plan of the book

The book is divided into two sections: *theory* and *application*. In the *theory* section, authors reconstruct and evaluate the work on salvation goods and religious markets by Max Weber (Merz-Benz, Stolz), Pierre Bourdieu (Schultheis) and rational choice (Bruce, Stolz, Merz-Benz).

Peter-Ulrich Merz-Benz reconstructs the concept of "salvation good" used by Max Weber. He argues that Weberian salvation goods

---

2   I thank all authors for agreeing to discuss and rewrite their contributions and for working so well together with our team and myself at the Observatory of Religions in Switzerland (ORS). In our team, I would like to thank Joëlle Sanchez and Eric Morier-Genoud for help in organizing the conference, Philippe Gilbert for fund-raising, Deirdre Canning for formatting the book and creating the index, and Christophe Monnot for shooting the cover photograph. I also thank Christine Rhone and Rachel Matthey for various translations and for correcting the english in different texts.

3   Apart from the vast literature on the rational choice of religion debate, other books attempt to give different points of view on the question, especially the very valuable ones edited by Lawrence A. Young (1997) and by Ted G. Jelen (2002). Both, however, focus closely on the current debate between pro-rational choicers and contra-rational choicers.

are not "objects" that may be passed from one person to another, but rather goods of a different kind. By comparing them with the Weberian notion of "culture good", (which is strongly influenced by the Neo-Kantian Heinrich Rickert), Merz-Benz shows that salvation goods are "goals of action", "presupposed values", "subjective conditions" and "emotional dispositions", which may underlie and guide actions. A central Weberian idea is that individuals try to "stabilize" salvation goods – they strive for a "permanent state of grace". Merz-Benz then describes in detail two salvation goods-dispositions: "asceticism" (in which the believer turns into God's tool), and "contemplation" (in which the believer turns into a "vessel" of the divine).

Franz Schultheis presents the Bourdieusian view on "salvation goods" and "religious fields". He shows that Bourdieu starts out by reconstructing Weberian ideas of competition between different religious roles (magician, prophet, or priest) and their market and authority relationships with the "laity". Bourdieu calls the ensemble of these both cooperative and antagonistic relationships a "field", and it was here – as Schultheis convincingly shows – that the Bourdieusian theory of social fields took off. Schultheis explains the workings and the differentiation of the Bourdieusian religious field. Such fields include market relations (with varying salvation goods, competition between providers and consumers of different social classes), but also important power relations between the "orthodox" and the "heterodox" religious specialists and different kinds of field-specific "habitus". An interesting part describes Bourdieu's idea of "dissolution" of the religious field in modern societies.

Jörg Stolz argues that it has remained unclear what "religious goods" really are and under what conditions such goods may be exchanged on "religious markets". To find a solution to this problem, he integrates different concepts from rational choice theorists and Max Weber into a new typology of individual and social religious goods. While individual religious goods are produced or consumed by a single person, social religious goods are produced or consumed jointly by a multitude of social actors, leading to interesting strategic problems of coordination, dilemma and conflict. The typology shows that markets are one possibility of producing, exchanging and allocating religious goods among others. It therefore suggests that arguing either for or against religious goods and markets in general does not make sense.

In contrast, *Steve Bruce* states, "an interest in religious 'markets' is largely pointless because the characteristics necessary for rational choice (in the economist sense) are absent when the goods in question are religious." He arrives at this conclusion by criticizing three points of rational choice approaches: the assumption of the defective hegemonic religion, the explanations by "religious human capital", and several general assumptions underlying the approach. As to the third point, Bruce argues that religious groups are not like economic firms, since they cannot (rationally) change products, and that believers are not like consumers, because they are often culturally constrained in their choices and cannot compare religious goods with respect to utility and costs.

In the *application* section, our contributors apply salvation goods and religious markets concepts to a wide range of religious phenomena.

Pierre-Yves Brandt compares first-century Christianity with present-day Christianity (in the West), and he asks why Christian salvation goods seem to have been more attractive in antiquity than they seem to be now. In order to do this, he draws on the work of Gerd Theissen and a host of sociological and psychological studies in the sociology and psychology of religion. His answer is that, due to different historical contexts, the salvation goods sought, the salvation means used, and the specific competition with non-Christian means of salvation differ radically in the two cases. In antiquity, individuals found Christian preaching attractive, since it promised a special kind of *integration*, leading to the salvation goods of status, power, wealth, wisdom, and holiness (all defined in transcendent ways). In modern, Western societies, individuals seem to look for *individuation* through Christian preaching, which may lead to salvation goods such as psychological equilibrium, well-being, cognitive control or good health. Modern-day Christianity seems less attractive, since the competition with other (especially non-religious) institutions promising the same salvation goods is very strong.

Using methods drawn from anthropology and the compared history of religions, *Silvia Mancini* compares two popular cults of southern Italy: the movement following the thaumaturgist Padre Pio and the followers of Giuseppina Gonella who, when possessed, took on the personality of her dead nephew Alberto of Serradarce. Mancini shows convergences and divergences in the types of salvation goods offered by both cults: Padre Pio, who is credited with a wide array of charismata, offers miracles and healings; Giuseppina Gonella (when possessed by Alberto) offers exorcism, healings, and blessings. According to Mancini, in both cases a specific technique of "mythico-ritual dis-historicization" is used in order to create these salvation goods, which can give a certain "psychological unity" to individuals faced with "periods of bereavement, illness, serious trouble and other conditions recurring in these underdeveloped socio-economic strata". Finally, Mancini explains why the cult of Padre Pio has been canonized, while that of Giuseppina (Alberto) remains unrecognized by the Catholic Church.

Enzo Pace argues that at least some religious goods have a side to them that defies the logic of the market. He makes his point by presenting a typology of religious goods, which distinguishes supply-side commodities, demand-side commodities and largely gratuitous commodities. While supply-side commodities may be analyzed with the market model, demand-side commodities and gratuitous commodities are either produced by individuals themselves or given freely. Pace then presents two case studies, one on the Universal Church of the Kingdom of God, the other on the Catholic Neo-Pentecostal movement. The comparison of the two cases shows how religious goods may be transformed from demand-side and gratuitous commodities to supply-side commodities through institutionalization.

Jean-Pierre Bastian applies the religious market model to the recent situation in Latin America. He shows that in Latin America a largely monopolistic religious landscape has been transformed into a strongly diversified situation, while the overall level of religiosity has stayed on a high level. Bastian argues that there already was a certain kind of "internal" religious competition during the times of the Catholic monopoly, but that the logic of religious entrepreneurialism virtually exploded when the monopoly was broken. He shows this with regard to the evolution of "religious products" as well as the use of modern media technologies. The economic perspective, however, does not explain the quest of religious groups to gain social legitimacy and political power. Bastian argues that we therefore have to complement rational choice theories with the Bourdieusian theory of the "religious field".

Terry Rey presents a case study of the Pentecostalist Ronald, a refugee, who "chooses" between a Baptist and a Pentecostal church (L'Armée Céleste) in Miami's "Little Haiti". Offering an ethnographic description of the religious landscape of little Haiti, as well as of the two churches in question, and depicting Ronald's state of mind and career as a refugee, Rey argues that a Weberian/Bourdieusian model, including the notions of "religious capital" and "habitus", can better explain Ronald's "choice" than a rational choice model. According to Rey, Ronald had been socialized to look for "worthiness" and "heat" in religion. This is why he "chose" the Pentecostal church instead of the Baptist one - even if there could have been evident social benefits from joining the Baptist church. Again according to Rey, Ronald was "'embedded' in his language, class, ethnicity, and race, just as he was 'situated' by his religious habitus in ways that in fact greatly limited his religious possibilities".

Véronique Altglas looks at salvation goods and religious markets with respect to Neo-Hinduism in the West by presenting two case studies: Neo-Hindu Siddha Yoga and Sivananda Centers in both France and England. The "salvation goods" offered by these two movements are, according to Altglas, not only transcendent (such as the ultimate awareness of the divine absolute), but very largely immanent. The movements promise success and better performance, individual fulfillment and self-realization in the here and now. Altglas shows that "Indian gurus have adapted their salvation goods to their new audience as they came to the West", tuning their "offer" strategically to the needs of an interested public, in order to maximize their market share. Finally, Altglas analyzes why predominantly the middle-classes seem interested in these kinds of Neo-Hinduism. She also discusses the evidence for the claims of deprivation theory, which argues that offers of spiritual growth especially attract the downwardly mobile middle class.

A second application of "salvation goods and religious markets" to the history of modern yoga is presented by *Maya Burger*. She shows that yoga has always included "salvation goods" in a Weberian sense, but that it has become a "good of the world market" only in the last one hundred years. Burger sketches the general renaissance of yoga in India and the world and then concentrates on the case of the yoga tradition established by Krishnamacharya and Pattabhi Jois. She shows that the market model highlights many interesting facets of the yoga tradition in question, for example, the importance of a "trademark" or tradition as a criterion of authority. However, she argues, the market model cannot totally describe or explain what is happening. For example, the ultimate salvation goods promised by yoga cannot be sold or bought; what is sold is only the "path". As an alternative model, Burger suggests using "pilgrimage" in order to describe and explain the observed phenomena.

Turning to an altogether different field, *Jean-François Mayer* asks if the concept of religious market may be applied to the "cultic milieu" (Campbell). His answer is straightforward. The concept may be applied not only in a metaphorical but also in a very concrete sense. In the cultic milieu, religious or spiritual goods are sold and bought; we find spiritual entrepreneurs and customers as well as the phenomena of standardization, competition, innovation and the like. Mayer makes his point by drawing on a host of concrete examples from the cultic milieu, among them the new "Mystery Park" by Erich von Daeniken, the esoteric fair "Lebenskraft" or the esoteric journal "Recto-Verseau" in Switzerland.

3. A new look at salvation goods and religious markets

Taken together, the contributions may well point to a new direction for our thinking about religious goods and religious markets. A Weberian view (Merz-Benz, Stolz, Burger) will direct our attention to the fact that we should distinguish salvation goals and means, that salvation goals/means are embedded in "world-views" and specific life-practices (habitus) and that salvation goods may be not only produced and consumed, but also used in power relationships. This view is extended and refined by *Bourdieu* (Schultheis, Bastian, Rey, and Altglas) who gives us the notion of "religious field", which includes both the idea of a "religious market" and a system of authority relations based on religious claims. These ideas might throw light on much of what has been called the "limits" of the concept of religious markets in the current rational choice versions (Bruce).

While all the authors in our volume would probably subscribe to the notion that "religious goods" in a Weberian sense exist and that at least some religious goods are *not* exchanged on religious markets, they clearly differ concerning the importance and scope attributed to the market concept. Bruce rejects the concept totally: in this view, religious goods are never exchanged on markets. Most other authors, however, opt for a limited use under special circumstances and involving special kinds of religious goods only. The concept clearly seems more easily applicable to the cultic milieu (Mayer), the success of Padre Pio in southern Italy (Mancini) or the competition between religious groups in Latin America (Bastian) than to a charismatic religious service (Pace) or the ultimate goals of yoga (Burger). Two authors try to react to this situation by distinguishing different types of religious goods, some being exchangeable on markets, others not (Stolz, Pace). The future will show if this is a successful way of thinking about religion.

Let me finish this introduction with a word concerning our title. We chose to speak of "salvation goods" (where we could also have talked of "religious goods") to demonstrate the importance we attribute to the work of Max Weber and Pierre Bourdieu. In addition, we decided to use the plural "religious markets" (instead of the singular "religious market") in order to suggest the usefulness of analyzing the *diversity* of religious goods and markets. It turns out that the authors in this volume do just that.[4]

References

Bourdieu, Pierre (1971a) "Genèse et structure du champ religieux", *Revue française de sociologie* XII 295-334.

–. (1971b) "Une interprétation de la théorie de la religion selon Max Weber", *Archives européens de sociologie* XII 3-21.

–. (1987) "La dissolution du religieux", in ders. (ed.) *Choses dites*, pp. 117-123. Paris: Editions de Minuit.

Jelen, Ted G. (2002) *Sacred Markets, Sacred Canopies. Essays on Religious Markets and Religious Pluralism.* Lanham, Boulder, New York, Oxford: Rowman & Littlefield Publishers.

Warner, R. Stephen (1993) "Work in Progress toward a New Paradigm for the Sociological Study of Religion in the United States", American Journal of Sociology 98 (5): 1044-93.

Weber, Max (1920/1978) *Economy and society. An outline of interpretive sociology.* Berkeley: University of California Press.

–. (1920/1988) "Die Wirtschaftsethik der Weltreligionen: Einleitung", in (ed.) *Gesammelte Aufsätze zur Religionssoziologie I*, pp. 237-275. Tübingen: Mohr UTB.

Young, Lawrence A. (Ed.) (1997) Rational Choice Theory and Religion. Summary and Assessment. New York: Routledge.

---

4   We would like to thank the 450ème Fund of the University of Lausanne as well as the Section des Sciences des Religions and the Départment Interfacultaire d'Histoire et de Sciences des Religions (DIHSR), for helping to finance the publication of this book.

Peter-Ulrich MERZ-BENZ

Salvation Goods and Culture Goods: An Interpretation of Max Weber

1. Introduction

According to the protagonists of rational choice theory, the term of "religious good" – or, as Max Weber called it, the "salvation good" – is a fairly straightforward one. Religious goods are what individuals want from religions or religious groups and the main point is that religious action is just as rational as any other action. However, it all depends on whether the concept of subjective rationality is properly applied (Boudon, 1993: 10). If this is the case, the degree of rationality in an action can be clearly determined. James S. Coleman states that "much of what is ordinarily described as nonrational or irrational is merely so because observers have not discovered the point of view of the actor, from which the action *is* rational" (Coleman, 1990: 18). As to religious action and the striving for salvation goods, Rodney Stark claims to have reached the following point of view: "Reliable evidence suggests that religious behavior is as rational as other forms of human action" (Stark, 1999: 286). In religious action, the "exchanges with god or gods" constitute the object of rational thought (Stark, 1999: 270). Humans seek to "utilize and manipulate the supernatural" (Stark, 1999: 269) and they base relative actions on what appears to them to be good reasons. Stark's article ends with the observation that: "in their dealings with the gods, people bargain, shop around, procrastinate, weigh costs and benefits, skip instalment payments, and even cheat" (Stark, 1999: 286). Religious ideals, principles, myths, visions etc. become an issue exclusively as the

objects of human wishes, desires, ideas or simply as "utilitarian"
action. Whether only humans are involved in these exchanges, or
whether one of the partners is a god, is irrelevant. Religious action
means estimating, calculating, weighting up advantages and disad-
vantages – almost as if the actor were at a market or, in this case, a
religious market, the market of salvation goods. The concept of
religious action as represented by rational choice theory is, however, –
in spite of the differentiations – limited with regard to one decisive
point. For the religious action is also determined, even primarily so by
presupposed religious values. It is these religious values which, as it
were, become apparent and validate this action. They direct and
influence the intention of the actor even before any reference is made
to the specific object. Religious action means exactly that: an action
that is, per se, of a religious character – and not just when god or
religious ideals or myths are the object of rational thought. This must
definitely be considered in the concept of religious action. For then,
and only then, does the rational structure of religious action become
evident.

What does such a concept of religious action look like? In order to
show this, I shall refer to the sociology of religion of Max Weber, or
more exactly to Max Weber's concept of the salvation good. In fact, in
my opinion, the concept of the salvation good was for Weber *the*
fundamental category in the analysis of religious action, in particular
of action within the framework of the religions of salvation. I shall
concentrate on these in the following paper.

2.   Salvation good and culture good

What, though, is the exact meaning of the category of the salvation
good? And what is its relationship to the culture good? The development of the religions of salvation is, according to Weber, an
"evolution towards the systematization and rationalization of the

methods for attaining religious sanctification" (ES[1]: 538). In particular, this includes "[eliminating] the gap between unusual and routine religious experiences" (ES: 538). Religious conviction is not only the conviction of a "religious virtuoso", paired with, as it were, the "psycho-physical states of extraordinary quality" (ES: 538; 538-540). Religious conviction is always something of this life. Religious values and goals of salvation come into effect *in the world*. This can occur in the form of active human performance, or the religious values can become part of a passive, but as such consciously organized, attitude to life. Religious values and goals of salvation lead to systematic regulation of everyday ethics and, thus, of everyday action, and in this way they gain an authentic form of appearance. Things and processes from the most different areas of life become objects of religion-oriented action or become "religiously infected". These objects incorporate religious values. A *salvation good* is the actual manifestation of religious values in human action and through human action – and in this point the concept of the salvation good corresponds in principle to that of the culture good.

What, though, is meant by "culture good"? I refer in my answer both to Max Weber – of course – and to Heinrich Rickert, Weber's philosophical source; this is done with the intention of bringing the respective arguments into a systematic context. "Culture good" is the epitome of all things, processes, objects, that were made by human action with reference to culture values. Culture values, though, are always social values too. And correspondingly "all the goods (...) that the members of a society should be concerned about and may demand to be maintained" fall under the concept of the culture good.[2] We are – so the famous dictum from Max Weber says – "cultural people, with the ability and the will to consciously take a *position* with regard to the world (to judge the world, PUMB) and to give it meaning" (WL: 180). In this way part of empirical reality "is coloured by our interests

---

1   Abbreviations, cf. References, p. 27, Works of Max Weber.
2   Rickert 1902, p. 577; cf. Rickert 1921, pp. 21-22; Merz(-Benz) 1990, § 10, especially pp. 209-210.

which are qualified by those value ideas" (here culture values are meant; PUMB; WL, p. 175). Furthermore, the things and processes, the objects, which belong to this part of reality, are brought into a relational context of meaning. In as much as it is the manifestation of culture values, this part of empirical reality is for us "culture". The analogy between the salvation good and the culture good is obvious: in both cases values are realized in action and thereby a part of empirical reality is "formed" in its own particular way.

3. Rationality in religious action: salvation goods and "conduct of life"

How far does this bring us towards understanding the category of the salvation good? In the concept of action to which the cultural human being is capable, Weber established – as we know – what is meant by rationality of action and by rationalization; in other words, the rational formation of reality by human action. If we apply this model to religious action – as suggested by the analogy between the salvation good and the culture good – we can uncover the special structure of rationality in religious action.

We shall proceed as follows: first of all, the specific aspects of the salvation good will be established and we shall show in which form the realization of values occurs in this case. Then, as already stated, we shall deal with the argument regarding the structure of rationality characterizing religious action.

For Weber it is clear: religious action should be understood according to the model of social and cultural action.[3] I should like to emphasize two characteristics. 1) Religious action is – as stated in the chapter "The sociology of religion" in *Economy and Society* – a "certain kind of community activity", oriented to the rules of the

---

3   ES, pp. 4, 22-26; WL, pp. 175-181; Merz(-Benz) 1990, pp. 337-352.

social world. 2) The "outer course" of social action – and consequently of religious action – "is a highly multifaceted one". Therefore, "understanding" of social action is only possible by considering the "subjective experiences, ideas, and purposes of the individual, in other words, the "motives", or "meaningful reasons".[4] What then does the concept of the salvation good refer to? The concept of the salvation good describes the influence that the goals and paths of salvation have on people's whole "conduct of life" in the case of the religious rejection of the world – as is characteristic for Catholicism and Protestantism, among others. The promise emanating from the religions of salvation – metaphorically speaking – "throws a shadow in people's minds".[5] It influences people's motivation and makes up the whole relationship between all meaningful actions. The crucial point is that this influence does not take place through single goals of salvation or through promises of a certain kind. Rather, it is concerned with the religious "control" of the conditions of action as such; this means, the disposition of consciousness in which the action per se occurs. The salvation good denotes a "subjective condition" (ES: 538) which is the basis of action of all sorts, and which gives it a kind of overall meaning. To follow a religious conduct of life is something different – and more fundamental – than to strive towards individual goals of salvation or single promises. The one is a prerequisite of the other.

With regard to the salvation good, one thing matters above all: the consciousness, or the feeling, of taking on a "permanent religious disposition" and thereby securing one's relationship with the divinity. It is this condition, which has to be continuously "created" in everyday religious action. "The assurance of grace", the highest salvation good, whether "characterized by a mystical or by a more active ethical coloration" – means "the conscious possession of a lasting, integrated foundation for the conduct of life" (ES: 538). The crucial term is that of "preservation". One must achieve continuity and uniformity in the

---

4   WuG, p. 245, 5 (My translation, PUMB); cf. ES, pp. 399-400, 11.
5   WL, p. 200; cf. ES, pp. 544-545.

possession of the religious good (ES: 538-541). And for this, it is necessary to develop a "methodology of sanctification", or a methodical set of rules for the acquisition of salvation goods.

The character of the preservation of salvation changes, however, according to the character of the specific salvation good. There are – as mentioned in a passage inserted by Weber in the second edition of "The Protestant Ethic" in 1920 – "deep-lying differences which apply to the classification of *all* practical religious activity" (PE: 113, my *emphasis*, *PUMB*); Weber also refers to this difference in the chapter on "The sociology of religion" in *Economy and Society*, but there he does not, in principle, assign meaning to it. Accordingly "the religious believer can make himself sure of his state of grace *either* in that he feels himself to be a vessel of the Holy Spirit *or* the tool of the divine will. In the former case, his religious life tends to mysticism and emotionalism, in the latter to ascetic action. Luther stood closer to the former type, Calvinism belonged definitely to the latter" (PE: 113).

4. Salvation through contemplation

It should be emphasized that – in accordance with earlier arguments – the salvation good consists in both cases of a subjective condition, an emotional disposition. Through the extrusion of everyday interests, which means through "contemplation", a mystical emotionalism is cultivated; on this basis God should be able to "speak within one's soul" immediately and undisturbed – that is the goal (ES: 544). Also linked with contemplation, a condition that aims to enjoy the "possession of the divine", is the gaining of knowledge. However, this is knowledge in which unexceptional contents are to the fore. Likewise, this knowledge has little to do with "new knowledge of any facts or doctrines". Knowledge, mystical knowledge means "perception of an overall meaning in the world". The relation, orientation and new orientation to the world are defined by the possession of this meaning.

In this respect, mystical knowledge denotes a "practical form of knowledge" (ES: 545). With reference to mysticism, Weber himself speaks of the salvation good as a "unique quality of feeling, or more concretely, the felt emotional unity of knowledge and volitional mood" (ES: 546). To what degree does this mystical emotionalism mean – as postulated earlier – the gaining of an overall meaning of action? In what way is contemplation connected with a systematically rationalized conduct of life? Even Weber himself explicitly puts contemplation on a level with a "flight from the world" and "inactivity". The answer is that the rationalized conduct of life is purely the *means* of reaching the goal of contemplation (ES: 545). The essential meaning of the world can be perceived, but cannot be comprehended in a rational form (ES: 548). For this reason, rationalization is mainly of a "negative kind". Principally it consists of nothing more than the "avoidance of interruptions caused by nature and the social milieu" (ES: 545-546*)*. But in no way does mystical contemplation per se resemble the "avoidance of every contact with the social milieu". Rather, a mystic, living in the inner-world, will strive to maintain his state of grace "against every pressure of the mundane order". This happens by "minimizing" his activity, i.e. "by 'resigning' himself to accept the institutions of the world as they are, by living with them, but nevertheless paying as little attention to them as possible. He submits humbly to the circumstances under which God has determined he should live. But his attitude towards the world is "characterized by a distinctive brokenness". The success of his inner-worldly action is irrelevant for salvation. For him only one thing counts: that his soul does *not* succumb to the temptations of the world (ES: 548). The systematic conduct of life of the mystic living in the inner-world serves just one goal: to realize the specific salvation good, the felt emotional unity of knowledge and volitional mood, through the reality of action and in coexistence with others. But that is not all. Something crucial must be added: the specific salvation good should be blended with the institutions of the world in such a way that they as little as possible affect it. And in this respect, in the systematic pursuance of this goal, the conduct of life of the mystic does, in fact, appear to be rational. The attitude of the inner-worldly mystic is expressed in an exemplary way in Luther's conception of vocation. For Luther, vocational work means nothing more than to obey unconditionally the objective historical order, in particular, the corporate vocational order. The believer lives in the world and overcomes it in himself by having no trust in it, but he nevertheless – as Ernst Troeltsch states – "humbly subjects himself to the course".[6]

5. Salvation through asceticism

The second possibility to assure a state of grace occurs in the form of "active ethical behavior performed in the awareness that God directs this behavior, i.e. that the actor is an instrument of God" (ES: 541). Weber calls this action and the related methodology of sanctification "ascetic". Asceticism means on the one hand "subjecting the natural drives to a systematic pattern of life" (ES: 542). On the other hand, asceticism is also connected with the religious and ethical criticism of the relationship with social community life. The world, in particular the social world, is a twofold temptation: firstly, as the "site of sensual pleasures which are ethically irrational" and – even more important – "because it fosters in the religiously average person complacent self-sufficiency and self-righteousness in the fulfilment of common obligations" (ES: 542). To be an instrument of God, in contrast, can only mean "concentration on the active achievements leading to salvation". For this, two ways are open: "world-rejecting asceticism" and "inner-worldly asceticism". "World-rejecting asceticism" is the active retirement from the world, or – in contrast to contemplative "flight from the world" – the conscious withdrawal from all areas of life. "Inner-worldly asceticism" involves the active confirmation of

---

6   Troeltsch 1906, pp. 26-27; cf. Max Weber's critique of Luther's term of vocational work, PE, pp. 85-88.

religious temper within the world (or more precisely: within the institutions of the world; ES: 542). Inner-worldly asceticism is known to be the "most important mean" to bring order, or a clear structure, into the Protestant conduct of life based on the Calvinistic ethic (PE: 119). It should be emphasized that a rationalistic conduct of life is suitable for both forms of asceticism; for example, in the case of world-rejecting asceticism, "the man who, par excellence, lived a rational life in the religious sense was, and remained, alone the monk" (PE: 120-121). Nevertheless, inner-worldly asceticism is more important, as in this the consistent realization of religious and ethical criticism of social community life is achieved. In inner-worldly asceticism, the world becomes a "duty" imposed on the religious person. This can mean that the world should be remodelled, or even revolutionized according to ascetic ideals. But more than anything else, it is combined with the task of maintaining the ascetic way of thinking in one's vocation. It concerns being within the institutions of the world and, at the same time, fighting these institutions as a natural vessel of sin (ES: 543). With vocation, Weber means that "work in the calling was a, or rather, *the* task set by God" – completely in contrast to Luther's interpretation of the term. Vocation effectively means calling; "everybody is called to some calling" to obey God.[7] But this vocation should be fulfilled rationally: first and foremost – according to the Protestant ethic – in terms of an economic conduct of life which is pleasing in the sight of God and successful according to all the rules of economics and management, but not oriented towards the enjoyment of riches.[8]

Weber follows this characterization with an argument which is decisive for understanding religious action as a rational act: "The person who lives as a worldly ascetic is a rationalist, not only in the sense that he rationally systematizes his own conduct, but also in his rejection of everything that is ethically irrational, aesthetic, or dependent upon his own emotional reactions to the world and its

---

7   PE, p. 85; PE, p. 216, n. 24.
8   For further variations regarding fulfilling vocational duty, cf. ES, pp. 543-544.

institutions" (ES, p. 544). Let us take a look at the first part of this argument: this refers to the inherently rational order of religious action – an arranged order, for example, according to the viewpoint of means/ends rationality. Furthermore, this order is simultaneously the order of the personal conduct of life. It represents that which, through all the individual actions, determines the identity of the actor. But it must be emphasized, that the identity of the actor is more than this. It also consists of (religious) values and value ideals, which, through these actions, are realized. This leads us to the second part of the argument. The ascetic who lives in the inner-world is also a rationalist with regard to bringing values and value ideals into effect in the world. The "rejection of everything which is ethically irrational, aesthetic, or dependent upon his own emotional reactions to the world and its institutions", or briefly, the effect of – or, better still, the ability to affect – the values and value ideals in the world is itself the object of rational thought.

6. Conclusion

In this article, I have shown that contemporary rational choice versions of "religious goods" are flawed in that they tend to forget not only the underlying value structure of religious action, but that Max Weber has presented us with a much more convincing model: The rationality of a religious conduct of life develops, according to him: 1) through the validity of religious values for the reality of action; 2) through the systematization of action based on these values; and finally 3) through thereby achieving religious control of the conduct of life overall. These elements comprise the category of the salvation good – by analogy with the culture good: values are realized by action in both cases. As we now know, for the salvation good, there is something more of crucial importance: the creation of a subjective condition, through which the overall meaning of his conduct is conveyed to the actor – the meaning of leading a religious life per se. To establish such a permanent religious disposition is the object of rationality.

Thus, little by little the complex rational structure of religious action crystallizes more and more clearly. At the same time, we come – once more – to see the value of "standing on the shoulders" of classic sociologists.*

References

Works of Max Weber

ES   Economy and Society. An Outline of interpretative Sociology. Edited by Guenther Roth and Claus Wittich. New York: Bedminster Press 1968.

PE   The Protestant Ethic and the Spirit of Capitalism. Translated by Talcott Parsons. Introduction by Randall Collins. Los Angeles, Ca.: Roxbury 1996.

WL   Gesammelte Aufsätze zur Wissenschaftslehre. Tübingen: J. C. B. Mohr (Paul Siebeck) 1973.

WuG   Wirtschaft und Gesellschaft. Grundriss der verstehenden Soziologie. Tübingen: J. C. B. Mohr (Paul Siebeck) 1972.

Boudon, Raymond (1990) "Toward a synthetic Theory of Rationality". *International Studies in the Philosophy of Science* 7, 1993, pp. 5-19.

---

* Translated by Rachel Matthey

Coleman, James S. (1990) *Foundations of Social Theory*. Cambridge: The Belknap Press of Harvard University Press.

Merz[-Benz], Peter-Ulrich (1990) *Max Weber und Heinrich Rickert. Die erkenntniskritischen Grundlagen der verstehenden Soziologie.* Würzburg: Königshausen & Neumann.

Rickert, Heinrich (1902) *Die Grenzen der naturwissenschaftlichen Begriffsbildung. Eine logische Einleitung in die historischen Wissenschaften.* Tübingen und Leipzig: J.C.B. Mohr (Paul Siebeck).

–. (1921) *Kulturwissenschaft und Naturwissenschaft. Vierte und fünfte, verbesserte Auflage.* Tübingen: J.C.B. Mohr (Paul Siebeck).

Stark, Rodney (1999) "Micro Foundations of Religion: A Revised Theory". *Sociological Theory* 17: 264-289.

Troeltsch, Ernst (1966) "Die Bedeutung des Protestantismus für die Entstehung der modernen Welt". Vortrag, gehalten auf der IX. Versammlung deutscher Historiker zu Stuttgart am 21. April 1906. *Historische Zeitschrift*, Der ganzen Reihe 97. Band, Dritte Folge - 1. Band. München und Berlin: R. Oldenburg, pp. 1-66.

Franz SCHULTHEIS

Salvation Goods and Domination: Pierre Bourdieu's Sociology of the Religious Field

1. Introduction

After the "breakthrough" of his work "Distinction: A Social Critique of the Judgment of Taste", there was a non-stop stream of contributions to the reception and interpretation of Pierre Bourdieu's theory of the social world. In countless variations, his central theoretical concepts, like habitus, capital, fields or illusio, were considered, the epistemological premises underlying his theory analysed, and comparative and theoretical perspectives presented; his work was situated either in the field of the contemporary social sciences or in the context of the great theoretical traditions. Bourdieu – according to the international citation index, the most quoted social scientist of the post-war era – is generally treated today as a classic and his praxeological sociology is not only respected and used by sociologists, but also by anthropologists, ethnologists, historians, pedagogues, art historians and, last but not least, scholars in the study of religion. His work is regarded as an important fund of knowledge on theoretical perspectives and methodology, and even as a theoretical coordinate system for the analysis of social reality.

Bourdieu's work covers a very wide number of topics – his theoretical positions were developed in constant interaction with empirical research beginning in the mid 1950s when, as a newly qualified philosopher and graduate of the Paris elite university, *Ecole Normale Supérieure*, he was sent to Algeria on military service and there taught himself the craft of field research in the social sciences. This led him from studies on the influence of Berber cosmology on architecture, through the reproduction crisis in the French farming community, to educational sociology, and the analyses of our dealings with photography, fashion, museums and consumer trends. Accompanying this were his pioneering analyses in the sociology of literature and art, as well as socioanthropological research on questions of symbolic order. Religion was also the object of Bourdieusian research and theory; in fact, this work led to a new paradigm, but astonishingly this remained unnoticed and unheeded at first. As will be shown, it was through the study of Max Weber's sociology of religion that Bourdieu was led to develop his theory of fields; and from the resulting structure and dynamic of the religious field, the basic pattern for the analysis of other social fields emerged.[1]

This contribution presents an approach to Pierre Bourdieu's theoretical construction and sociological analysis of religious fields and covers several stages and aspects. Firstly, the concept of the field is explained in the context of Bourdieu's theory on social space and his sociotopographical approach. Then follows a brief description of his sociogenetical reconstruction of the emergence of the religious field using the logic of his "genetical structuralism". This leads, in the third part, to a look at the structure and dynamic of the religious field which closely follows Weber's sociology of dominance. Finally, the Bourdieusian concepts of "field" and "habitus" are presented in their complementarity.

---

1   It should be remembered that Bourdieu in his concept of "capital", as used in "religious", "cultural" or "symbolic capital", clearly adopts Weber's concept of "salvation goods" (Biens de salut) borrowing at the same time Weber's pointed hypermaterialistic view of religion.

2. The social space and its fields: Bourdieu's sociotopographical approach

When seeking systematical access to Pierre Bourdieu's theory of social fields in general, and his analysis of the religious field in particular, one must first examine his thinking on social space.

The concept of "space" plays a central, systematic role in Pierre Bourdieu's theory of the social world. Visualized as an ideal type, and made plausible by Bourdieu using the Calder Room Compositions,[2] the "global social space" presents itself in an abstract way as a "field, i.e. at the same time as a field of force, the necessity of which is imposed on the agents who move in it, but also as a battlefield in which the agents confront each other with varying means and goals, according to their positions within the structure of the field of force, thereby contributing to maintaining or transforming that structure."[3] For Bourdieu, social space also means in concrete terms an ensemble of positions which coexist at varying distances from each other, and these distances are describable and measurable by means of a multi-dimensional coordinate system. In this way, for instance, two cities on the globe can be clearly situated by means of longitude and latitude, the distance between them can be exactly determined and there is no quibbling about the fact that one can only be in one place at one time.

The concept of "space" is in Bourdieu's view of the social world primarily of heuristic importance, in that it forces one to think in relations and structures; in particular, it offers the possibility of avoiding

---

2   "I remember that many years ago I sometimes said to my students: Take a sheet of paper and draw me a social world". Almost all drew a pyramid. Since then, I see, to use another picture, the social world like a perpetuum mobile from Calder, where there are small universes, which turn and change in a multidimensional room with and against each other." In Bourdieu, P. (2002) "Lire les sciences sociales, 1989-1992", quoted from: *Sciences Humaines*, N° special: L'oeuvre de Pierre Bourdieu, p 94.

3   Bourdieu, P. "Espace social et champ du pouvoir", in *Raisons pratiques*. Paris, 1994, p 55.

spontaneous substantialistic or essentialistic theory.[4] First and foremost, the task of sociology for Bourdieu is to study the forces and
conflicts involved in the relationship between individual and collective agents in a space that is created and developed by these forces;
social reality manifests itself for him mainly in the form of mutually
dependent and exclusive elements, which produce this space through
their interactions.

In this relational view, the elements that populate the space of social reality, i.e. individuals or groups, exist primarily by means of their
difference, that is, they take relative positions in a space of relations,
which is not immediately visible as such, but nevertheless constantly
proves the effectiveness of its reality through the manifestation of its
elements. This idea of difference and distance is decisive for Bourdieu's concept of social space.[5] The latter is comprised of mutually
exclusive positions, and their proximity also corresponds to their va-
lency in the hierarchy of positions which are either next, under or over
each other. In this ensemble of interdependent positions, an individual
can take only one place at any one time and Bourdieu's sociology
aims to analyse the correlation between the position of an individual
and his or her disposition to judge and act in specific ways.

With regard to Bourdieu's view of individual agents, this relational
thinking leads to them always being seen as occupying a social position – an epistemological assumption incompatible with the premises
of methodological individualism. In Bourdieu's theory of habitus this
point is decisive; each individual finds himself in a specific place in

---

4   In the common-sense perspective of an individual, "society" is as a rule a system
     of circles, which surround the individual at varying distances, from the family
     through the local community to the state or world society. Here "society" is too
     often understood as anthropomorphous and "holistic", or as a kind of "super
     subject", which thinks, wishes, does etc. Bourdieu's field perspective tries to
     break with this objectivistic misjudgment of "society". Society is perceived
     purely as relational or structural: it is the ensemble of relationships, which are
     maintained by the individuals who belong to society, it "is" this structure of
     interactions, no more and no less.

5   This view reminds us, not without reason, of the structuralistic theory of
     language.

social space at a certain time in his biographical flight path and perceives the social world from that standpoint's perspective, whereby previous standpoints are revealed more or less distinctly in relativizing or reflective attitudes (views and expectations).

For Bourdieu's view of social classes, this relational view of the social world also leads, by way of the space paradigm, to desubstantialization (building on, but also criticizing Marx).[6] The sociological perspective should not dissect the social world into classes – a too rigid, objectivistic and unhistorical way of thinking – but rather conceptualize social spaces, in which individual and collective elements emerge in various configurations. Then, according to the sociohistorical context, classes can in fact be portrayed and analysed. Bourdieu's theory of social fields is empirically based and historically specific – whether we are referring to the literary field at the time of Flaubert, the debate about impressionism surrounding Manet or the attempt to objectify one's own biographical flight path sociologically. For any concrete empirical analysis, the aim is to identify the forces that work and compete in that field at a certain point in time and to investigate the dynamic of these competitive struggles. For this, Bourdieu often uses the game metaphor, in order to make the idea of the field more tangible. To put it simply, each field can be seen as a "game", in which "players" fight according to specific rules for a specific "stake", which appears to them "worth" the time and energy that have to be invested in the competition. For each of these "games", from capitalist market competition to the contest for academic reputation, from competitive sport to the struggle to find religious truths, the belief in the meaning of the game is a prerequisite and each game has its own logic, as well as being relatively independent of the other games which are "played" in parallel by other agents according to other rules. In each specific case, it is then possible to establish whether certain demographic factors (gender, age, ethnic affiliation) or sociological characteristics (occupational position, education,

---

6   Schultheis F. and Vester, M. "Soziologie als Beruf. Hommage an Pierre Bourdieu", in *Mittelweg*, 36, No. 5, 10/2002: 41-58.

income) are of importance in the dealing of the "cards" or not. But this question has to be addressed when analysing a specific field. It is important from Bourdieu's viewpoint to discover, or theoretically construct, the constitutive logic of inclusion and exclusion in such a field.

3. On the sociogenesis of the religious field: processes of inclusion and exclusion regarding access to religious goods and processes of domination

Following Bourdieu's way of looking at the structure and dynamic of the religious field, which is influenced by Weber but at the same time goes further, it is advisable to start from a very simple idea. Religious practice (rituals, symbols, doctrines, etc.) has no limitations, as long as it is not subject to monopolization but is in general freely available to everyone for everyday use; thus one is happy or unhappy according to one's own taste and needs for religious things. If necessary, anyone can recite a magic formula or say a prayer, kneel down, honour a totem or anything furnished with extraordinary powers (charmisma), as well as develop symbols or rituals, etc. However, as soon as a group of individuals claims, and enforces, the exclusive rights to legitimate transactions with these goods and meets with active approval or passive toleration from those excluded (in fact "dispossessed"), then an interesting elementary form of associative relationships *(Vergesell-schaftungen)* emerges. The result is the dialectic between inclusion and exclusion, whereby one group claims, or usurps, the monopoly of the legitimate use of religious objects, constituting a corps of "chosen" people, of religious experts or virtuosi. In this same process, but on the opposite side, those excluded from this monopoly are (dis)qualified, institutionalized and negatively defined as the social category of the "laity", the religiously untalented or the profane.

The religious field emerges through these processes of monopolization in two ways:[7]

– firstly, through social differentiation on the level of agents, their roles and functions. The "holy"/"profane" dichotomy is reflected here by the opposition between "priest" and "layperson", representing an elementary form of the religious field's structure.

– and also through the differentiation or specialization of social facts. According to the social anthropology of Marcel Mauss, it can be assumed that social facts are "total" in their archaic or elementary form, i.e. that material and symbolic, economic and religious meanings and functions appear to be merged. This linkage or interpenetration of the spheres or "fields", so typical of simple societies, was broken only in the course of societal differentiation and complexification (according to Durkheim, particularly through the increasing division of labour); it then finds expression in the juxtapositions of different societal "games", each with different societal rules and stakes, but always showing the same basic patterns. From the viewpoint of the sociology of dominance, developed by Bourdieu and based on Weber, their common denominator is the monopolization or control of goods by social groups.

Characteristic of the religious field is the dichotomy between the positively qualified persons, the "experts" with extraordinary qualities (gifts and talents), and the mass of unqualified; this is, therefore, the basic structural pattern of all social fields, even if it is not always visi-

---

7   In one of our discussions about the reconstruction of his theory of the social world, Bourdieu related that he became aware of his model of the religious field, as it is represented here in the annex, during a lecture at the University of Lille, as he was introducing his students to Weber's sociology using self-translated passages from Wirtschaft und Gesellschaft and thereby came to speak of the aspect of sociology of religion. As he, for didactic reasons, drew on the blackboard the structure of relationships between the people on the one hand and the various religious expert groups on the other hand, he suddenly became aware that these relationships could not simply be understood as interaction structures which realised themselves in the interaction, but rather completely in contrast represented an "objective" structure which provided, so to speak, the "elementary form" of all fields.

ble with the same clarity. This is due, among other things, to the fact that the religious field displays an extreme form of power concentration and its organization is hierarchical and authoritative, so that long before the emergence of modern states it represented a kind of prototype of the dominant order. While this "mother" of all dominant orders was able to penalise disobedient members by excommunication (and in the case of the inquisition by even more terrible punishments) – to use a common and apt example from Christendom's medieval history, institutions from the artistic and intellectual fields, for instance, have far fewer powers of direct sanction. Whoever grasps the chalice or performs consecration without authorization, whoever questions the doctrine or preaches his or her own religious truths, will be punished for this sacrilege.

4. Class and religion: from Weber to a Bourdieusian theory of fields

Bourdieu's theory of class-specific salvation needs is very strongly influenced by Max Weber's writings.[8] At the stage where fundamental differentiation between the qualified and unqualified, the experts and the profane, the elite and the masses takes place, this elementary form of the field is already similar to a market, in which producers and consumers of "salvation goods" confront each other. Those who have the monopoly of legitimate transactions with religious symbols and rituals offer their expertise to the religiously "untalented"[9], who can request

---

8   See Weber (1922/1985), (1920/1988).

9   The status of the non-expert or untalented and "simple-minded" emerges with the claim for the monopoly of competence and virtuosity on the part of the self-appointed elite of the chosen in the dominant group. As soon as this claim of a minority finds the acceptance of the majority – an act of subjugation, which Bourdieu describes as symbolic violence – then autocratic usurpation becomes a legitimate claim to power. With this recognition of their superiority and having

religious goods of varying quality according to their "salvation needs"; and offer the producers something in return for their religious services (e.g., sacrifices, gifts, the buying of indulgences, alms, church taxes, etc.). Interestingly, Weber's sociology of religion, similar to that of Gramsci, differentiates between class-specific salvation needs, "habitus" and life styles of the population, which lends the idea of a market for salvation goods additional plausibility. This sociological conception can be transferred without too much trouble to other areas of social practice and everyday life, as well as, for example, to the class-specific way of furnishing one's house, where the connection between class position, need, taste, and kind of life style points to a very similar structural pattern.

4.1 Social classes and their salvation needs

According to Weber, salvation needs differ according to the actual class position and the functions of religious representation corresponding to that position: for instance, the dominant classes seek justification of their privileges, the dominated classes the promise of salvation, and the intellectuals are looking, in particular, for religious knowledge and convictions which meet their needs for rational investigation and organisation of fulfilment in earthly life – a disposition which expresses itself prototypically in the search for systematic, aesthetic stylization and "design" *(Gestaltung)* of everyday life.

Because of its strong dependence on the forces of nature and its contingencies, the rural/popular milieu is, according to Weber, much less open-minded about rational religious convictions than urban occupational categories and remains to the present day particularly susceptible to magical or pagan practices. The religious dispositions

---

at their disposal the monopoly for production of legitimate symbolic goods (religious, scientific, artistic etc.), this elite is then optimally equipped to prove this superiority and to continually increase the distance between themselves and the mass of laypeople or the profane.

and practices of the upper social classes, on the other hand, are as a rule clearly more "rational", i.e. free of magical connections and oriented towards specific social and ideological functions (the theodicy of their privileges and claims to power). However, the salvation needs of the educated classes in general, and intellectuals in particular, seem to tend towards a strategy of, as Nietzsche would put it, "self-deification" *qua* systematic stylization and aesthetization of their everyday way of life. One aspect common to the religious dispositions of the dominant classes is that they see its key function in the symbolization of distinction vis-à-vis popular (vulgar) religious attitudes and practices. This pattern of elite differentiation between their own and the common taste of common people is in no way limited to the magical and religious domain, but is characteristic of the whole spectrum of symbolic action.

4.2 The differentiation between religious specialists: priests, prophets and magicians

First of all, the emerging religious field was structured along the polarization of "experts versus laity", followed by the development of class-specific salvation needs and demands for religious goods. This led on the side of religious experts to almost simultaneous differentiation between the three positions struggling for monopoly of the legitimate definition and handling of religious goods, as is clear from Bourdieu's sketch showing the structures of the religious field in the appendix,

In the centre of this field we find the church; which has crystallised into an institution after lengthy processes of assertion and monopolization. During such processes a religious movement of "chosen people" around a charismatic leader can develop, through the intermediate stage of a sect, into a multinational concern for the production and administration of salvation goods. Once achieved, this position of monopoly permitted the church to claim universal validity of its truths and the right to assert these both outwardly against the resistance of "other believers or non-believers" (crusades or compulsory conversion) and inwardly (the fight against heresy of all kinds). Its claim to truth is, on the one hand, questioned by the figure of the magician, on the other hand by that of the prophet – both of whom struggle with the church for the monopoly of religious truth, and all strategically turn to the laity or certain categories of laypeople, in order to give emphasis to their teaching. Bourdieu's sketch of the religious field makes clear that religious experts, if they want to be successful, have to take into consideration that receptivity to religious messages of prophetic or magical provenance will vary for each social class.

Thus, a magician offers salvation goods which precisely meet the practical, magical and religious needs (dealing with the contingencies of life, exorcism of fate …) of uneducated strata (the key clientele of the church) and he therefore stands in direct competition with the salvation goods offered by the church. Prophets, in contrast, deliver salvation messages that are in competition with the church's orthodoxy and the monopoly of interpreting god's will. Prophet and magician have in common that both their salvation competence and their salvation claims are person-specific, i.e. are charismatic, while those of the church, and that is its main constitutive characteristic, are commonplace and ordinary, institutionally embedded in the "charisma of office". This "charisma of office" is partially passed on to the representatives of the church, the clergy; however, whether or not this "embodiment" is convincing relies to a great extent on the personal charisma of the individual.

4.3 The religious field as a model for other social fields

The configuration outlined here of the competition for a monopoly is characteristic of the structures of other social fields, and a lot points to the fact that, here too, we are dealing with elementary forms of associative relationships (Vergesellschaftung) and their dynamics. In the field of medicine, for example, faith healers as well as alternative medicine question the monopoly of orthodox medicine. Similar processes apply to the practice of other sciences, where the claim to truth of universitarian knowledge and the "charisma of office" of homo academicus can be attacked by competitors from outside and inside. In fields like those of artistic production, these processes are much less clear due to the lower degree of institutionalization, but here too struggles are well known between established (legitimate) positions and the heretics and prophets (popular or avant-garde artists), who question the former's monopoly. Here again, the positions that confront each other claim legitimacy of varying quality and origin: on the one hand, there is the institutionalized cultural capital in the form of codified and documented competencies, in the same pattern as the church's "charisma of office", which offers the respective agents participation in the accumulated symbolic capital of their institution. On the other hand, there is the personal charisma that stems from the extraordinary competencies of specific individuals, who, thanks to these qualities, are able to create and satisfy demand on the market of symbolic goods. We are dealing here, therefore, with elementary forms of society, which can appear, like transformational generative grammar in Chomsky's sense, in a theoretically unlimited number of possible, empirical, concrete cases in constantly new variations of the same theme. Here it is advisable to make a short detour and look at the social-anthropological perspective of the field. From very early on, Bourdieu was extremely interested in the sociology of Marcel Mauss, for whom he felt an affinity and with whom he shared many basic perspectives on social theory. One of these was the conception that specific social parts, which were later perceived of as "autonomous" and "auto-logical", crystallised during the social differentiation process out of a preceding ensemble of undivided "total social facts", to use Mauss's words. On the basis of the theory of "the gift", Mauss had made plausible in a modest but brilliant way that archaic societies definitely did not differentiate between economic, social, cultural and religious realities and functions, but regarded them all as simultaneously active "dimensions" of one and the same act or object. The "splitting" of the more or less autonomous parts of the social world during the social transformation from archaic to historical and, later, to modern societies is in itself part of a double process of domination – of people over nature and of people over people. This process is manifest in the structure of the emerging fields of religion, economy or politics through the concrete processes of monopolization and appropriation. Therefore the perspectives gained by Bourdieu following Weber's thinking on the religious field can also be applied to all other fields, as they describe the logic that is the basis of this differentiation process.

5. Field and habitus: social reality in subjective and objective form

In the above-mentioned sociogenetic and field-analytic perspectives, we have directed our attention primarily towards the objective social structures and have neglected the fact that Bourdieu's term, "field", must always be regarded as complementary to that of "habitus", that is, as an ensemble of subjective dispositions, positions and attitudes. The sociogenetic view of the emergence of a field should, therefore, always be accompanied by a psychogenetic reconstruction of the habitus of its agents. For we can only understand a specific social game if the following are made comprehensible: what drives the players who get involved, what strategies do they follow and what investments are at stake for them?

The main question here is: how and under what conditions can people be led to accept an ensemble with more or less compulsory norms and practice, which have a great effect on their physical, psychological, affective and cognitive positions, and which gradually become so "deep-rooted" that they seem like second nature and are taken for granted?

Confronting objective and subjective structures, we find field and habitus, codification and deep-rootedness, canonization and convictions as complements and affinities. In conceptualising "habitus" as the "structured and structuring principle" of social practice, as the "generative grammar" of forms of practice, Bourdieu was influenced by Weber, who employed this term in his sociology of religion systematically and in a way mostly compatible with Bourdieu's use.[10] However, there were other influences, for Bourdieu interpreted "habitus" in the tradition of Durkheim and Mauss's sociology of religion and knowledge, in as much as with *practical meaning* he means "objective meaning without subjective intention".

It is important to note that Bourdieu's heuristic concepts of field and habitus both resist any substantialization, because he always emphasizes the practical content of the "structure". Therefore, the term "field" only serves to elucidate the "objective" relationships which give action "meaning" and are *shown* in it, without necessarily expressing real relationships. This is a "repeat" of what habitus manages to do as the generic principle of "objective meaning without subjective intention". The "field" is not real, but people's behavior, perception, feeling, thinking and action all take place as if they obeyed its "forces".

6.   The dissolution of the religious field?

Bourdieu's pioneering discourses on Weber's sociology of religion and theory of the religious field originated in the early 1970s. At that time, there was an intense debate going on in France on secularisation and the crisis of religion. The discussions on the so-called people's religiosity (religion populaire) and the modernization of Catholicism,

---

10   The concept of habitus is unfortunately missing in the register of Weber's "Wirtschaft und Gesellschaft" (posthumously published). If one takes the trouble to track it down and to analyze and interpret it in the way it is used, then the enormous affinity between the two sociologists becomes obvious.

triggered by the II Vatican Council, were also heated. Bourdieu himself understood these two articles not so much as studies on the sociology of religion but as a contribution to general, sociological theory. Max Weber's work was for him to the fore – Weber being little known in France at the time or "unrecognized" because of a one-sided reception of his work. However, this does no harm to the interest these articles should have for the sociology of religion. On the contrary, Bourdieu's contribution has led to a situation where questions in the sociology of religion have become of paradigmatic importance for the whole discipline of sociology.

Exactly ten years after the publication of these studies, Bourdieu spoke on the topic of "The dissolution of the religious" at a conference on the sociology of religion (cf. Bourdieu 1987b). In the face of the deep crisis of this specific, sociohistorically rooted and institutionalized form of the religious – as it was described and debated at that time, he was confronted with the question concerning the "new clergy". In answer to this, Bourdieu used his theory of fields in order to find a sociologically plausible answer. As the religious field was the venue for struggles regarding the monopoly of the legitimate interpretation of the religious, we found ourselves, according to Bourdieu, in a process where both the market for salvation goods and the suppliers were increasing and becoming more complex. The boundaries between fields like medicine, philosophy and those of specific physical techniques (free dance, martial arts or yoga) as well as areas like psychoanalysis or sexology, which up to then had been relatively clear, were opening up – as Bourdieu says – to an increasingly liberal exchange. Faced with this wide choice of goods for care of the soul and body (goods, techniques, instruments for producing the salvation state), the individuals were helping themselves, to a certain degree, in order to put together their own eclectic or syncretistic forms of representing transcendence and related practices. A decisive contribution to this was made, according to Bourdieu, by the fact that the composition of the clientele for religious salvation goods was radically changed by the sociostructural transformations of the postwar era (tertiarization, decline of the agricultural industry, the gain in importance of the middle classes and, above all, the education explosion of the 1960s). Expert religiosity, up to then reserved for a relatively small elite, would now be made available to the growing new middle class, which would become the central pillar of the new syncretistic religiosities – a hypothesis which was to be confirmed in the following decades.

7. Future perspectives

Bourdieu's theory of fields, influenced by Weber, has one advantage which should not be underestimated: no specific definition of religion is given and this avoids the risk of having to universalise the socio-historically specific, institutionalized form of religion. Moreover, this approach suggests that the religious field should be regarded as the place of permanent conflict over the monopoly of the legitimate definition of what can, and should, be recognised as religion, and that this should be made the object of specific empirical research.

A great deal of empirical research on the sociology of religion has used Bourdieusian concepts; for example, F.-A. Isambert's important study "Le sens du sacré" has proved the strength and usefulness of this approach. On the other hand, some – like Swartz (1996) – point to the fact that this perspective is less suitable for an analysis of concrete empirical objects, like congregations or religious leading figures, than for the examination of more complex social constellations around the struggle for the monopoly of the legitimate determination of religious truths. Another critique (see, for example, Rey 2004) claims that the perspective of Bourdieu's field theory is too rigid, a critique which is greatly relativated if not dispelled completely, by an apt tribute to the theoretical, methodological and empirical merits of this approach.

Through his view of religion, which is not substantialistic but structural and open to concrete historical variation, Bourdieu's approach in the theory of fields also offers added value in the form of epistemological vigilance against ethnocentric generalizations and anachronistic stereotypes. A further advantage lies in the fact that the field theory view of the religious is suitable for a comparative approach and can be used to describe similar or divergent structural changes in varying societal domains. The large number of contributions in the journal *Actes de la Recherche et Sciences Sociales*, which was founded by Bourdieu, give evidence of this.

On the other hand, this kind of objectivization of the religious has inevitably been condemned as profanization and a materialistic reduction of the holy. Another reproach is that there is absolutely no "concept" or clear definition of religion and even that the concept of religion is systematically destroyed, in that it mixes such incompatible items as going to church and the sacrament, East Asian meditation techniques, Körperkult (body modification) or reading horoscopes; a reproach which was also mentioned in connection with the field theory analysis of literature and academia.[11] Bourdieu would probably answer this by saying that religion was historically created by people and during the different stages of this long-term historical process of self-creation varying empirical manifestations were revealed. At the same time though, he would also agree with the anthropologically oriented hypothesis that, beyond the phenotypical variability of religious conceptions of belief and practice, on the genotypical level we must assume that there is a basic motive for the religious, like an anthropological constant. Thus, from the sociological viewpoint, religion is by no means banished from the social world, rather, the sociohistorical complexity and driving force of this human practice is taken very seriously.*

---

11   It should be remembered that popular religiosity has always been syncretistic and pragmatic, pointing to its usefulness in concrete matters of concern, a circumstance that incidentally has always been condemned, and even openly fought, by religious institutions and experts.

*   Translated by Rachel Matthey

References

Bourdieu, Pierre (1971) "Une interprétation de la théorie de la religion selon Max Weber", *Archives européennes de sociologie*, vol 12, pp. 3-21.

–. (1971) "Genèse et structure du champ religieux", *Revue Française de sociologie*, vol. XII, no 2: 295-334.

–. (1982) *Ce que parler veut dire*. Paris: Fayard.

–. (1984a) "Haute culture et haute couture", in *Questions de sociologie*. Paris: Édition de Minuit, pp. 196-206.

–. (1984b) "Quelques propriétés des champs", in *Questions de sociologie*. Paris: Éditions de Minuit, pp. 113-120.

–. (1987a) "Sociologues de la croyance et croyances de sociologies", in *Choses dites*. Paris: Éditions de Minuit, pp. 106-111).

–. (1987b) "La dissolution du religieux" in *Choses dites*. Paris: Éditions de Minuit, pp. 117-123.

–. (1994) "Propos sur l'économie de l'Église", in : dres. : *Raisons Pratiques – Sur la théorie de l'action*. Paris: Seuil, pp. 215-217.

–. (1994) "Piété religieuse et dévotion artistique", *Actes de la Recherche en Sciences Sociales*, décembre, no 105: 71-74.

–. (2000) *Das religiöse Feld. Texte zur Oekonomie des Heilsgeschehens*, UVK, Konstanz.

Bourdieu, Pierre and Saint-Martin, M. de (1982) "La Sainte Famille : l'épiscopat français dans le champ du pouvoir", *Actes de la Recherche en Sciences Sociales*, no 44-45: 1-53.

Dianteill, E. (2002) "Pierre Bourdieu et la religion. Synthèse critique d'une synthèse critique." *Archives des Sciences sociales des Religions* (118): 5-19.

Ebertz, M.N. and Schultheis, F. (1986) "Populare Religiosität in der modernen Gesellschaft. Kontinuität, Pluralität, Visibilität." in *Österreichische Zeitschrift für Soziologie*, 3: 62-79.

–. (1986) "Populare Religiosität", in Ebertz, M.N./ Schultheis, F. (Hg.): *Volksfrömmigkeit in Europa. Beiträge zur Soziologie popularer Religiosität aus 14 Ländern*, München, pp. 11-52.

Rey, T. (2004) "Marketing the goods of salvation: Bourdieu on religion." *Religion* 34 (4): 331-343.

Schultheis, F., Egger, St. and Pfeuffer, A. (2000) "Vom Habitus zum Feld. Religion, Soziologie und die Spuren Max Webers bei Pierre Bourdieu", in Pierre Bourdieu: *Das religiöse Feld. Texte zur Oekonomie des Heilsgeschehens*, UVK, Konstanz, pp. 131-176.

Swartz, D. (1996) "Bridging the Study of Culture and Religion: Pierre Bourdieu's Political Economy of Symbolic Power". *Sociology of Religion* 57(1): 71-85.

Weber, Max (1973) *Wirtschaft und Gesellschaft*. Tübingen: Mohr.

–. (1922/1985) "Religionssoziologie (Typen religiöser Vergemeinschaftung)", in (ed.) pp. 245-381. Tübingen: J.C.B. Mohr.

–. (1920/1988) "Die Wirtschaftsethik der Weltreligionen: Einleitung", in (ed.) *Gesammelte Aufsätze zur Religionssoziologie I*: 237-275. Tübingen: Mohr UTB.

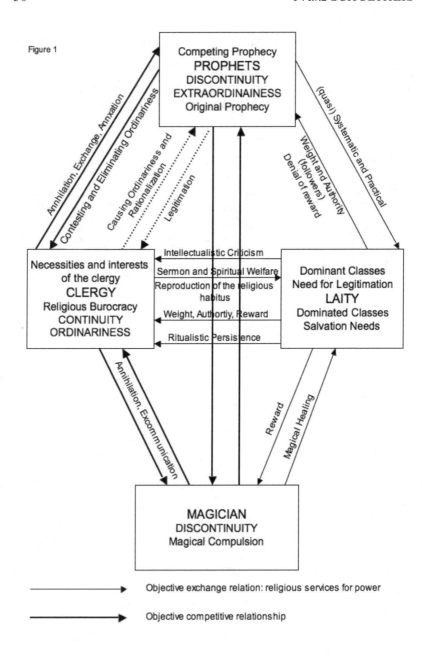

Figure 1

Jörg STOLZ

Salvation Goods and Religious Markets: Integrating Rational Choice and Weberian Perspectives

1. Introduction

The concept "religious market" is presently enjoying a tremendous success. Not only sociologists, but also journalists, politicians and, interestingly, some of the religious actors themselves, are beginning to use the term more frequently. Even one of the most prominent critics of the theory of religious markets concedes that modern societies are characterized by "a largely novel situation in human life: the possibility of choosing a religion" (Bruce, 1999: 3). The theoretical enterprise that has developed and defended the theory of religious markets – rational choice – has, however, been strongly criticized. Just about everything rational choicers have said about religion has been questioned (Ammerman, 1997; Bruce, 1999; Chaves, 1995; Hamilton, 2001; Lechner, 1996). Two of the most important theory-immanent criticisms are that rational choicers have not really worked out their model well enough and have not stated clearly, first, what kind of "goods" we are faced with, and second, under what conditions such goods might be said to be traded on a "market" (Bruce, 1999: 30ff.; Hamilton, 2001: 220ff.).

This article argues that these two problems concerning the rational choice approach can be solved by distinguishing different types of religious goods and integrating them into a larger rational choice framework. In this framework, markets are only one type of "social system" among others in which religious goods may be produced and allocated. In order to create this new framework, I show, first, that rational choicers have so far – and without really acknowledging it – used at least four different types of concepts of "religious goods". Second, I go back to the work of Max Weber who is the most important classic author for the concept of "religious goods" (a fact that so far has not been recognized by rational choicers).[1] Weber gives us the important notions of institutionalized salvation goals and salvation means, as well as the idea of religious goods as a means of religious authority, all of which I can integrate into my framework. Finally, I draw on ideas from James S. Coleman, Siegwart Lindenberg and Hartmut Esser, in order to create a new typology of religious goods. Specifically, I will show the following:

1. Religious goods are only one of the elements of religions (religious symbol systems). Religions institutionalize various types of religious goods, linking them into "chains" of salvation means and salvation ends.
2. There are different types of religious goods. Specifically, we have to distinguish individual religious goods (consumer, membership and personal goods), where individuals find themselves in parametric situations, from social religious goods (communal, collective and positional goods), where individuals produce religious goods interdependently.
3. The type of religious goods determines how they are produced and allocated. Exchange on a "market" is but one possibility. Specifically, religious goods may be transferred by socialization, produced by individuals themselves, produced together with others or used in authority relations.

---

1   This point is missed by Collins (1997) who presents an otherwise very interesting comparison between Stark and Bainbridge, Weber and Durkheim.

2. Religious goods and religious markets: rational choice

The concepts "religious goods" and "religious markets" are at the very heart of the theories of "rational choice of religion". It may therefore come as a surprise that there is some confusion as to what religious goods really are in the rational choice literature. In my view, rational choicers have so far given us (but not clearly distinguished) four different versions of what religious goods might be.

2.1 Religious goods as compensators and other-worldy rewards

In an early version of their theory, Stark and Bainbridge (1985, 1989) define religious goods as supernatural, general and non-verifiable *compensators*. By the term "compensator" Stark and Bainbridge (1985: 6) mean "the belief that a reward will be obtained in the distant future or in some other context which cannot be immediately verified". Rewards are "anything humans will incur costs to obtain" (1989: 27). Since human beings regularly strive for rewards they cannot immediately have, they often settle for a substitute, a compensator. Compensators may be secular or based on supernatural assumptions. The supernaturally-based compensators can be either specific and falsifiable – which makes them "magic"; or they may be general and non-falsifiable – which makes them "religion". Examples of magical compensators are promises such as being cured of cancer, getting a good grade at school or winning back one's unfaithful lover. Examples of religious compensators are the meaning of existence, an afterlife, illumination or the coming of the savior at some unspecified time (1985: 7, 30). It is interesting to note that, in this version of Stark and Bainbridge's theory, compensators are the sole element of their definition of religions: Religions are "systems of general compensators based on supernatural assumptions" (Stark and Bainbridge, 1989: 81). Religious firms can then be seen as organizations that produce two things: on the one hand, supernaturally-based compensators, on the other, "secular" goods (rewards) such as friendship, social ties or social identities that may be produced by any kind of social group. In a revised version of his theory Stark drops the term "compensator", and talks instead about "otherworldly rewards", which are "those that will be obtained only in a non-empirical (usually posthumous) context" (Stark, 1999: 268). Looking at the examples that Stark and Bainbridge give in the two versions of their theory, we see that they focus on (at least some) of the *final goals* that religions often propose. Below we will see that Max Weber describes the same phenomenon as "salvation goals".

2.2 Religious goods as religious membership

A second version of the "religious good" (like the next two versions) can be found in the work of Laurence R. Iannaccone. Here, *religious membership* and the opportunity to participate in collective religious action are treated as a commodity:

> At the heart of any economic theory of religion is the notion of religion as a commodity, an object of choice (...) Consumers *choose* what religion (if any) they will accept and how extensively they will participate in it. Nor are these choices immutable – people can and often do change religions or levels of participation over time (Iannaccone, 1991: 158, his emphasis).

While the Stark and Bainbridge version suggested that religions were made up of or included religious goods, here the fact of *belonging* to a religious group itself seems to be the religious good.[2] Being a Catholic or a Mormon, a Wiccan or a Jehovah's Witness, a Buddhist or a Scientologist seems to be what individuals "choose" on the "market". Iannaccone then gives us two main attributes of the goods thus defined. First, they are linked to the *supernatural* (Iannaccone, 1992: 125), supposing the existence of gods, transcendent forces, and the

---

2   Iannaccone does not make this distinction between membership and personal religious good as I do.

like. Second (and linked to the first attribute), they are inherently *risky*. This is because individuals cannot evaluate the goods. They have to trust and believe, both as to the means and the promised ends that come with the membership. They cannot have security but are asked to have faith.

2.3 Religious goods as collective goods

A third definition, also found in the work of Iannaccone, sees religious goods as *collective goods*. This is the case when it comes to "group activities such as listening to sermons, scriptural studies, testimonial meetings, liturgies, worship, hymn singing, and sacramental acts" (Iannaccone, 1994: 1183). In these situations "religion is a 'commodity' that people produce *collectively*" (1994: 1183, his emphasis). The interesting thing about these collective religious goods is, following Iannaccone, that a free-rider problem emerges. Since the religious good (such as a high level of enthusiasm) is produced collectively, all participants can benefit from it, regardless of the degree of their personal involvement. Rational individuals may therefore be tempted to "free-ride", that is, enjoy the public good without contributing personally. This in turn may lead to the non-provision of the collective good. Iannaccone argues that religious groups are routinely endangered by such a collective-good problem and that they often solve this problem by penalizing or prohibiting "alternative activities that compete for members' resources" (1994: 1186). Some religious groups thus forbid involvement in activities such as secular entertainment and education or they "demand of members some distinctive, stigmatizing behavior that inhibits participation or reduces productivity in alternative contexts – having shaved heads, wearing pink robes, or being in an isolated location does the job quite effectively" (1994: 1188). In this way, participation in the group becomes more costly and free-riders are deterred. Rational individuals will decide either to really join or to leave. According to Iannaccone, this theory explains why conservative and "strict" churches often seem to be doing better than their more liberal competitors. In fact, their strictness allows them to weed out free-riders and thus to create overall a "better" collective religious product.

2.4 Religious goods as household commodities

Finally, we can find in the work of Iannaccone the idea of religious goods as "household commodities":

> Religious commodities are not physical goods like cars or computers that can be manufactured, packaged and sold in stores. Nor are they services like haircuts or banking that we have others do for us. Rather, they fall into a third category that economists call "household commodities" – valued goods and services that families and individuals produce for their own consumption (Iannaccone, 1992: 124).

Iannaccone takes up the important idea of Becker (1976/1990) that households may be seen not only as consumers but also as producers, using market goods, time and human capital in order to produce more basic "household commodities". These commodities may be "as concrete as meals and laundry or as abstract as relaxation and love" (Iannaccone, 1992: 124), and they are "consumed by family members rather than being sold" (1990: 297). The abstract commodity that is thus produced is "religious satisfaction" (1990: 299). For example, a family may decide to produce a certain amount of "religious satisfaction", by praying before meals, thus using a certain amount of time, human capital (they have to know the prayers) and energy. Evidently, this commodity is not "bought" on a market, but is produced by the family themselves.

2.5 Religious markets

Rational choicers are convinced that it is useful to conceptualize the religious domain of any society as a religious economy (Stark and

Iannaccone, 1994: 232). A religious economy consists of all the religious phenomena in a given society and includes a religious market. On this market, religious firms produce and sell "religious goods" in order to satisfy the "religious needs" of the "consumers" (Iannaccone, 1991, 1992, 1995; Stark and Iannaccone, 1994). Consumers, on the other hand, choose the religious goods according to their preferences and budget constraints. Rational choicers do not simply treat the market concept as an analogy or even as a metaphor. They are convinced that we can talk just as well about a religious market as of a market for cars or washing powder.

Since religious markets function like other markets, practically all major insights from economics can be used to analyse and explain religious phenomena (Iannaccone, 1991: 159). The laws of supply and demand, for example, apply. *Ceteris paribus*, a religion which is cheaper or which allows us to obtain the other-worldly good more easily has a higher probability of being consumed,[3] and if the amount of religious goods on the market rises, prices for religious goods will fall. A second example is the law of the invisible hand: unregulated markets produce more welfare than regulated ones. Thus, religious monopolies, oligopolies or mixed regimes (with state churches and free churches) will not work as efficiently as unregulated religious markets. In the latter we will find higher-quality religious products with lower prices, leading to higher aggregated religiosity.

2.6 Critique

There are many texts that criticize the rational choice approach to religion, its views on religious goods and religious markets (e.g. Bruce, 1999; Chaves, 1995; Hamilton, 2001), but I will not repeat their arguments here. In spite of all the (often) valuable critical points,

---

3   It makes the finding all the more interesting that strict or costly religions might
     have more success than "cheap" ones. But this may be explained equally in rational choice terms, albeit with a more complex model. See Iannaccone (1994).

I am personally convinced that the rational choicers have produced some of the most innovative approaches in recent sociology of religion and that it might well be advisable to build on at least some of their work. Not everything, though, is acceptable. For my purposes, three points of criticism – which I have not yet found in the literature – will suffice. First, rational choicers have, to my knowledge, not yet acknowledged the fact that they themselves talk about different types of religious goods. After all, the four types presented above differ quite sharply. In one version, they are promises of transcendent events, in another, membership, in yet another, participation in a collective enterprise (such as a religious service), and in the final version religious satisfaction. Consequently, rational choicers have not made it clear when to use which concept of the religious good. This is why I venture to give a new typology of religious goods which clarifies the relation between the types as well as the question of application. Second, rational choicers assume that religious markets are the main model for the production and consumption of religious goods. But markets are only one type of "social system" and a very special one at that, with various structural conditions. Rational choicers thus overlook the existence of other ways in which production and allocation may take place (e.g. individual production, production in social groups and organizations). This means that, depending on the type of religious good, rational choice models not of markets but of these other types of social systems have to be applied in order to reach a satisfactory description and explanation. Finally, rational choicers have not yet fully taken into account the work of Max Weber, who is, after all, the most important classic author discussing religious goods. This is why we will turn to Weber now.

3. Salvation goods and authority relations: Max Weber

In his sociology of religion, Weber's main aim is to compare the world religions (e.g. with regard to their salvation goods or their religious ethics) in order to explain how the specific elements of ascetic Protestantism have helped to produce modern capitalism (Boudon, 1998). It is Judaism, Hinduism, Buddhism, Christianity, Confucianism and Taoism that Weber treats, using his methods of comprehension *(verstehen)* and explanation *(erklären)*, ideal-type construction, and historical comparison.

3.1 Salvation goods

The term "salvation good" *(Heilsgut)* is a central one in the works of Max Weber (Weber, 1920/1988, 1922/1985; Schluchter, 1991: 80). The fact that this has gone unnoticed in the Anglo-Saxon world is probably due to translations that did not quite know what to make of the term, translating it by "state of salvation", "substantively divine salvation", "highest bliss available" or even "sacred value".[4] All these translations lose the sense which interests us here, namely, that Weber talks about "goods", which can be striven for, supplied and consumed. Instead of salvation goods, Weber also uses the terms "salvation goals" *(Heilsziele)*, "salvation means" *(Heilsmittel)* and "promises of the religions" *(Verheissungen der Religionen)*.

Since Weber does not define the term "salvation good", I venture to reconstruct the definition he might have given. A salvation good is an end or a means to an end which is offered by a religion, embedded in a specific world-view and a system of life practices, and which may be aspired to or used by an individual or a social group. Salvation goods may be confined to certain points in time or lasting; set in the

---

4   All these translations of *Heilsgut* can be found in the same text: Weber (1920/1978).

future or the present; transcendent or immanent; individual or collective; ascetic or contemplative; aspired to actively or given to the individual by an external power (Weber, 1922/1985: 321ff.; 1920/ 1988: 237ff., 536ff.). For our purposes, four aspects of Weber's conception of salvation goods are worthy of mention.

Salvation goods are either *goals* or *means*. Weber thinks that religions propagate salvation goals that may be reached through certain "salvation means". This is an important point: individuals can use salvation means in a calculating, rational way in order to reach future salvation goals, thus allowing for sociological explanation. A further point is the fact that the means to an end may become the end in itself. If "belief" is a means of being rewarded later by eternal life, the state of being a true believer may itself become a salvation goal. Salvation means such as rituals, good works, mystic or ascetic self-perfection, sacraments or faith may therefore also all be seen as "salvation goals" themselves. Striving for future goals gives the individual a special "way of living", a "habitus" which produces immediate emotional gratification (and is therefore a "good"). Note that we are not in a market-type situation. The individual is not buying a "product" on a "market", but using culturally embedded means of action in order to reach certain goals.

Salvation goods should not be thought of as isolated entities. Rather, they imply a specific *world-view* and specific *life practices* of the respective religion. As to the world-view, the religious symbol system determines what sad state of affairs the individual or group is to be saved from and, therefore, what the state of salvation looks and feels like. If, for example, the world-view sees the main problem as one of social and political servitude, the salvation goal may well be a promised land and the domination of political enemies; if the world-view constructs the problem as one of an endless stream of reincarnations, the final state may be one of stepping out of this circle (nirvana).

Salvation goods *satisfy different psychological and social needs*. Following Max Weber, psychological needs may be either compensatory, legitimating or intellectual (Weber, 1922/1985: 285ff.). Felt deprivation, misfortune and suffering lead the individual to search for compensation; he or she may look for a salvation good which promises release from misfortune, deliverance from evil, or bodily healing in the near or distant future. Individuals, however, who find themselves in privileged positions will mainly look out for salvation goods that will legitimize their position. They feel the need for justification of their well-being. Finally, Weber tells us, there may arise an inherent intellectual need to make sense of the world and to rationalize existing worldviews; this need, too, may lead to the acceptance of a very specific kind of salvation good. All these psychological needs differ depending on the historical situation and the social class in which the individual finds himself. This is why different social classes tend to accept and produce different kinds of religiosity.

Salvation goods may be *this-worldly* or *other-worldly*. Weber tells us that many salvation goods of the different religions were not, and are not, other-worldly (such as an afterlife in paradise), but this-worldly. They may be formulated positively, as the attainment of good health, long life, happiness, riches, fertility, a large number of descendants, a good name, high social status (for example, caste status), political power, land, and victory in war; or they may be formulated negatively as the liberation from illness and death, unhappiness, poverty, sterility, shame, defeat in war, slavery, exploitation, etc.

In his famous typology of salvation means, Weber focuses mainly on individual possibilities of being saved, distinguishing three "active" and three "passive" types (1922/1985: 321ff.). His idea is then to say that in one of these cases (asceticism in the world), there is a greater chance of modern capitalism emerging.

3.2 *The battle for religious authority*

Although Weber clearly distinguishes between "producers" and "consumers" of religion, analysing much interaction between "supply" and "demand", he does not treat salvation goods within the framework of a "market theory" but primarily within that of the sociology of

authority relations *(Herrschaftssoziologie)*. Religious groups are defined as "authority units" *(Herrschaftsverbände)*, controlling their
members by providing or withdrawing salvation goods depending on
whether or not individuals comply with group demands. A church, for
example, is seen by Weber as a "hierocratic organization", that is "an
organization which enforces its order through psychic coercion by
distributing or denying religious benefits" (1920/1978: 54).

A church thus enforces its orders on all individuals with specific
characteristics (e.g. geographical unit, origin) independent of whether
these individuals agree with the teachings and norms or not (Weber,
1922/1985: 28). Churches use "charisma of function" *(Amtscharisma)*:
the authority of priests lies not in their personal qualification, but in
the fact that they occupy certain positions of power within the church
hierarchy (1922/1985: 692). State support aside, churches have their
own important means of power that enable them to enforce their
orders, especially excommunication and economic boycott (1922/
1985: 693). However, ruling religious groups like churches are, in
Weber's view, often challenged by other "producers" of religious
goods: by prophets and magicians who base their claims on personal
charisma. These actors are "deviant", "heterodox" and are often
fiercely attacked by the religious establishment. One of the central
features of Weber's sociology of religion then is the description of this
"battle" of orthodox and heterodox religious specialists (priests,
prophets, magicians) for religious monopoly (1922/1985: 268ff.).
Bourdieu (1971) has reinterpreted Weber by calling this game of
power a "religious field", suggesting it to be one among many other
"social fields" with similar power struggles.

3.3 Critique

Again, I will not go into a detailed critique or appraisal of Weberian
salvation goods and authority relations (see, for good critiques,
Schluchter, 1991; Tyrell, 1992). For my purposes the following points
will suffice. Weber is clearly the most important classic author re-

garding theory of religious goods. He has not, however, given us a complete sociological theory of religious goods. His typology of salvation means and ends does not tell us what kinds of goods may be produced in which types of social situations. For a new, integrated theory of religious goods, there are two Weberian points in particular that have to be taken into account. First, Weber indicates that religions give their adherents "chains" of salvation means which eventually lead to "salvation ends". Religious goods may thus lie on different "planes" of abstraction. Second, Weber shows us that religious goods may be the basis for authority relations, religious authority being itself a "good", over which ferocious battles may flare up among religious specialists.

4. Integrating the approaches into a larger framework

In what follows, I will link Weberian and rational choice approaches, showing that they are special cases of a larger, more encompassing approach.

4.1 A new typology of religious goods

In order to construct a new typology, I combine different elements: definitions of religion and religious goods, rationality assumptions, the different concepts of religious goods proposed by rational choice authors and Weber, as well as ideas about frames and private and social goods developed by James S. Coleman, Siegwart Lindenberg and Hartmut Esser. All the usual disclaimers concerning typologies apply: empirical cases are often more complex than the typology would suggest and "mixed types" are possible; generally, this typology is only a tool which has to prove its usefulness in future research.

First, in order to be able to distinguish religious goods from other types of goods, I need a definition of *religion*. By this term I denote the ensemble of cultural symbol systems that respond to problems of meaning and contingency by alluding to a transcendent reality. Religious symbol systems normally comprise mythological, ritual and ethical elements which may or may not be presented as salvation ends and means (salvation goods). As can be seen, I opt for a definition where religion does not consist entirely of salvation goods, but includes them. A *religious good* may then be defined as a goal, or a means of reaching a goal, which is proposed by a religion. Religious goods may be transcendent or immanent, future or present, individual or collective. Since religious goods are part of the religious symbol system, they are normally *institutionally and culturally given*. They are a part of the culture and the institutions (roles, norms, scripts) of a given social group or society. The social group – or the whole society – thus teaches the individual, first, which religious goal should be aspired to, and, second, what means should be used to reach that goal.[5]

Second, I accept the assumption of (bounded) *rationality*: I suppose that individuals act rationally, that is, they act in a way that furthers their own interests. However, I specify the model in the following way. Since there are costs attached to calculating and comparing expected gains, individuals switch between different "frames", of which the "rational frame" is but one. Often, individuals use a "traditional frame" in which they follow given "everyday recipes". It is only in unusual situations, in the case of surprises or if special symbols lead to the expectation of important possible losses or gains, that the individual switches to other frames, for example, the

---

5   It is interesting to note that a group of rational choicers have produced a theory (which has not yet been applied to religion) exactly along these Weberian lines: the theory of social production functions (Lindenberg, 1989, 1990; Esser, 1998, 1999, 2000b). This theory assumes that individuals have some very basic human needs (e.g. physical well-being, social esteem). These needs can, however, be met in extremely varied ways. Cultural and institutional systems therefore provide individuals with goals and legitimate means to reach the goals (and means to reach the means).

rational, the hedonistic or the evaluative frame (Lindenberg, 2000). When individuals switch to a rational frame, this implies calculating the costs and benefits of given religious goods and choosing the best alternative.

Third, I make a distinction between *parametric* and *strategic situations* (Elster, 1986: 7). In parametric situations, individuals "play against nature". In strategic situations, individuals play "against" (or with) each other, thus having to take into account each other's actions and interests. Parametric situations can be treated with decision theory; strategic situations have to be explained with the tools of game theory. In parametric situations we find individual religious goals; in strategic situations we find social religious goals. Esser (2000b: 55ff.) distinguishes the three strategic situations of coordination, dilemma and conflict.

Fourth, different religious goods have different attributes, the most important ones being: *divisibility, exclusiveness, rivalry* and *alienability* (Coleman, 1990: 33ff.; Esser, 2000b: 166ff.).

Fifth, since one of the uses of the following typology is to show under what circumstances markets are involved in the production and allocation of salvation goods, I will define the term "market" at this point. *Markets* are an ensemble of bilateral exchange relationships between (individual or collective) actors, who supply and demand goods. From a sociological point of view, markets are a special type of "social system" that may be distinguished from other types, for example, interaction systems, social groups or organizations (Esser, 2000a: 31ff.). Compared to these other social systems, markets are special in that they function in an unplanned and anonymous way. Market participants follow their own interests and are interested in other market participants only insofar as they are potential exchange partners. Since suppliers and consumers have common interests, one may say that markets solve a coordination problem. If conditions allow, a market will produce market equilibrium. I will argue that markets are a useful model mainly for two of the following six types of religious goods (consumer and membership goods).

Figure 1: A typology of religious goods

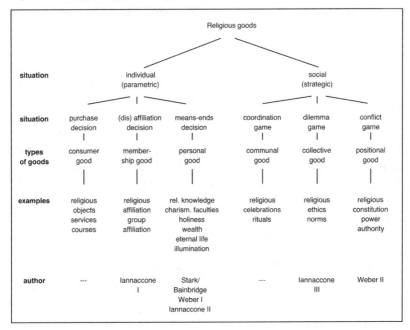

The new typology (Figure 1) distinguishes three individual religious goods (consumer, membership and personal goods) as well as three religious social goods (communal, collective and positional goods). In the following, I present them one by one.

4.2 Religious consumer goods

Religious consumer goods assume a parametric situation where the individual normally acquires the good from somebody else and then has the sole rights over its consumption. The goods are transferable, divisible and exclusive and there are no external effects involved. Examples of such goods are religious books, magazines, CDs, DVDs, devotional objects and the like. Obviously, these goods are transferable, divisible and exclusive: Buddha statues can be bought (transferred), if I buy one, another customer cannot buy the same one at the same time, he may, however, buy another one. These goods are clearly divisible and exclusive, which is why we do not encounter special "strategic" problems. The situation is parametric and the individual may rationally choose and consume the product by maximizing (or satisficing) his or her preferences. As we see from the above examples, often these goods are not directly linked to membership in a group and they may be paid for directly with money. In close proximity to these "perfect" consumer goods we find other goods which are more "social", but which are still divisible, transferable and exclusive, such as religious courses and therapies (e.g. Alphalive, meditation courses, therapy sessions) where individuals pay for the education or service they demand. Consulting a magician or fortune-teller may, depending on the breadth of one's definition of religion, also fit in here. Finally, even "religious services" such as marriages or funerals may be acquired with money (often for nonmembers of a group). These are cases of markets and market behavior which perfectly resemble the anonymous and unplanned economic market. Surely, nobody would want, in these cases, to speak of an "economic metaphor".

4.3 Religious membership goods

The second type of good is the *membership* of a religious group. These goods consist of the fact that the individual may consider him or herself to be a member of a group, giving him or her certain rights to the resources (such as knowledge, rituals, friendship) of the group. Among these resources we normally find "chains" of salvation means leading to salvation ends. In return, the individual normally gives up control over certain actions or resources (e.g. agrees to follow certain rules, subscribe to certain beliefs, support the group financially, etc.). Memberships are normally indivisible, and not alienable. They are often exclusive; the group thus forbids membership of other religious groups. They may also have important externalities. One good example for externalities can be seen when individuals convert to "New Religious Movements" which then often leads family members to challenge the religious groups' demands on their children or spouses (or even to claim that the groups have used "brainwashing"). For our purposes, we may construct the situation of the choosing individual as a "parametric" one. If the group accepts him (which may be seen as a sort of "capital"), the individual can decide rationally if he or she wants to join.

So, are religious memberships goods that are "traded" on "religious markets"? In my view, this question cannot be answered generally. The answer depends almost completely on the social context. Two variables are especially important in this respect. First, religious membership may be socially institutionalized as a matter of choice or not. In certain historical and geographical contexts, freedom of religion is guaranteed, religious plurality is given, and religious choice is socially well accepted. In such a society, religious membership markets may well exist. In other contexts, however, we have neither freedom of religion nor religious plurality. This is not to say that we have a "regulated market" (which assumes that there always has to be a market, either unregulated or regulated). Religious membership in a certain group may be transmitted from parents to children and be just a matter of fact. Religion may be fused with morality and citizenship and society in general. Here, then, we do not find a "religious market", although we may well find individuals who rationally use salvation means in order to acquire salvation ends.

Second, different levels of choices concerning memberships have to be distinguished. It is a very different thing to choose between being a Catholic or a Muslim or between going to the Reformed Church in one's hometown or the one in the next town. Choices may thus refer to different religions, different denominations (e.g. in the same religion) or different local churches or groups (e.g. in the same denomination). For empirical work, it is important to clearly see just where the majority of choices actually take place. To give an example, in Switzerland, there are almost no converts from Protestantism to

Catholicism or vice versa. On this level, there is no "market". We do see, however, quite important internal mobility between the Protestant state church and free church youth groups, leading to quite an interesting amount of competition, copying of "methods", etc

4.4 Religious personal goods

Religious personal goods are goods that are normally not exchanged on a market. They are (mostly) not divisible but may be exclusive due to the possibility of excluding individuals from a religious group. We can distinguish:

- *religious human capital* such as religious knowledge, religious techniques (meditation, exercises, etc.) and charismatic and magical faculties (speaking in tongues, gifts of prophecy, levitation, etc.);
- *physical, psychic and social well-being* in the present as well as in the future, such as good health, inner peace, material wealth, a long life, high social status (e.g. being among the "chosen" ones), an eternal life in paradise;
- *ethical faculties and states of being* in the present as well as in the future, such as the fact of being without sin, without "thirst", without "negative feelings", in a state of complete accord with religious laws, etc.;
- *religious experiences and states of being* in the present as well as in the future, such as experience of conversion, illumination, union with the divine, states of grace, unshakeable faith, or the "religious habitus" (Weber) in general.

Some of these goods are transferred to the individual by primary or secondary socialization (such as religious human capital). Some are produced by the individual him or herself (such as certain magical faculties acquired through asceticism, holiness acquired – partly – through self-control, or nirvana through the practice of yoga). Some are administered by religious specialists (such as sacraments), and some are "given" by transcendental forces (such as the gift of speaking in tongues, justification in faith or eternal life). While these goods are very often linked to membership of a religious group, this is not necessarily the case. Sometimes an individual may produce them or receive them without membership or discipleship (e.g. the enlightenment of Shree Rajneesh or an individual creating his or her own Wicca rituals). We may in a certain sense say that individuals are rational in that they use "salvation means" efficiently in order to reach "salvation goals". But they are not "customers" who "buy" something, exchanging it for money or some other valued good.

If membership of a group can give access to salvation means and (ultimately) salvation goals, shouldn't we say that religious personal goods are "exchanged on markets" too? I think not – for the following reasons. First, individuals often choose religions for reasons other than the primary personal religious goods (e.g. because of friendship with a member, psychological disarray) or for other aspects of the religion which do not touch explicitly on the "religious goods" of the religion's ideology. Religious goods of the personal or communal type are one reason among others why membership may be attractive and they may be put more or less into the foreground by the group when trying to attract members (if it does). They are, however, not the same thing as membership. Second, individuals often use personal religious means in order to reach religious goals without having consciously chosen their religion (e.g. because they were brought up in it or because everyone else follows this religion).

4.5 *Religious communal goods*

I now turn to religious social goods, that is, goods which are in some way or other "produced or consumed in interdependence with other actors or have external effects" (Esser, 2000b: 195). Social goods are either not perfectly divisible or not completely exclusive, and they typically imply some sort of "strategic situation". Due to their social nature, they are not produced and allocated on markets but in other types of social systems such as interaction systems, social groups, organizations or whole societies. The first type I present is the *relig-ious communal good*; these are defined as religious goods whose production is only possible by being with others. "Communal goods originate in the sociable cooperation of actors. And they originate only and *directly* through this act of cooperation" (Esser, 2000b: 170, his emphasis). In a way, communal goods are a goal in themselves; their performance is the product. Thus the actors who produce and con-sume, who are in control of and who are interested in the goods, are the same. Therefore, these goods are internally neither divisible nor exclusive and normally do not have allocation problems. Where is the "problem" in such situations? It lies in the *coordination* of efforts. To take a non-religious example: when dancing a tango, the problem is not one of "production" or "allocation" – it is one of coordination, of how to bring the dancers' bodies into synchronicity. The solutions to coordination problems are normally found in culture and institutions: conventions, rules, scripts, roles and the like are used to organize the joint production of the good. Examples in the religious sphere abound. Religious celebrations and customs such as Easter, Dong Zhi or Ra-madan, rituals and sacraments like the Shabbat, Wiccan fertility cults, Raëlian "baptism", ecstatic Pentecostal dancing or the singing in a religious choir may all be seen as communal goods in this sense. They may have the most diverse religious "meanings" and the sociologist may find different functions (e.g. with Durkheim the "integrative" one), but in general there is no doubt that the "product" of the activity lies in the performance itself. We can also easily see how coordination problems with these goods are solved in different cases. Religious celebrations often have liturgies (scripts) which prescribe the sequence of events. Also, there is often someone with a special role who super-vises the process, a master of ceremony (e.g. priests). Note that a market theory may explain why a better communal good attracts a larger crowd of participants. But it may not be applied to the situation of the interaction system itself, in which the good is *jointly produced and allocated*.

4.6 Religious collective goods

Another type of social good is the *religious collective good*. These goods are again produced and consumed in interdependence with other actors. The difference with communal goods is, however, that cooperation is not the goal in itself, but a means to an end. Also, the "producers" and the "consumers" are not necessarily, as in communal goods, the same individuals. This is because religious collective goods are neither internally nor externally divisible or exclusive. Powerful external effects and important incentives to free-ride results. The problem of these religious goods is, therefore, not one of coordination but of *production*. Everybody would be better off if the good was produced, but equally everybody has an incentive to free-ride, thus endangering the very same production. A nonreligious example is the provision of a strong students' association which defends students' interests. Since the benefits of such an association are available to all the students, regardless of whether they enter and support the association or not, rational individuals will tend to free-ride. The effect may be the non-existence of the association. There are different ways of solving this problem, and important ones are small sized groups, enforceable norms or selective incentives (Olson, 1977; Esser, 2000b: 199ff.). In his famous article, Iannaccone (1994) explained why strict churches are strong, by showing that strictness is a public good problem. We can generalize this idea to an even larger array of phenomena by using the concept of religious collective goods. The first example is the sheer material existence of the religious group, which enables the individual to join in celebrations (communal goods) or reach some sort of personal religious good. The group, however, has to be financed, its religious specialists have to be paid, buildings have to be rented or bought, etc. In order to prevent free-riding, many religious groups institutionalize enforceable norms for financial contributions from members (e.g. tithes, church taxes). Individuals who do not honour their obligations may then be excluded from the group. The second example of a religious collective good may be seen in the cultural strength of the religious group. An impressive emotionality, deep conviction and consensus about the existence of gods and high participation of members may all further the possibilities of their members to reach their own personal salvation goods. If the group believes strongly, I myself may believe more easily. Such cultural strength, however, is only to be attained by important contributions from the members in terms of time, energy and deference to the group consensus. Rational individuals may thus try to free-ride. They like to be members of a strong group, but may not necessarily be prepared to "pay" their contributions in terms of time and energy. This is why we often find strong and enforceable norms in terms of participation and belief. Turning to our question of the applicability of the market model, we see that collective religious goods are not "sold" on markets but are jointly produced in *social groups or organizations*. They may, however, have an important effect on the attractiveness of group memberships on religious markets.

4.7 Religious positional goods

The final type of good I will discuss is the *religious positional good*. These are goods and resources that are – for logical or technical reasons – scarce and cannot be multiplied. They are exclusive, that is, they create utility for their user only if other individuals are excluded from their use. The strategic game that results is not one of coordination or dilemma, but of *conflict*. Non-religious examples would be: winning a game of chess, getting the last seat in a lifeboat on a sinking ship or being a member of the ruling social class in a country. The problem with these situations is that they cannot be solved by coordination or cooperation. There is no way the actors can find an agreement. Battles are bound to take place until one of the participants emerges as the winner. In order to solve these conflicts, repressive norms, authority relations and strong sanctions are often the only means possible (Esser, 2000b: 104f.). Important religious positional goods can be found on different levels. At the individual level, we find the fact that several contestants may fight over high-powered positions in religious groups, such as being the leader of the group, the successor of the prophet, the pope, etc. This is especially so when clear rules of succession are not established. Good examples can be found in the early histories of Islam and the Jehovah's Witnesses. At the societal level, we find the phenomenon that there may be formal or informal "religious constitutions" which state which religious means and ends are legitimate and which are deviant. Some religious consumer, membership, personal and social religious goods are legitimate. Others are deviant and negatively sanctioned. The ruling classes or groups defend the constitution against competitors who offer different salvation means and goods in an effort to gain legitimation. This is the eternal fight of "established" religion against "non-established" religion, of "churches" against "sects", of "priests" against "prophets" and "magicians", which Max Weber shows us in his work (e.g. the conflict between Sadducees or Pharisees and the historical Jesus). Note that positional goods are not produced in markets but in interaction systems, social groups, organizations or even whole societies.

4.8 Placing Max Weber and rational choice authors in our framework

Where do we find the different types of religious goods discussed in the work of Stark and Bainbridge, Iannaccone and Weber? Figure 1 shows that when Iannaccone and Stark (in his newer work) talk about "religious markets", they often seem to mean "membership goods": the fact of choosing a certain religion or religious group. Stark and Bainbridge with their concept of "compensators", as well as Weber with his concept of "salvation good", can be found under the column "personal good". Here, the individual uses institutionally given salvation means in order to reach salvation goals. Religious personal goods are also close to the idea of "household commodities" in Iannaccone's work, since individuals often try to produce these goods themselves, using their own time, energy, and religious capital, as well as institutionally given salvation means. Iannaccone's concept of religious goods as collective goods can be found in the fifth column; we reconstruct these goods as one type of religious social good. Finally, Weber's concept of power conflict between religious specialists is a case of the struggle for religious positional goods in the sixth column. Interestingly, two cases have not been described either by the rational choicers or by Weber (in terms of goods): (1) the case of religious consumer goods where religious goods are exchanged for money; and (2) religious communal goods where the strategic problem lies mainly in the coordination of participants' efforts.

4.9 Religious goods and religious symbol systems (religions)

Following our definition of religions (or religious symbol systems) it is important to note that religions consist of a lot more than just religious goods. They incorporate a large array of world-views and life practices that may not themselves be seen as religious goods. On the other hand, religions normally do not offer just one type of the religious goods mentioned. In fact, often, they incorporate all of them in some way or another. In Catholicism, for instance, we find consumer goods such as devotional objects (e.g. pictures of saints), membership goods (the fact of officially being a Catholic), personal goods (e.g. sacraments like baptism, the Eucharist, penitence and reconciliation, grace and justification, a saintly life), communal goods (e.g. the mass), collective goods (e.g. the church in its financial, structural and cultural aspects) and positional goods (e.g. according to whether the Catholic Church is a dominant or marginal group in a given country). Obviously, these different types of goods are often closely intertwined. For example, an individual may acquire personal goods such as a saintly life only by being a member (membership good), taking part in the mass (communal good) and paying the church tax (collective good). He or she may do all this without thinking of him or herself as being on a "market". The strength of the proposed framework lies in showing that religious goods are not all produced in the same way and that different situations and logics underlie different religious goods.

4.10 Religious goods and religious markets: Summary

We have defined markets as an ensemble of bilateral exchange relationships between (individual or collective) actors, who supply and demand goods. Markets function in an unplanned and anonymous way and market participants follow only their own interests. If we start with the proposed typology, where are markets used to exchange religious goods? A market of the idealtype can be found with regard to *religious consumer goods*. These goods may indeed be exchanged in an unplanned and anonymous way. *Membership goods* are "exchanged" on markets only in a few cases. There may indeed be historical situations where individuals searching for new membership roles are "matched" with groups who offer such roles by what we call the "religious market". Given other historical contexts, however, membership roles in a religious group may be simply seen as "given", excluding the usefulness of the market model. *Personal religious goods* are normally acquired by socialization, produced by the individual or "received" from religious specialists or transcendental forces. While their production may include religious goods acquired on markets (e.g. consumer goods and membership goods), they themselves cannot be "bought". They are often (but not always) produced or received by individuals who are already members of a religious group (by upbringing or joining). *Religious social goods* all involve rational actions, but cannot be described by the market model. Religious communal goods involve not an anonymous and unplanned bilateral exchange of resources, but the joint production of a religious good which is normally well planned (even when there are "improvised" elements, as in Pentecostal religious services), and which involves close personal acquaintance. *Religious collective goods* and *religious positional goods* are by nature indivisible, producing strong external effects. Their special functioning cannot therefore be described by the market model. However, the way the respective problems of coordination, dilemma or conflict are solved may have effects on the "attractiveness" of the social group on the membership market (if there is one). Groups with impressive meetings, a good infrastructure and high power in the religious field may be more attractive to those searching for a religious group.

5. Conclusion

I have attempted to show how Weberian and rational choice concepts of religious goods, religious markets and religious authority structures may be integrated into a larger theoretical framework. By distinguishing individual religious goods (consumer, membership and personal goods) and social religious goods (communal, collective and positional goods), a more complex theoretical structure is provided than in previous theories. This structure enables us to understand the circumstances under which the different kinds of religious goods may be produced, the typical problems that may arise and the solutions found. Specifically, it allows us to see that markets are only one of the types of social system which govern the production and allocation of religious goods. Depending on the type of goods, we can ascertain whether or not markets represent a useful explanatory tool for a given religious phenomenon. This model also suggests that positions which argue in a global way "for" or "against" the market model seem to ignore the complexity of the production and allocation of religious goods.

References

Ammerman, Nancy Tatom (1997) "Religious Choice and Religious Vitality: The Market and Beyond", in Lawrence A. Young (ed.) *Rational Choice Theory and Religion: Summary and Assessment.* New York: Routledge, pp. 119-132.

Becker, Gary (1976/1990) "The Economic Approach to Human Behavior", in Gary Becker (ed.) *The Economic Approach to Human Behavior.* Chicago: The University of Chicago Press, pp. 3-16.

Boudon, Raymond (1998) "L'Ethique protestante de Max Weber: le bilan de la discussion", in Raymond Boudon (ed.) *Etudes sur les sociologues classiques.* Paris: Presses Universitaires de France, pp. 55-92

Bourdieu, Pierre (1971) "Genèse et structure du champ religieux", *Revue française de sociologie* 12: 295-334.

Bruce, Steve (1999) *Choice and Religion: A Critique of Rational Choice Theory.* Oxford: Oxford University Press.

Chaves, Mark (1995) "On the Rational Choice Approach to Religion", *Journal for the Scientific Study of Religion* 34(1): 98-104.

Coleman, James S. (1990) *Foundations of Social Theory.* Cambridge, MA: The Belknap Press of Harvard University Press.

Collins, Randall (1997) "Stark and Bainbridge, Durkheim and Weber: Theoretical Comparisons", in Lawrence A. Young (ed.) *Rational Choice Theory and Religion: Summary and Assessment.* New York: Routledge, pp. 161-180.

Elster, Jon (1986) "Introduction", in Jon Elster (ed.) *Rational Choice.* Oxford: Basil Blackwell, pp. 1-33.

Esser, Hartmut (1998) "Why are Bridge Hypotheses Necessary?" in Hans-Pete Blossfeld and Gerald Prein (eds) *Rational Choice Theory and Large-Scale Data Analysis.* Boulder, CO: Westview Press, pp. 94-111.

–. (1999) *Soziologie: Spezielle Grundlagen,* vol. 1: *Situationslogik und Handeln.* Frankfurt: Campus.

–. (2000a) *Soziologie: Spezielle Grundlagen,* vol. 2: *Die Konstruktion der Gesellschaft.* Frankfurt: Campus.

–. (2000b) *Soziologie: Spezielle Grundlagen,* vol. 3: *Soziales Handeln.* Frankfurt: Campus.

–. (2000c) *Soziologie: Spezielle Grundlagen,* vol. 4: *Opportunitäten und Restriktionen.* Frankfurt: Campus.

Hamilton, Malcolm (2001) "Religion and Rational Choice", in Malcolm Hamilton (ed.) *The Sociology of Religion: Theoretical and Comparative Perspectives,* (2nd edn). London: Routledge, pp. 215-228.

Iannaccone, Laurence R. (1990) "Religious Practice: A Human Capital Approach", *Journal for the Scientific Study of Religion* 29(3): 297-314.

–. (1991) "The Consequences of Religious Market Structure: Adam Smith and the Economics of Religion", *Rationality and Society* 3(2): 156-177.

–. (1992) "Religious Markets and the Economics of Religion", *Social Compass* 39(1): 123-131.

–. (1994) "Why Strict Churches Are Strong", *American Journal of Sociology* 99(5): 1180-1211.

–. (1995) "Voodoo Economics? Reviewing the Rational Choice Approach to Religion", *Journal for the Scientific Study of Religion* 34(1): 76-89.

Lechner, Frank J. (1996) "Secularization in the Netherlands?", *Journal for the Scientific Study of Religion* 35(3): 252-264.

Lindenberg, Siegwart (1989) "Social Production Functions, Deficits, and Social Revolutions: Prerevolutionary France and Russia", *Rationality and Society* 1(1): 51-77.

Lindenberg, Siegwart (1990) "Rationalität und Kultur: Die verhaltenstheoretische Basis des Einflusses von Kultur auf Transaktionen", in Hans Haferkamp (ed.) *Sozialstruktur und Kultur.* Frankfurt am Main: Suhrkamp, pp. 249-287.

–. (2000) "The Extension of Rationality: Framing Versus Cognitive Rationality", in Jean Baechler, François Chazel and Ramine Kamrane (eds) *L'acteur et ses raisons: Mélanges en l'honneur de*

Raymond Boudon. Paris: Presses Universitaires de France, pp. 168-204.

Olson, Mancur (1977) *The Logic of Collective Action: Public Goods and the Theory of Groups*. Cambridge, MA: Harvard University Press.

Schluchter, Wolfgang (1991) *Religion und Lebensführung*, vol. 2: *Studien zu Max Webers Religions-und Herrschaftssoziologie*. Frankfurt am Main: Suhrkamp.

Stark, Rodney (1999) "Micro Foundations of Religion: A Revised Theory", Sociological Theory 17(3): 264-289.

Stark, Rodney and Bainbridge, William Sims (1980) "Towards a Theory of Religion: Religious Commitment", *Journal for the Scientific Study of Religion* 19: 114-128.

–. (1985) *The Future of Religion*. Berkeley: University of California Press.

–. (1989) *A Theory of Religion*. New York: Peter Lang.

Stark, Rodney and Iannaccone, Laurence, R. (1994) "A Supply-Side Reinterpretation of the 'Secularization of Europe' ", *Journal for the Scientific Study of Religion* 33(3): 230-252.

Stolz, Jörg (2007) "Secularization theory and rational choice. An integration of micro- and macro-theories of secularization using the exemple of Switzerland", in Pollack, Detlef and Olson, Daniel V.A. (ed.) *The Role of Religion in Modern Societies*. New York: Routledge, pp. 249-270.

Tyrell, Hartmann (1992) " 'Das Religiöse' in Max Webers Religions-soziologie", *Saeculum* 43: 172-230.

Weber, Max (1920/1978) *Economy and Society: An Outline of Interpretive Sociology*. Berkeley: University of California Press.

–. (1920/1988) *Gesammelte Aufsätze zur Religionssoziologie I*. Tübingen: J.C.B. Mohr (Paul Siebeck).

–. (1922/1985) *Wirtschaft und Gesellschaft*. Tübingen: J.C.B. Mohr.

Steve BRUCE

The Social Limits on Religious Markets

1. Introduction

Until recently most attempts to explain differences in the power, presence and popularity of religion between and within societies have concentrated on the supposed causes of popular demand. Thus the various authors whose work might reasonably be viewed as part of a secularization thesis (Wilson, 1966; Berger, 1969 or Bruce, 1996, for example) have concentrated on explaining why one group of people might be more or less receptive to religion than another. Although those who work in the secularization paradigm often refer to features of religious institutions that might make them more or less successful in inculcating religious belief and satisfying such faith as exists, they suppose that changes in the popularity and power of religion are to be explained by changes in the extent and nature of belief.

Since the 1980s there has been an alternative that eschews talk of demand in favour of observations about supply.[1] In their theory of religion, Stark and Bainbridge (1985; 1987) argue that there are aspects of the human condition (essentially the scarcity of "rewards") that mean people are always in the market for "compensators". Somewhat confusingly compensators can be explanations of why rewards have not been obtained, promises of future rewards, and lesser rewards. As religions can invoke the supernatural, they are superior to

---

1   A book-length presentation of my criticisms of rational choice theory can be found in Bruce (1999). Similar points are made more briefly and elegantly by Bryant (2001). For a collection of essays sympathetic to the approach see Young (1997). For a more balanced assessment see the essays in Jelen (2002).

secular philosophies and therapies in the supply of such compensators. Communism can promise improved standards of living in the next decade; Russian Orthodoxy can promise that the meek shall inherit the earth. Hence the demand for religion should be reasonably high and constant. Thus the large variations we see in the rates of church attendance, church membership, and other indices of interest in religion must reflect differences in supply.

In his association with Roger Finke and Laurence Iannaccone, Stark has since elaborated a more obviously economistic "supply-side" theory of religious behaviour. Taking as his paradigm the supposed virtues of the free market over the regulated economy in meeting and stimulating needs for such consumer goods as cars, Stark argues that differences in religious vitality (usually measured by church membership or church attendance) can be explained by structural features of the religious economy. Where there is a free and competitive market, religious vitality will be high. Where one supplier of religious goods enjoys a monopoly or hegemony, religious vitality will be low. This will especially be the case if the unevenness in market share is caused by state regulation (Finke and Iannaccone, 1993; Finke, 1992; Finke and Stark, 1992; Iannaccone, 1991).

The supply-side model has been subject to considerable testing. Not surprisingly, Finke, Stark and Iannaccone find much evidence to support it, mostly in contemporaneous comparisons of levels of religiosity in parts of the USA with apparently different degrees of religious diversity. Many others have tried to replicate the results and failed: Breault (1989), Bruce (1992; 1995), Chaves and Cann (1992), Land, Deane and Blau (1991), and Olson (1998) fail to find support for what Warner has called the "new paradigm" (1993). In a specific challenge to the supposed supportive findings of early papers which correlated religious diversity and vitality, Voas, Olson, and Crockett (2002) have shown that those results were very largely a statistical artefact. Those who wish to avoid technical statistical arguments can criticise the Stark approach much more simply by noting that the general supply-side claim of a positive connection between the variety of religious products on offer and the amount of "take-up", taken at the level of

European societies, fails to fit the two obvious tests. Generally speaking, are the countries with the greatest variety of religion, the most religious? No. Generally speaking, as countries have become more liberal and more religiously diverse, have they become more religious? No. Stark and his associates make their case with weak correlations between statistics of dubious validity. The counter-case stands on much larger foundations. The differences between contemporary societies run the wrong way: for example, the more homogenous Catholic societies are more religious than the more diverse Protestant ones. The differences over time run the wrong way: Britain has a much freer and much more diverse market in Christian churches in 2000 than it had in 1800 but the proportion of the population at all involved has fallen from at least 60 per cent to about 8 per cent.

In this essay I will consider two specific bodies of work in the US rational choice approach: the supposed defects of hegemonic religion and the treatment of religious as a form of human capital. To summarise my case before I make it, I will argue that the economistic propositions are either implausible or, when they are plausible, they are as easily or better explained by more conventional approaches. In the third part of the essay, I will critically consider the basic principles of economistic analysis and argue that religion has features which make it unsuitable for treatment as a commodity.

The recent extensions of economics into sociology have largely been inspired by the work of Chicago economist Gary Becker, who argues that:

> the economic approach is a comprehensive one that is applicable to all human behavior, be it behavior involving money prices or imputed shadow prices, repeated or infrequent decisions, large or minor decisions, emotional or mechanical ends ... Support for the economic approach is provided by the extensive literature developed in the last twenty years that uses [it] ... to analyse an almost endlessly varied set of problems, including the evolution of language, church attendance, capital punishment, the legal system, the extinction of animals and the incidence of suicide (1986: 112 and 114).

It is also worth repeating Becker's succinct summary of the assumptions underlying the economistic approach to human behaviour. It
assumes first that people engage in "maximising" or "economising"
behaviour: if we can buy an identical product in two shops at different
prices, we will buy the cheaper; second, that there are "markets that
with varying degrees of efficiency co-ordinate the actions of different
participants (...) so that their behavior becomes mutually consistent";
and third, that "prices and other market instruments allocate the scarce
resources within a society" (Becker, 1986: 112).

2. The defects of hegemonic religion

Central to the supply-side model is the belief that, for a wide variety
of reasons, hegemonic religion, especially when it is state-provided,
depresses take-up. Because it derives its power from something other
than popularity (land taxes, for example) hegemonic religion is unre-
sponsive to needs. For example, it is slow to move its resources as
population shifts. And it is slow to change its products as the wishes
or needs of its people change. Because there are no popular checks on
its costs, it is inefficiently expensive (building big cathedrals instead
of small wooden churches, for example). Its officials have little incentive to become or remain popular. In an open market those defects
would be remedied by the formation of dynamic, cheap, and ambitious
religions, keen to serve unmet demands. But hegemonic religion, especially when it is supported by the state, prevents the emergence of
competing and potentially more popular brands of religion. The
existence of a state church will impose artificially high "start-up"
costs on potential alternatives.

There is undoubtedly an element of truth to these general
propositions. It is, for example, not hard to find evidence that the state
churches of England and Scotland (and, contrary to the views of US
rational choice theorists, these were two very different organizations)

were sometimes slow to shift resources as population shifted. Crockett's work on the England and Wales Census of Religious Worship of 1851, pioneering in its statistical sophistication, shows the lowest rates of church attendance in the most urban and the remote rural parishes (1998). While the first finding fits with the secularization expectation that features of modernization undermine religion, the explanation of the second is obviously the sparseness of population and the greater distance from churches; or, to put it in supply terms, the relative scarcity of opportunities to go to church. Where churches are few and very far between, people will find it hard to attend them.

However, when presented as universal laws, the supply-side propositions run into some obvious difficulties. One is that they assume that the laity is passive and can only consume religious goods that are provided for them by the state church. This misses entirely the fact of auto-provision. In the Catholic, Orthodox and Lutheran strands of Christianity (which lay great stress on the church) auto-provision is difficult but in Reformed Protestantism there is no such obstacle. Indeed the history of Christianity in Europe is replete with examples of people engaging in what, if we must maintain economistic metaphors, we could call "subsistence religion". In the highlands of Scotland in the early nineteenth century, people made up for the lack of churches by worshipping in the open air. When Gaelic-speaking ministers were in short supply, prayer meetings were led by lay catechists.

The supply-side case needs to explain why self-provision is less likely to occur in a hegemonic setting than in a free market and here the notion of artificially increased costs becomes central. People are discouraged from meeting their own religious needs by state regulation. This can take a variety of forms from the relatively mild constraints of the current requirements in Russia for religions to be approved by the local government to the severe constraints on personal liberty imposed by on non-conformists by the British state at times in the seventeenth and eighteenth centuries. Again, as with so much of the supply-side story, the point about costs has a certain degree of plausibility but fails to meet so many examples that we cannot accept it as a general principle. It is true that the French drove out the Huguenots. It is true that repression discouraged some waves of British dissent (the more radical sects during the English Civil War, for example) but we can also find many examples of repression back-firing. Far from discouraging his supporters, the treatment of George Fox, the founder of the Quaker movement in England, only made them more determined. That repression in the end failed is clear from modern British history. At the time of the restoration of the Stuart monarchy in the mid-seventeenth century almost all English and Scots people adhered (with varying degrees of enthusiasm) to their state churches. In the 1660s a series of laws were enacted to restrain dissent. The Corporation Act made it impossible for dissenters to hold municipal office, the Act of Uniformity silenced their ministers, the Conventicle Act outlawed meetings of more than five people who were not members of the same family. The Five-Mile Act kept dissenting ministers that distance from any corporate borough and the 1673 Test Act made all civil, naval and military employment dependent on having taken the sacraments in a parish church (Bebb, 1980: 69-71). Yet by the time of the Census of Religious Worship in 1851 dissent had grown to the point where more than half of those who attended a Christian church in England attended something other than the state church.

To summarise, in some circumstances repression works; in other cases it backfires and produces a high degree of commitment. As with so much in economics what looks like a universal law from which predictions can be derived turns out to be a tautology.

One particular lever in the supply-side model is worth considering in some detail because it draws our attention to the difficulty of treating religion as a commodity. One of the major supposed defects of state-provided religion is that security of tenure and income gives the clergy no particular reason to attract a congregation, or having got one, to try to keep it. Stark (1997) says of the German Lutheran clergy that they lack recruiting zeal because, as they are paid out of taxes irrespective of congregation size, they are better off with few adherents, because they get paid the same but have to do less work. It is certainly not hard to find some examples that fit the bill. The figure of the idle cleric who viewed holy office as a sinecure and who regarded flattering his social and ecclesiastical superiors as far more important than meeting the spiritual needs of his flock is familiar from the novels of Jane Austen or Anthony Trollope. Some clerics accepted a large number of offices, took the income and used a very small part of it to pay curates to do their work for them. The general point that the structure of funding and the routes to promotion may lead to goal displacement obviously has some application. But again, we have to doubt that it can stand as a general law.

Consider for a moment the position of a tenured university teacher; Rodney Stark can himself serve as an example. That he is paid irrespective of how many students sign-up to take his classes should, if we apply the general supply-side principles, cause him to teach badly, to discourage potential students, and to be pleased when he becomes so unpopular that his classes are cancelled for lack of demand. If we search our own experience of our colleagues we may find one who fits the self-serving model posited by Stark in his comment on Lutheran pastors. And we will find ten teachers whose pride in their work, whose professionalism, and whose commitment to their discipline leads them to work hard to do their jobs well and to attract students, even when such popularity forces them to work harder for the same returns.

Now let us add the ideological component. Some clergy are doubtless attracted by the secular aspects of the job. Far more are motivated by a sincere religious calling. We can see clear evidence of this in the responses to radical changes within the state churches in England and Scotland. From the Reformation the Christian Church in the British Isles went through periodic upheavals as factions within the Church competed to define its theology and liturgy and as political powers sought to use the Church as an instrument of social control. In Scotland, between the Covenant in 1638 and the Restoration of the Stuart monarchy in 1660, some 210 Episcopalian ministers were deprived of their livings. Under Charles II it was the turn of the Presbyterians to be kicked out of their charges; by 1684, 312 had been deposed (along with a further 63 who lost their parishes under the Test

Act of 1681). Many of those were Episcopalians, penalized by a badly drafted act, but among the Presbyterians was John Veitch of Westruther. He had been deprived in 1662 and then reinstated under the Indulgence and then deposed again in 1681: his humanity and his philosophical attitude to such changes in his employment are well reflected in his remark to successor as he left for the second time. He pointed to the large stack of dried peats (the main source of domestic fuel) and asked him to leave as good a pile when he in turn was deposed (Drummond and Bulloch, 1973: 5). A close knowledge of British church history shows very large numbers of clergy who refused to abandon their beliefs and principles to accord with each change in policy and polity and who suffered repeatedly as a result yet who never lost their faith or their calling. We cannot prove statistically that hegemonic state churches have been staffed far more often by men like Veitch than by men like Stark's caricature Lutheran but we know of enough Veitchs to reject Stark's general principle.

3. Human capital

The presumed connections between the rational choices of actors and the resulting societal patterns are laid out in Laurence Iannaccone "Religious practice: a human capital approach" (1990). He claims that an economistic approach can explain denominational mobility, the typical age of converts, the typical pattern of inter-religious marriage, and the levels of participation found in different sorts of marriages.

The notion of "investment" is used to explain why most American stay in the churches in which they were raised, return to that church if they have drifted away (as they typically do in early adulthood), and, if they move, ideologically travel only short distances. People who have invested a certain amount of human capital (time and effort) in acquiring the beliefs of one tradition and mastering its liturgical or ritual procedures will be reluctant to lose that capital. To move a long way requires a lot of new investment and wastes previous effort. Hence there are not many Baptists becoming Catholics.

Here we have the common phenomenon of a body of data fitting an alternative explanation every bit as well as its fits a human capital approach. We could suppose, as most sociologists of religion have done previously, that beliefs sediment so as to shape our receptivity to future alternatives and that beliefs are associated with enduring identities and supporting communities. That you have held for some time a Baptist view of religion may not stop you ceasing to be religious but makes it likely that, if you remain religious or wish to return to a supernatural faith at some later stage of your life, you will find most *plausible* beliefs that accord with the residues of the earlier stage of belief. Having been a Baptist for a while is likely to make you feel like a Baptist and to be emotionally attached to that identity and community. Using conventional sociological ideas, we can explain the pattern identified by Iannaccone perfectly well without recourse to the contentious idea that religious attachments are shaped by a wish to maximise the return on investment.

Iannaccone believes that data on the typical age at which people experience religious conversion also supports his model:

> The human capital model predicts that religious switching, like job changing, will tend to occur early in the life cycle as people search for the best match between their skills and the context in which they produce religious commodities. Across time, the gains from further switching will diminish as the potential improvement in matches diminishes and the remaining years in which to capitalize on that improvement decrease (1990: 298).

Again, the presented data fit the prediction but the prediction does not test the theory because the same data are readily compatible with a quite different explanation: that the plausibility of beliefs is a product of social interaction with other like-minded believers and the extent to which those beliefs produce a satisfactory understanding of the world and one's place in it. Both of these are likely to produce increased plausibility over time. Fifty-year old Scottish Presbyterians do not become Moonies, not because they have few years left in which the recoup their new investment but because their long involvement with Presbyterianism and with Presbyterians makes them ill-disposed to believe Moon and his representatives.

Like so much of the rational choice approach, the human capital propositions sound plausible in the abstract and unlikely when put into claims about specific people and actions. Iannaccone assumes that beliefs and liturgical practises are hard to learn. Mastering the entire Presbyterian Shorter Catechism will take time but most Christian churches are similar and, as researching sociologists regularly prove, their rituals can very quickly be picked up by imitating the person in the pew in front. Furthermore, Iannaccone regards learning as a cost, which misses the point that it can be viewed as an enjoyable challenge. After all, the main consumers of evening classes are the elderly and retired. Knowing that they do not have enough life left to become another Picasso does not prevent thousands of old people taking up painting.

The explanation of data on the effects of inter-religion marriages is even less persuasive. We know from a variety of sources that where a couple belong to the same church or religious tradition, they are more likely than "mixed" marriages to be regular church attenders, to give money to religious work, to raise their children in the faith, and so on. Iannaccone claims;

> A household can produce religious commodities more efficiently when both husband and wife share the same religion. Single-faith households benefit from "economies of scale": the same car drives everyone to church; there is no question as to how time and money contributions will be allocated to different religions; it is not necessary to debate the religion in which one's children will be reared (1990: 301).

There is no doubt that conflict between spouses about religious beliefs and affiliation can be painful and hence no surprise that people tend to marry within the same denomination: people can imagine the disputes and act to avoid them. But a much simpler explanation of the pattern is that churches provide an excellent venue for meeting young people who are similar not only in religion but in social class, culture and ethnic background.

Better evidence for Iannaccone's model are data that show that shared-faith marriages have higher rates of church attendance than inter-denominational marriages but again, nothing in this especially supports the claim that the pattern arises because partners of the same religion can produce religious commodities more efficiently. When fuel in the US is often cheaper than soft drinks can we really believe that it is the saving that results from the whole family being able to go to church in one car that explains this? There is an obvious alternative. An axiom of sociology is that reality is socially constructed, maintained and changed. To add to one's own internalized beliefs a significant other who reinforces such beliefs will have a profound impact on the strength of one's faith and hence on the enthusiasm with which one participates in collective expressions of such beliefs.

Furthermore, there is a problem with the direction of causality. Iannaccone's data do not establish which of (a) couples sharing the same faith, and (b) extensive religious involvement, comes first. For his model to work, (a) must precede (b) but the reverse is equally, if not more, likely. It is precisely those people who are most committed to their faith who will make a point of considering only fellow-believers as suitable marriage partners.

4. General problems

In the third part of this essay, I want to question the appropriateness of extending the classic assumptions of economics to religious action. I will first identify some central difficulties with the economistic model of human behaviour as being driven by a desire to maximise utility and then consider what distinguishes those fields where the market model works well from those where it does not. To state my conclusion at the outset, I will argue that a rational choice model of religious action would work well only in a largely secular culture.

4.1 Conditions for maximising utility 1 : Comparability

A basic requirement for maximising utility is that we be able to compare alternatives. In choosing between rival brands of soap powder, we can compare the weight in the box or the strength of the powder and thus decide which offers the greatest return. Or we can subscribe to a consumer association which performs such tests for us. But how do we do this with religion? How can we compare the value of being a Jehovah's Witness and being a Catholic? As the veracity of the competing claims made by religions can only be known after death, or on the Day of Judgement, in this life we have no way of knowing which, if any, is correct.

Certain peripheral and secondary aspects of church-going could perhaps be tested against secular alternatives. Going to church could be compared with going to concerts as a way of making friends or meeting potential spouses. We might even be able to test the evangelist's assertion that "getting right with Jesus" will have greater benefits for our mental health than would buying sessions of secular psychotherapy. But even here comparison is difficult because presumably only those who genuinely are converted enjoy the psychological benefits of religious conviction. We cannot pretend to salvation in order to test its this-worldly benefits. So even with peripheral aspects of religious behaviour one of the conditions for maximising utility is absent.

And it is certainly absent for the core of religion. Until death we cannot be sure whether any religion is correct. Or to put it another way, we cannot hedge our bets by buying small amounts of different religions. We can manage soap powder uncertainty by buying some of each of rival brands; we cannot diversify our religious portfolios as a hedge against choosing the wrong God (which, by the way, is why Pascal was wrong about his wager; it assumes there is only one God!).

The obvious difference between soap powder and religion can be seen clearly if we consider the power of ideology to shift perceptions fundamentally. When we change from Daz to Omo, we are not required to believe that Daz is not a soap powder but is actually cement powder. Although many religious adherents can be polite about other religions and it is sometimes the case that one religion will allow that another has an incomplete vision of the truth, most religions require that the claims of competitors be rejected. There is no God but Allah. To an orthodox Catholic, Calvinism is not a comparable alternative: it is the work of Satan.

4.2   The conditions for maximising utility 2: Pricing

If comparing the value or benefits of rival products is one necessary condition for maximising utility, a second is the ability to compare costs. The price of soap powder is expressed and exacted in a common currency. My box of Blobbo soap sachets conveniently tells me how many I will need for what weight of dirty clothes; it also tells me the price. I can thus calculate the cost of using Blobbo. But to talk of the price of religious involvement is stretching a metaphor too far. The metaphor is not salvaged from shipwreck by substituting the shadow price of time for money. How "costly" time spent on some activity is to us depends on the extent to which we find that passage of time rewarding. To one potential member of a Pentecostal church a two hour prayer meeting may be a huge cost; to another it may be a great pleasure.

In brief, the economistic model of human behaviour requires that we be able to assess costs and returns from some neutral standpoint before we make a commitment to one religion rather than another. But the nature of religion does not allow such comparisons and measurements.

4.3 The irrationality of the ideologue

Economists often justify the inaccuracy of their simplistic models of human behaviour by saying that the virtue of assuming maximising utility is that it identifies interesting deviations from the expected but I would argue that in the case of ideologues the extent of deviation is too great to sustain the metaphor.

One obvious deviation is that ideological organizations do not resent free riders; they encourage them. Most churches and denominations welcome people who attend sporadically and make no contribution. Some sectarian movements operate an exclusive notion of membership but they do not do so to prevent their resources being wasted on those who wish the benefits of membership without the costs. They do it to ensure ideological rectitude. The Exclusive Brethren has very few weakly attached associates but this is not because the organization is behaving economically rationally by excluding free riders; it is because the Brethren believe that failure to maintain the right "walk with the Lord" will endanger the salvational status of existing members and misled outsiders as to what is required of the Lord's people.

A further illustration of the deviation from the maximising expectation can be seen in the inflexibility of ideologues. A distributor of Massey-Ferguson tractors who finds sales drying up can switch to selling John Deere tractors. If the agricultural sector collapses, he can get out of tractors altogether, sell his real estate, and invest in foreign currency. In all activities there is inertia but the inertia involved in economic activity is far less than the ideological constraints on what churches can do to become more popular. Lutheran churches may envy the success of Pentecostalism but they cannot readily change their beliefs.

The radical difference between ideologies and consumer products is clearly seen in the way that ideologues respond to failure. Small sects often console themselves by some version of the assertion that their unpopularity just proves they are right. When a supermarket chain's sales fall, the directors did not say "Well, that just proves our clothes are too good for ordinary people" and carry on regardless. Instead, they hire new design teams, change their pricing policies and do their best to win back market share from their competitors.

4.4 *Cultural contraints on consumers*

It is also the case that maximising behaviour of consumers is also constrained by culture (and its embodiment in social relationships). Religious affiliation is so often closely associated with other forms of social identity that most people are not free to maximise by switching. In Kosovo or Bosnia, religious affiliation is not a matter of personal preference that you can alter at will and in which you can seek opportunities to maximise your utility. It is a matter of communal identity and those who change religion will often find themselves ostracised from their community or worse. People are not shunned or murdered for changing car brands; in many countries they are shunned, expelled or killed for switching religion.

There are few religious cultures where switching is commonplace and even in extremely tolerant societies radical alternation of religion is likely to threaten social relationships. Even in Scotland, such a secular society that little hangs on religious affiliation, leaving the Free Church for the Free Presbyterian Church may cause family members to shun each other. But for a Protestant to become a Muslim will require that most of his social world be restructured: which is why such conversions are extremely rare.

The point seems so obvious one feels almost embarrassed to spell it out but as it is central to the religious market model, we should do so: in most societies religious affiliation is not an individual preference.

To prevent misunderstanding, I should state at this point that I am not arguing against the idea that human behaviour is rational. It is unfortunate that the Starkian approach to religious behaviour has been dubbed "rational choice" because it makes opponents appear to be arguing against the rationality of human action. It is perfectly proper that we should assume action to be minimally rational until we have very good grounds for arguing that, in any particular case, it is not. We can go further and argue that, were social action not minimally rational, we would not be able to identify, comprehend, and explain it. What I am questioning is the narrow assertion that economic rationality, with utility maximising set at the level of the freely choosing individual, provides a useful model for understanding religious belief and behaviour. There is nothing at all irrational about conforming to social mores, obeying laws, or supporting communal traditions.

To summarise thus far: economistic or rational choice models of behaviour depend on us knowing what is the rational choice. When faced with the possibility of buying the same breakfast cereal from two outlets, it would be economically irrational not to compare the prices and buy the cheaper. But, as Jon Elster puts it: "To the extent that we cannot tell, or cannot tell uniquely, what the rational choice would be, the theory fails ... In a word rational-choice theory can fail because it does not tell us what rationality requires" (Elster, 1986: 17).

5. Where do markets work?

The rational choice model explains well some forms of action. I am persuaded that it offers a viable approach to understanding the sales of automobiles, for example. So we can return to the observations I have just made and put the same points in positive terms. The model of the maximising individual works best when there is widespread and general demand for a product; when costs and values can be assessed from a neutral standpoint that does not change fundamentally at the point of choice; and when there is very little brand loyalty: that is, when the matter in hand is a personal choice that is little encumbered by enduring and powerful social identities. For example, almost everyone wants personal transportation. We can assess the costs and rewards of one model of car against another. And, although my friends might poke fun at me if I swapped my dull saloon car for a flash sports model, my class, tribal, religious, ethnic, or national identities are not dependent on a particular car brand. Now it may well be that religion in the United States is like that: a strong general preference for people having a religion but within very broad limits (even Mormonism is now mainstream) no one much cares what it is. That might explain why American scholars are much more attracted to the rational choice approach than their European counterparts.

But most religion is not like that. Most people are born into a faith at the same time as they are born into a nation, a race, and a language group. In very many settings changing religion is not possible because it means being disloyal to your family, race and nation. We only have to consider the recent example of the wars in the former Yugoslavia to appreciate why very very few Slovenes and Croats see conversion to either Islam or to the Orthodox strand of Christianity as a maximising opportunity. Where religion, ethnicity and nationalism are closely linked (and that is generally the human condition) religion cannot be treated as a consumer preference.

Even where a change of religion does not necessarily involved defecting to the enemy, religious monocultures may treat deviation as a mark of disloyalty. Eileen Barker's case studies of new religious movements in Armenia offer a clear illustration of this point. She tells the story of Armenian friends dismissing as "aliens" those who join NRMs. When she pointed out that they had Armenian surnames and Armenian parents, she was told: "They are no longer Armenians!".[2]

And even in the USA religious choice is somewhat constrained by powerful social identities. One of the major faults of Stark, Finke and Iannaccone's claimed demonstrations of a positive correlation between religious diversity and religious commitment is that they exaggerate diversity by counting black and white versions of sects and denominations as alternatives. In a world that is still sufficiently ra-

---

2   I am grateful to Eileen Barker for telling me this story and for many years of inspiration.

cially divided for only some 6 per cent of marriages to cross the racial divide, this is a mistake. They make a related mistake in treating ethnic and linguistic variants of a single tradition as alternatives. Adding a Swedish language Lutheran church to a town does little or nothing to increase the options for non-Swedes.

6. Conclusion

All of this brings me to an ironic conclusion. The proponents of the rational choice or economistic model of human behaviour believe that it can explain both the micro-social behaviour of individual religious belief and behaviour and comparative societal patterns of religiosity. If the observations I have made above are at all plausible, we must conclude that it is only when it is least needed that the model works. It is only in a fairly thoroughly secular society that religion can be treated as a commodity, the consumption of which can be explained by the assumption of maximising utility. The validity of rational choice models of religion is not a small methodological quarrel but goes right to the heart of the nature of religious belief and of social science. If we consider what sort of society it would be in which economic models of religious behaviour worked well, the answer must be one in which religion (the supreme producer of cultural limitations on economizing) no longer matters much.

References

Bebb, Evelyn D. *(1980) Nonconformity and Social and Economic Life, 1660-1800.* Philadelphia, PA: Porcupine Press.

Becker, Gary (1986) "The Economic Approach to Human Behavior", in J. Elster (ed.) *Rational Choice.* Oxford: Basil Blackwell, pp. 108-122.

Berger, Peter L. (1969) *The Social Reality of Religion.* London: Faber.

Breault, Kevin D. (1989) "New Evidence on Religious Pluralism, Urbanism, and Religious Participation", *American Sociological Review,* 54: 1048-53.

Bruce, Steve (1992) "Pluralism and Religious Vitality", in S. Bruce (ed.) *Religion and Modernization.* Oxford: Oxford University Press, pp. 170-94.

–. (1995) "A novel reading of nineteenth century Wales: a Reply to Stark, Finke and Iannaccone", *Journal for the Scientific Study of Religion* 34: 520-22.

–. (1996) *Religion in the Modern World: From Cathedrals to Cults.* Oxford: Oxford University Press.

Bryant, Joseph M. (2001) "Cost-benefit Accounting and the Piety Business: Is Homo Religiosus, at Bottom, a Homo Economicus?", *Method and Theory in the Study of Religion,* 12: 520-48.

Chaves, Mark and Cann, David E. (1992) "Regulation, Pluralism and Religious Market Structure", *Rationality and Society* 4: 272-290.

Crockett, Alasdair (1998) "A Secularising Geography? Patterns and Processes of Religious Change in England and Wales, 1676-1851", unpublished Ph.D. thesis, University of Leicester.

Drummond, Andrew L. and Bulloch, James (1973) *The Scottish Church 1688-1843.* Edinburgh: St Andrew Press.

Elster, Jon (ed.). (1986) *Rational Choice.* Oxford: Basil Blackwell.

Finke, Roger (1992) "An Unsecular America", in S. Bruce (ed.), *Religion and Modernization: Sociologists and Historians Debate the Secularization Thesis.* Oxford: Oxford University Press, pp. 145-169.

Finke, Roger and Iannaccone, Laurence (1993) Supply-side explanations for religious change. *Annals of the American Academy of Political and Social Science* 527: 27-39.

Finke, Roger and Stark, Rodney (1992) *The churching of America, 1776-1990: winners and losers in our religious economy*. New Brunswick: Rutgers University Press.

Iannaccone, Laurence (1990) "Religious Practice: a Human Capital Approach", *Journal for the Scientific Study of Religion,* 29: 297-314.

–. (1991) "The Consequences of Religious Market Structure", *Rationality and Society,* 3: 156-177.

Jelen, Ted G. (ed.) (2002) *Sacred Markets, Sacred Canopies: Essays on Religious Markets and Religious Pluralism*. Lanham, MD: Rowan and Littlefield.

Land, Kenneth C., Deane, Glenn and Blau, Judith R. (1991) "Religious pluralism and church membership", *American Sociological Review* 56: 237-49.

Olson, Daniel V. A. (1998) "Religious pluralism in contemporary US counties", *American Sociological Review* 63: 757-61.

Stark, Rodney (1997) "German and German-American Religiousness", *Journal for the Scientific Study of Religion* 36: 182-193.

Stark, Rodney and Bainbridge, William S. (1985) *The Future of Religion*. Berkeley: University of California Press.

–. (1987) *A Theory of Religion*. New York: Peter Lang.

Voas, David, Olson, Daniel V. A. and Crockett, Alasdair (2002) "Religious Pluralism and Participation: Why Previous Research is Wrong", *American Sociological Review* 67 (2): 212-30.

Warner, R. Stephen (1993) "Work in progress toward a new paradigm for the sociological study of religion in the United States", *American Journal of Sociology* 98: 1044-93.

Wilson, Bryan (1966) *Religion in Secular Society*. London: CA Watts.

Young, Lawrence A. (1997) *Rational Choice Theory and Religion*. London: Routledge. 26.

Pierre-Yves BRANDT

Integration or Individuation: Are the Salvation Goods Promised by First-Century Christian Preaching Still Attractive?

1. Introduction

Christianity expanded very rapidly at the beginning of our era. Today, in the West, Christianity is contracting. How can we explain this contrast? In terms of salvation goods, the question concerns understanding what could have comprised the attractiveness of Christian preaching. In addition, it concerns understanding what could have increased its attractiveness compared with other religious trends of the first-century Greco-Roman world, so that Christian communities experienced such growth in the first and second centuries[1], while many are declining today in our industrialized societies.

In the present paper, firstly, my purpose is to make evident the salvation goods that made Christian preaching especially attractive in the first-century. To clarify this point, I will take support from the sociological analyses led by Gerd Theissen, a specialist of the socio-cultural context where Christianity emerged. His works are, in my view, the most complete on this subject, because based on the most recent sociological theories and firmly rooted in the examination of classical sources documenting what we can know of the various trends present in Greco-Roman antiquity and, more specifically, in the Hellenistic world. On this basis, I will pay special attention to the

---

[1] Even if Stark (1996: 3-13) rightly shows that the numerical presence of the Christians must not have become tangible in the Empire until the beginning of the third century.

psychological benefits ensuing, for the individual, from the appropriation of the salvation goods promised by these different trends.

This will lead me, secondly, to discuss the contextual character of the attractiveness of a good: what could appear as a salvation good in the first century does not necessarily do so today. The explanation for this shift between the beginning of the Common Era and the present begins with the observation that the manner of constructing individual identity has changed. The salvation goods conveyed by first-century Christian preaching promised a gain in social integration. These salvation goods retain their attractiveness today for a good many people on the planet, including in the West. However, in our secularized societies, the majority of citizens, most of them coming from traditionally Christian families, can access these salvation goods without having to belong to a religious institution. That is why, for them, a Christian preaching that offers increased social status through belonging to a religious group has lost a great deal of its attractiveness.

My aim, thirdly, is to identify those salvation goods sought today, chiefly in the West. Without any claim to exhaustivity, I will in the process mention some psychological benefits found in the religious by our contemporaries. This paper thus adopts an approach that combines historical, comparative, sociological and psychological viewpoints to clarify how the social milieu influences whether or not a salvation good is desirable for a given individual at a given time.

2. Salvation goods promised by the first-century Christian preaching

Gerd Theissen sees in the preaching of the original Christianity the expression of a humanist view of the human being in the sense that it "confers on the latter an intangible value independent of his or her social role" (1996: 228). In the first and second centuries, such an approach was not exclusive to Christian preaching. Sharing it were certain strands of Judaism, from which Christianity issued, and Stoic philosophers of the imperial period such as Seneca, Musonius, Epictetus and Marcus Aurelius, together with peripatetic philosophers of cynical tendency such as Dio Chrysostom or the Platonist Plutarch.

Theissen notes that the humanism of biblical origin (Jewish or Christian) and philosophical humanism "were relatively independent from one another", while each remained "in tension with important antagonistic forces" (1996: 230) both within Judaism, where ethno-centric withdrawal and a rejection of Hellenism found expression, and among supporters of the imperial institutions based on the devalorisation of barbarians, slaves and women.

The common point between these different humanist currents is that they offer their followers access to values and status reserved, according to the principles of Greco-Roman civil society, for a few very restricted elites. In terms of the religious market, these different trends can therefore be considered competitors. However, they do not all have the same understanding of the discriminative barriers that can be crossed, nor do they all have the same concept of the conditions to fulfil in order to cross them. Four separations are pertinent: one, be-tween a member of the population and a foreigner (i.e. Greek opposed to barbarian, or Jew opposed to pagan); two, between a free man and a slave; three, between a man and a woman; and four, between the privilege of divinity attributed to the emperor and the common mortal. Let us briefly consider these four areas.

Concerning *acceptance of foreigners*, philosophical humanism, while affirming that any human being is a citizen of the world, retains strong prejudices with regard to barbarians (Theissen, 1996: 239). In parallel, in Judaism, Philo can say that he who obeys the *Torah* "obeys the natural law common to all men and is henceforth a true citizen of the world" (1996: 241), while affirming that "the dispersal of men among many peoples can be overcome only if all turn toward this one God and toward his Law" (1996: 241).

Concerning *attitude to slaves*, Seneca grants them family commu-nity on condition that they are worthy of it, while for Paul "it is not the morality of man, but his redemption, that founds the equality of principle of any man" (1996: 234-235). Practically, the Christian communities offer slaves social integration not only inside the family community but also outside it, in the ecclesial community. In Judaism, the Essenes go even further since, it seems, they refuse to perpetuate the status of slave within their community (1996: 236).

Furthermore, "the rejection of the divinization of the emperor is firmly rooted only in the biblical traditions, while Stoic philosophy shows only some reservations. Inversely, gender equality finds more convincing expression in philosophy" (Theissen, 1996: 244).

Beyond these differences, the main characteristic that emerges from the analysis of salvation goods promised by first-century Christian preaching is that this preaching offers *broad social strata of the population* salvation goods that remain reserved for privileged circles by other strands of Judaism or philosophers of Greco-Roman antiquity. In other words, if these other trends offer an opening, it remains limited. According to the case, women or slaves gain access to certain prerogatives, but only if they are Jews; slaves and foreigners gain acceptance, but only if they show proof of great morality; or again, women gain some status, but only if they are part of the social elite. Compared with other minor sub-cultures like Judaism or certain philosophical schools, Christianity appears in contrast as "Judaism for non-Jews" or "philosophy for the uneducated" (Theissen, 1996: 269). This permitted Paul to write, "There is neither Jew nor Greek, there is neither slave nor free, there is neither male nor female; for you are all one in Christ Jesus. And if you are Christ's, then you are Abraham's offspring, heirs according to promise".[2]

In this line, first-century Christian preaching proceeds to attribute status that obviously contradicts the social reality of its members. The fact that it can allow itself this, according to Theissen, results from a major difference between philosophical and biblical humanism. Philosophical humanism establishes the value of the human being

---

2   Gal 3: 28-29. *The Holy Bible, Revised Standard Version: An Ecumenical Edition.* Glasgow: Collins, 1973. Biblical abbreviations and quotations in the present paper come from this translation.

intrinsically. "Each person contains part of the divine reason that makes him capable of moral action" (1996: 245). The value of the human being is already given; it need only be recognized and implemented. Nevertheless, the effective attribution of the status that flows from this value depends on its implementation. The degree of (moral) attainment of the individual will enable him to gain access to an elite status.

In contrast, Jews and Christians establish the value of the human being extrinsically: it is God-given. Consequently, it "can be claimed independently of the effective state of man and even in clear contradiction to this state. Even the value of a sinner can equal that of an honest man if God so wills. Love can address even the enemy, because God shines his light on both the good and the bad. Precisely this attribution of value, contrary to the real, characterizes the biblical traditions. It concerns not only the inner (moral and religious) value of man, but also his social status. It permits attributions of status that run counter to reality" (Theissen, 1996: 245).

That is why, in primitive Christianity, we find at the same time a conformist tendency to make Christians "the best citizens, wives and slaves by the standards of the time" and "indications of a 'revolution of values' in which small people appropriate values and attitudes of the upper class." (Theissen, 1999: 10).

These attributions of status running counter to reality comprise an essential part of first-century Christian preaching. Borrowed from the biblical tradition as understood by various strands of first-century Judaism, this vision was to be very widely generalized by Christian preaching, in particular the Paulinian current, and reach many types of the underprivileged. For this reason, the first Christian communities[3] in Greco-Roman society "grew deep roots in the lower classes" (Theissen, 1996: 276) and "remained very distant from the imperial elite that judged the new faith in an unanimously negative manner" (Theissen, 1996: 277). Yet they penetrated the local elites in a qualified manner, in that "most high-ranking Christians nevertheless

---

3   Theissen (1996: 276) draws these conclusions from studying the three
    communities: Corinth, Rome and Carthage.

belonged to the periphery, fringe of the local elite, that was excluded from the communal duties because it included women, foreigners or freed slaves"[4] (Theissen, 1996: 277). Adherence to Christian preaching provided these marginalized people with the promise of salvation goods that in principle were forever inaccessible.

This preaching of course takes support on that of Jesus, which already promised the Kingdom of heaven to the poor (Mt 5: 3), children, and even foreigners, who will, Jesus announces, sit at the table with Abraham, Isaac and Jacob (Mt 8: 11f). This attribution of status to those socially excluded from it goes together, in the preaching of Jesus, with a call to those who have status to renounce it and make themselves the servants of all. This did not fail to create some tensions in the nascent Christian communities, because the high-ranking Christians, who came from the fringe of the local elite and comprised a minority in these communities, nevertheless exerted a strong influence on the majority, who came from the lower social classes. This situation thus reproduced inside the community the discriminations that Christian preaching presented as overcome.

Therefore, these salvation goods promised by the Christian preaching of the first and second centuries are primarily those accompanying access to a status hitherto reserved for the elites. In context of the Greco-Roman world, this mainly concerns power, wealth and wisdom (Theissen, 1996: 246, 1999: 81-107). To these we can add holiness, in context of the Jewish subculture. Considering the barrier between Jews and non-Jews, we can understand it as separating the chosen people who enjoyed the privilege of membership in holy elite and the significance of eliminating that barrier (Theissen, 1999: 107-117).[5]

We can show in detail how Christian preaching promises all these goods to those who follow its message. As for access to power, be-

---

4   Should we perhaps say "public duties" rather than "communal duties"?

5   This concerns four goods: "History can be regarded as a struggle over the distribution of opportunities in life, which time and again is about four goods: the distribution of rule and possessions on the one side and the distribution of education and normative power on the other" (Theissen, 1999: 82).

lievers are declared citizens of heaven (Phil 3: 20), the adopted sons and heirs of God (Rom 8: 14-17), and members of his family; for wealth, they are the keepers of the treasures in heaven; for wisdom, they are the wise, while the wise of this world are declared mad (1 Cor 1: 26-31).

The promised access to these goods goes together, in Christian preaching, with justification of the deviant forms of behavior that ensue from support for its preaching. Deviant behavior necessarily expresses the gain in power received from inclusion in God's family. Theissen insists on this point: "The interpretation the Christians gave of their deviant behavior plays a decisive role: it was allegiance to a celestial *polis* of which they were citizens and which, like an earthly city, had the right, in case of conflict, to demand their life. Here below, that is, in the given society, Christians were *by principle* 'foreigners' or metiks" (Theissen, 1996: 289).[6]

Just as the emperor had his social clientele, all the Christians, in fact, knew they were bound by a special allegiance (personal charismatic) to their Lord. They are his *familia*, his 'house', his 'soldiers', his 'slaves' and his 'freed slaves' (Theissen, 1996: 278). In the Empire, to eat at the table of the *kurios* gave access to the privileges of the imperial family. When the new member of a Christian community experienced welcome to the "Lord's supper" (1 Cor 11: 17-34), the equivalence is clear.[7] Similarly, in the relationship with Judaism, the table fellowship associating Jews and non-Jews illustrates very well that "Over wide areas primitive Christianity is universalized Judaism" (Theissen, 1999: 13).[8] "His table fellowship with the marginalized among the people anticipates the great eschatological table fellowship of the restored people in which Gentiles from all over the world will

---

6 The emphasis is mine.

7 For more details on this analogy, see also Theissen, 1999: 53-54.

8 Regarding themes common to Judaism and Christianity, one mainly concerns the question of status: neighborly love. "If love of neighbor is love between equals, it can be realized only by a renunciation of their superiority by those who are superior and a revaluation of the status of the lowly, in other words by humility and renunciation of status." (Theissen, 1999: 14). On the expansion of neighborly love, cf. also Theissen, 1999: 64-66.

take part – contrary to nationalistic expectations (Mt 8: 11f.)"
(Theissen, 1999: 36-37).[9]

3. Psychological benefits of support for first-century Christian preaching

In his work on the religion of the first Christians, Gerd Theissen offers
a definition of religion. There he specifies the place of the psychological dimension: it comprises an aspect of the function of religion.

> Religion is a cultural sign system which promises *a gain in life by correspond-
> ing to an ultimate reality.*... In religion, a gain in life is often to be understood in
> a very tangible way, above all as health and help. One need think only of the
> miracle stories and healing charisma in primitive Christianity. However, often
> religions promise something more sublime in addition: a life in truth and love, a
> gain in identity in the crises and changes of life – even the promise of eternal
> life. The study of religion investigates above all the psychological and social
> gain in life, i.e. the function of religion in individual and social life. In the *psy-
> chological* function of religion, we can distinguish cognitive, emotional and
> pragmatic functions (Theissen, 1999: 7).

Without going into detail, let us simply note that Theissen insists
on the fact that "It is important for us to rid ourselves of any one-sided
definition of the function of religion. It does not just serve to stabilize
thought, feeling and action; it does not just serve to surmount crises.
There can also be 'a gain in life' in the exposure of people to serious
upheavals, in their being purified by 'trials' and 'temptations' and
achieving a new life" (Theissen, 1999: 9). In other words, religion
operates in a triple manner: it is an ordering force, it helps to surmount
crises, and it provokes crises. These three manners are, moreover,
distinctly applicable to the cognitive aspect, the emotional aspect, and
the pragmatic aspect of the psychological function of religion
(Theissen, 1999: 7-9). Besides the psychological functions of religion,

---

9   See also Theissen, 1999: 27, point 2.

Theissen further distinguishes two social functions: the function of socialization and the function of conflict regulation (1999: 9-10).[10]

My paper, until now, has striven to identify the people *for whom* belonging to the Christian faith was attractive in the first century of our era: strata of the population who thereby gained symbolic social status. Let us now consider the psychological benefits of this gain. From a psychological viewpoint, this gain of symbolic social status results in a gain of identity and self-esteem (slaves ate at the same table as masters; they are called citizens of heaven, etc.). If we return to the three aspects of the psychological function, the gain in identity concerns simultaneously the cognitive and pragmatic aspects. In other words, on the cognitive plane, the individual accesses new self-understanding. The various metaphors borrowed from the sphere of the political elites and that of the Jews, applied generally to all the faithful, provide a conceptual system enabling the individual to construct a new self-image. On the emotional level, the increased self-esteem helps construct feelings of confidence and security. On the pragmatic level, a new *ethos* is legitimated. This *ethos* results in attitudes and behaviors that, outside this context, would appear transgressive, such as, for example, a certain familiarity with people who belong to another social category but are members of the same Christian community.[11]

These gains, however, are not acquired on an individual basis. In this sense, their access is not dissociated from social function. These gains are simultaneously acquired by all supporters of Christian preaching. In other words, the psychological benefits are mediated by

---

10   In Theissen, 1999: 305, the author describes potential tasks for a psychology and sociology of the primitive Christian religion. For the psychological approach, see especially Theissen, 1999: 79-80.

11   Theissen insists on the fact that, contrary to pagan religions or to Judaism, which appear as established on ancestral tradition, "Christianity developed an autonomous sign system which was international, exclusive and new." (1999: 209). This system is particularly new in the sense that it gives access to "… a new form of social life to which one converted by departing from the ancestral traditions" (1999: 209). This form of social life is characterized by its radical ethos.

belonging to a specific group. This results from a fundamental difference between how an individual's construction of identity was considered during the classical period in the Mediterranean area and how it is conceived today in the West.[12] Overall, the antique model of the world in which Christianity emerged, a model characterizing most of the Christian groups, is that of a specific identity characteristic of the group and access to this identity by belonging to that group. Therefore, the group gives identity; gaining a new identify is by access to the group possessing it. Today, in the West, the dominant model is that of a specific identity attributed to the individual. This opposition has consequences that have been analyzed in detail elsewhere (Brandt, 2002).

3.1 Different types of life gains

In his definition of religion, Theissen also mentions, among the life gains that a religion can promise, a life in truth and love or the promise of an eternal life. In addition to the more sublime realities on which we cannot linger here, he discusses the promise of more tangible realities like the promise of health and help. Moreover, he comments on this point by explicitly referring to the miracle stories and the charisma of healing in primitive Christianity. However, contrary to what may characterize, in a more recent period, the success of certain Christian charismatic groups, we must not see in the healing received by some of those who met Jesus or his disciples a salvation good specifically sought by the followers of the Christian faith. Two reasons account for this. First, healing is a salvation good offered by different religious currents of the period and not necessarily more accessible in the Jesus movement. Secondly, in the teaching of Jesus,

---

12   Thus, I am here discussing the dominant models of personality in these two
      contexts. There are, in each context, alternative, marginalized models. It would
      be necessary to analyze in detail the disputes of certain classical philosophical
      schools. Similarly, today in the West, there are minority groups that adopt
      modes of organization of a traditional type.

the emphasis is not on healing; whenever healing is granted, it signifies the surpassing of social exclusion.

4. Do the salvation goods attractive in the first century still offer the same psychological benefits today?

Let us now focus on the contemporary period and see if the salvation goods promised in first-century Christian preaching still have attractiveness today. To treat this question as a whole, it would be necessary to consider different areas of the world in succession in order to appreciate the differences. I shall remain content with some brief general remarks and then provide in detail some observations of a psychological nature that relate principally to Western societies.

4.1 General remarks

1) In contemporary Western societies, the groups that convey Christian preaching are often more conservative in maintaining barriers of discrimination than society as a whole. This is especially true of discrimination between men and women. With regard to accepting foreigners or mixing people who come from the upper elites with those who come from the lower social strata, the Christian communities of our Western societies do not appear as distinctly more capable of offering ways to abolish these discriminations. Under these conditions, the preaching has no chance of having the same type of attractiveness as in the first-century.

2) On the other hand, there are regions in the world where support for Christian preaching permits surmounting certain discriminative barriers through access to a new social status. This can certainly explain, for example, that religious congregations (Benedictines, Franciscans, Hospitallers, etc.) which have difficulty surviving in the

West include, in parallel, a high number of vocations in their estab-
lishments in Africa or Asia. Through this, young women can
legitimately gain freedom from family obligations; men and women
can gain access to studies and, for some of them, the right to pursue
their life in Europe or the United States. In other words, where the
social situation shows analogies with that of the first-century, the attractiveness of Christian preaching can function on the model that
presided at its beginning.

3) In addition, this may explain the success of certain Black
American evangelical groups, where racial discrimination combined
with economic discrimination seems to place access to higher social
status completely beyond reach. Here we meet again a mode of functioning certainly characteristic of many marginalized groups in
Western societies.

Let us now concentrate on salvation goods that, in the dominant
contemporary discourse of the West, take on a function comparable to
that of goods promised in the first century by Christian preaching.

5. Salvation goods sought today in the West

In my attempt to characterize these desired salvation goods, I will
essentially underline those sought in the religious sphere and the psychological benefits expected of them.

To appreciate the cultural gap in this respect that separates our
modern societies from those of the first-century Mediterranean area,
the analyses developed by anthropologist David Le Breton starting
from a study of risk-taking behaviors, in particular among contemporary young Westerners, are very informative. "To put oneself through
a trial, in an individual way, is one of the modern ways to crystallize
identity, when everything else is slipping away" (2002: 117), he
writes. He reads in what he calls "an unusual passion for risk" (Le
Breton, 1994: 81) an attempt to construct, in our Western societies, the

equivalent of new rites of passage, whose significance would be attributed individually. "To speak of an individual rite of passage for today's young generations is to speak of recourse to a clandestine and solitary form of symbolization of the taste for living. This is an individual rite of passage, to the extent that the act is unique, that it has value only for the person who dares it, that the individual is not always clear about the goal of his quest, and that he in no way changes, if he survives, his social status" (Le Breton, 2002: 116). All these characteristics distinguish these individual rites from the rites of passage practiced in traditional societies.

This analysis of risk-taking conduct pinpoints the profound transformation produced when the social structure leaves the traditional mode and adopts an individualistic one. At that time, "the actor increasingly tends to determine on his own initiative the values on which he wants to base his existence.... Each actor is then projected into a strongly individualized quest for meaning" (Le Breton, 1994: 81). We can then understand that, in our Western societies, the individual does not primarily expect a religious system to provide him with the means to gain social status and its associated values, but rather to reassure him of his own worth.[13] "The sacred as created by contemporary societies is an untamed energy that the Churches, losing influence, no longer govern. It is a type of raw material to tame, still free, whose spirit can fill the actor with a pervasive feeling of fulfillment and exaltation, producing an intense experience giving a taste for transcendence and perfection. The sacred is an individual value and projection, subject in this sense to the hazards of personal peculiarities" (Le Breton, 1994: 85).

In this sense, salvation does not first appear, for the majority of our Western contemporaries, as an offer enabling them to access individual and social status from which they would otherwise be excluded, but as the range of resources that can be put at the individual's disposal to construct the self. Where the sacred "released from

---

13   "Producer of his own identity, the individual is nevertheless subject to the approval of others in order to assure himself of his own worth." (Le Breton, 1994: 82).

the great systems ... begins to fragment according to the rhythms of contemporary individualism" (Le Breton, 1994: 85), the individual must confront the obligation to self-determine what can preserve the cohesion of his identity. To the extent that such a task puts intensive demands on individual skills, the analysis of these skills includes an obvious psychological dimension: they depend on both the intra-psychological structuration and the manner of belonging to a network of social relationships. The intra-psychological structuration supports the capacity to maintain internal psychological cohesion (emotional contents, affective conflicts, contradictory ideas) and the capacity to be in relationship with another who is not oneself (communication abilities, including the perceptive, expressive, and linguistic, and more broadly, mastery of a cultural system, together with the capacity to manage an object investment in a psychodynamic perspective). As for the manner of belonging to a network of social relationships, it is determined by the individual and the group. To describe it, one must consider conjointly both the individual and the group that includes him.[14]

Let us now consider what has just been said by means of the concept of salvation goods (and rational choice). Based on the analysis of the main problem facing our Western contemporaries, as soon as they support the individualistic structure of society, and insofar as this analysis is correct, salvation appears as *access to a stable individual construction of the self.* (Here we are not concerned about whether such a construction can indeed be the result of an individual rather than a collective undertaking. Whether we consider that we are here dealing with a pure fantasy or an achievable task manifesting the autonomy made accessible by modernity, the important thing is to know if the belief in the possibility of attaining such an individual self-construction is socially shared and desired. The following thoughts take the latter as an established fact.) From this angle, we can designate as salvation goods a set of means or resources that permit

---

14   For this task, the viewpoint of the psychologist is indissociable from that of the anthropologist (in the sense of cultural anthropology).

achieving this goal, this salvation: *the individual construction of a stable self.*

Let us try to designate what could be considered salvation goods from this viewpoint. This list is not exhaustive, but only shows how the psychology of religion can contribute to identifying these salvation goods. More precisely, and to remain in the context of a study related to religious markets, we will limit ourselves to goods explicitly characterized, by those referring to them, as religious. Various recent publications mention the psychological advantages associated with the fact of belonging to a religious group or following religious beliefs, and this precisely when, as the works published by Campiche show (2004), institutional religiosity is giving way to universal religiosity (in particular 2004: 41-48). These advantages can be interpreted as reinforcing psychological integrity, supporting or favoring individuation, where social integration is no longer enough to guarantee a stable identity. To mention a distinction put forth by Max Weber, we can locate advantages of this type at the level of common religiosity and at the level of religiosity for virtuosos (1920: 260).

5.1 At the level of common religiosity

The advantage can be considered from the standpoint of health. Several studies on ageing foreground this aspect. Thus, in a study on the factors favoring the health of older individuals, Lalive d'Epinay and Spini (2004) observe the importance of the religious factor. Similarly, McNamara, Andresen and Gellard (2003) confirm earlier works according to which older individuals who pray feel they are in better health. Previously, Atkinson and Malony (1994) had already shown that religion tempers the psychological distress resulting from stressful events in older individuals. In other words, religion helps older individuals to meet the problems connected with ageing. The fact of this help was established much more broadly by many studies on coping (Pargament, 1997), in other words, the set of strategies implemented by individuals and their social environment to deal with trials.

Among these strategies, we can mention recourse to beliefs. A review of several studies on the role of beliefs during a period of bereavement shows, for example, that religious beliefs reduce stress and facilitate acceptance of the loss by enabling the individual to understand the death more coherently (Benore and Park, 2004). In the context of our analysis of the current attractiveness of the religious, we could say that certain religious beliefs can appcar as salvation goods for people in bereavement.

This does not mean that it is easy to predict which beliefs will be perceived as helpful for a given person. A set of theories and works on the relationships between faith and health (Plante and Sherman, 2001) indicates that we must take into consideration great interindividual variability. Indeed, flowing from these works is that, in terms of "rational choice", individual differences must be taken into account (life stage, personality type) along with contextual factors (culture, socioeconomic status, crisis): according to the combination of these factors, aspects characterizing faith (i.e. motivations, behaviors, personal commitment) either favor or do not favor health. Research in progress (Huguelet, Mohr, Borras, Gillièron and Brandt, 2006) on the connections between religiosity and psychological health leads to the same conclusion. Considering this interindividual variability, it nevertheless appears that religious belonging or the fact of having religious convictions is, in certain situations, an advantage to getting through a crisis or problem.

In other words, in terms of salvation goods, we are here at the most elementary level of the goods stated by Weber: health, longevity and wealth (1920: 249); or, as Theissen puts it, "health and help" (1999: 7). The association between health and help is explained to the extent that help includes the means received to deal with stress and thus guarantees psychological health. From this angle, the religious dimension is primarily considered as helpful. However, helpful for what? We could say, in this context of coping in the contemporary West, for maintaining psychological equilibrium. Salvation would be, in this sense, to escape madness or, at least, psychological suffering (depression, decompensation).

5.2 At the level of religiosity for "virtuosos"

Moreover, certain works address forms of religiosity that Weber describes as reserved for people who make an intense personal investment in them. Here, the salvation goods correspond rather to seeking a 'life surplus'. Two examples will serve as illustrations. Each case concerns attaining a feeling of well-being.

First, in their study Byrd, Lear and Schwenka (2000) ask whether mysticism predicts the subjective feeling of well-being. The idea is that one advantage, the feeling of well-being, could be associated with the fact of having previous experiences characterized as mystical. This mystical dimension is measured by means of three distinct scales. Extroverted mysticism covers the experiences of the unity of everything, including the self with everything. Introverted mysticism covers the experiences of being absorbed into a great whole or of everything disappearing from thought until conscious of nothing but emptiness. Mysticism understood as a religious interpretation covers the situations where people claim to have experienced that ultimate reality was revealed to them or that they themselves were sacred. One hundred and fifty students from the University of Nebraska were invited to fill in questionnaires on these three aspects of mysticism together with questionnaires on their feeling of well-being (they are asked if they are satisfied with their life as a whole, their life orientation, and their religious life). When the three measures of mysticism are taken as a whole, the prediction is rather positive. However, once we examine the results in detail, the situation becomes more complex: for example, extroverted mysticism is negatively associated with life satisfaction, while mysticism understood as religious interpretation is positively associated with life orientation and satisfaction with religious life. In other words, a religious experience can just as well reassure and help stabilize what is being constructed as, on the other hand, destabilize it by emphasizing its unsatisfactory aspect in relation to the mystical experience.

Second is the study of Leak & Fish (1999), who are interested in religious maturity. They propose the construction of a scale to measure this maturity. The article describes how this scale is developed. Its validity is tested with the aid of correlations to other scales. The data are gathered from 180 students coming from two universities in the United States, one Jesuit and the other public. According to these data, religious maturity would be correlated with religious relativism, with religious reflexivity (self-awareness), with the acceptance of change within the Church, with a positive attitude to ecumenism, with the fact of having personal religious experience, with the frequency of personal prayer and with the perception that religious beliefs are a product of personal experience. What interests our study more precisely is that religious maturity is thus correlated with a feeling of religious well-being. Therefore, if at the level of common religiosity, the purpose of the sought-for salvation goods is to preserve health, at the level of religiosity "for virtuosos", the purpose is to obtain a "life surplus" which results in the attempt to guarantee for oneself a general and permanent feeling of well-being.

6. When psychological benefits become specifically sought-for salvation goods

In antiquity, as we have described it, psychological benefits appear as consequences of obtaining salvation goods. These psychological benefits, an increase of identity and self-esteem, are not considered salvation goods as such. They are not sought in themselves, if only because access to these benefits is mediated by belonging to a particular group. The salvation goods sought as such are power, wealth, and wisdom. For a whole series of excluded people, these goods, hitherto beyond reach, become accessible through following Christian preaching.

Today, in the West, access to these salvation goods is uncoupled from adherence to a religious discourse and an institutional religious membership. This is why the simple reproduction of first-century Christian preaching has lost much of its attractiveness for a substantial number of Westerners. The salvation goods promised in the first century are no longer those sought primarily in the religious context today. On the other hand, the psychological benefits that had a secondary status in antiquity appear today to have become salvation goods directly sought as such.

Granqvist and Hagekull (2000), for example, make this very evident. They conducted an enquiry on religious coping on a population of one hundred and fifty-six students of the University of Uppsala (Sweden). Defending the theory of the compensating function of religion, they show that single people, compared with those engaged in pair relationships, are more active religiously, have a more intense personal relationship with God, have greater experience of changes that imply increasing importance of religious beliefs, and have a religiosity more widely based on a regulation of affects. Attachment theory is the context for interpreting these results: the primary mother-child relationship shifts to the religious dimension (God), providing a safe base where the individual feels in security. Let us note that here we are rather distant from the predominant trend of primitive Christianity, where the prime function of the figure of God, as such, was not to be a figure of attachment: the substitute for the attachment was to a fellowship of belonging, called the "body of Christ", the Church, and so forth, rather than a divine figure. Belonging to the fellowship establishes the relationship to God, a paternal figure rather than a substitute for maternal attachment.

If we examine another function, cognitive this time, of religion, which consists in responding to questions which otherwise cannot be answered, we arrive at a conclusion that completes what we have just said. According to the observations gathered by Deconchy, Hurteau, Quelen and Ragot (1997), in a situation of cognitive "non-control", the subjects tend to resort to causal explanations of an irrational type. This fact leads these authors to question whether it is necessary to call these explanations "beliefs" or even "religious beliefs". For our purpose, it is sufficient to retain that a "rational choice" of the religious type can be to adopt an irrational explanation with religious content, when any other explanation is lacking. The psychological benefit is then to preserve a sense of cognitive control when rational coherence fails. The offer of a possibility of "control" precludes the experience of mental distress (Kirkpatrick, 1992: 21). This way of protecting the individual from psychological distress contrasts once again with the first-century, when the threats were different. In the context of antiquity, the narcissistic cohesion of the individual was preserved at the level of the group, but it was necessary in contrast to face impenetrable barriers on the plane of social exclusion.

Let us add to these two examples the results of a review of researches on conversion to new religious movements in German-speaking countries (Kraus, 1999) indicating that the benefits accrued in such a procedure are a more coherent and stable sense of identity, sense of personal value, and sense of life. Psychological benefits therefore assuredly appear today as salvation goods that can make religious groups attractive.

7. Conclusion

In antiquity as today, salvation can be characterized as integration into the human community along with the right to enjoy the privileges granted those who are fully-fledged members of it. Inversely, perdition would mean exclusion, being prevented from enjoying the availability of these rights, and indeed, at worst, no longer being considered as a member of the human species. Salvation goods of course designate not only the privileges whose availability is enjoyed by fully-fledged members (power, wealth, wisdom, holiness, to mention the four categories formulated by Theissen), but also the prior means that enable escape from perdition by effecting the transformation of one state to another (healing, rehabilitation, various helps). In antiquity, this transformation operated largely through a change of belonging. Identities, status, and values are strongly associated with well-recognizable social groups. The possibility of becoming a member of the group permits enjoyment of the psychological benefits of belonging to the group. The first figures of attachment shift to the group, which confers identity and self-esteem, and which assures the type of destiny after death, in fact everything favoring the construction of a stable and well-recognized relationship to self and to others.

Today, in the West, the responsibility for such a construction rests much more on the shoulders of the individual, along with all the anxieties that this can generate. The share of membership or non-membership in a given group is smaller than in antiquity, even if the inability to be independent is often intensified, according to the case, by a form of organized social exclusion. These forms include institutionalization (psychiatric hospital, prison and so on)[15], placement into the care of a guardian, or more extreme forms of exclusion leading to loss of employment (status of unemployed) or vagrancy (non-status of homelessness).

In this context, anything that can help preserve psychological integrity can take the value of salvation goods. Moreover, in this sector we can recognize an expectation with regard to the religious or, at least, a questioning of its impact and the legitimacy of the possible persistence of its offer. This is how I understand the interest of researchers in the place of the religious dimension in coping. Do religious systems have something to offer in this sector? They are not alone on the market: the bio-psycho-social model (Engel, 1977) of taking charge thematizes other dimensions from which help may be sourced. The representative of a religious offer enters into competition with the doctor (and more widely all the practitioners of the medical system), the psychologist, and the social worker. However, there are "market shares" to take when the combination of these participants shows insufficiencies. Like in the first-century, when various religious or philosophical trends offered alternative ways to access values managed by the imperial organization, today various religious trends can attempt to offer access to a stable and preserved psychological integrity. Must we then posit as a testable hypothesis that if they succeed in doing so, they will have success (in terms of attractiveness)?

---

15   This is why certain aged individuals may feel anxiety about their status as soon as they enter the Emergency Medical Services.

In brief, what do our contemporaries need to be saved in the West? From a social exclusion resulting from the inability to take responsibility for oneself as an individual. This does not concern an *a priori* exclusion, like in the first century of our era, where the fact of non-membership in a given group officially prohibited access to certain prerogatives. This concerns an *a posteriori* exclusion, resulting from a failure, namely, the inability to face successfully the test of being oneself (Ehrenberg, 1998). The Christian preaching that will be attractive to such excluded people today will be one that can transpose its message. In the world where Christianity emerged, the dominant system, comprising the imperial institutions and the emperor cult, remained reserved for an elite. This system, with which minority currents collaborated, such as, for example, the Sadducees in Judaism, generated many excluded people. In this context, where salvation could be described as "salvation by belonging", alternative trends began to construct competitive elites. Philosophical schools offered "religiosity for virtuosos" (such as salvation by developing a morality). Most Judaic currents, the Pharisees, Essenes and Baptists, continued to identify the elite by the election of the Jewish people (salvation by belonging). In this context, most of the currents of primitive Christianity offered "democratization" of the elite status and thereby enjoyed great attractiveness. Today, in the West, the dominant system that dispenses salvation through stable and preserved psychological integrity encompasses social institutions founded on the bio-psycho-social model (with which, for example, the State-recognized Churches collaborate). This system in principle does not produce many excluded, but it conveys a very demanding model of the individual. Alternative trends construct, on their side, ways to reinforce identity, which attract those who fear destabilization. Thus, certain schools or personal development trainings offer "religiosity for virtuosos", costly both in terms of personal commitment and in terms of finances. In this context characterized by a type of "psychologization of salvation goods", the Christian preaching of the institutional churches has difficulty in remaining attractive within the dominant system. That is why certain Christian trends seek other avenues in one alternative model of personal development or another, which nevertheless remain reserved for a small number of people. In parallel, various trends within the traditional religions continue to offer salvation through belonging to closed circles. At this point, the question is whether Christian preaching or other currents (religious or non-religious) will better know how to "democratize" access to the preservation of psychological stability.*

References

Atkinson, Bruce E., and Malony, Newton H. (1994) "Religious Maturity and Psychological Distress Among Older Christian Women", *The International Journal for the Psychology of Religion* 4(3): 165-179.

Benore, Ethan R. and Park, Crystal L. (2004) "Death-Specific Religious Beliefs and Bereavement: Belief in an Afterlife and Continued Attachment", *The International Journal for the Psychology of Religion* 14(1): 1-22.

Brandt, Pierre-Yves (2002) *L'identité de Jésus et l'identité de son disciple: le récit de la transfiguration comme clef de lecture de l'évangile de Marc* (NTOA 50). Fribourg: Editions Universitaires; Göttingen: Vandenhoeck & Ruprecht.

Byrd, Kevin R., Lear, Delbert, and Schwenka, Stacy (2000) "Mysticism as a Predictor of Subjective Well-being", *The International Journal for the Psychology of Religion* 10(4): 259-269.

Campiche, Roland J. et al. (2004) *Les deux visages de la religion: fascination et désenchantement.* Geneva: Labor et Fides.

Deconchy, Jean-Pierre, Hurteau, Chantal, Quelen, Florence and Ragot Isabelle (1997) "The Psychology of Religion and Cognitive Models (The 'Learned Helplessness' Case)", *The International Journal for the Psychology of Religion* 7(4): 263-268.

---

*   Translated by Christine Rhone

Ehrenberg, Alain (1998) *La fatigue d'être soi: dépression et société.* Paris: Odile Jacob.

Engel, George L. (1977) "The Need for a New Medical Model: A Challenge for Biomedecine", *Science* 196 (4286): 129-136.

Granqvist, Pehr and Hagekull, Berit (2000) "Religiosity, Adult Attachment, and why 'Singles' are More Religious", *The International Journal for the Psychology of Religion* 10(2): 111-123.

Huguelet, Philippe, Mohr, Sylvia, Borras, Laurence, Gillièron, Christiane and Brandt, Pierre-Yves (2006) "Spirituality and Religious Practices among Outpatients with Schizophrenia and their Clinicians", *Psychiatric Services* 57(3): 366-372.

Kirkpatrick, Lee A. (1992) "An Attachment-Theory Approach to the Psychology of Religion", *The International Journal for the Psychology of Religion* 2(1): 3-28.

Kraus, Daniel (1999) "Psychological Studies of New Religious Movements: Findings from German-Speaking Countries", *The International Journal for the Psychology of Religion* 9(4): 263-281.

Lalive d'Epinay, Christian J. and Spini, Dario (2004) "Religion and Health: a European Perspective", in K. Warner Schaie, Neal Krause, Alan Booth (eds.), *Religious Influences on Health and Well-being in the Elderly.* New York: Springer, pp. 44-58.

Leak, Gary K. and Fish, Stanley B. (1999) "Development and Initial Validation of a Measure of Religious Maturity", *The International Journal for the Psychology of Religion* 9(2): 83-103.

Le Breton, David (1994) "Passions modernes du risque et fabrication du sens", in Thierry Goguel d'Allondans (ed.). *Rites de passage: d'ailleurs, ici, pour ailleurs.* Ramonville-Saint-Agne: Erès, pp. 81-86.

–. (2002) *Conduites à risques: des jeux de mort au jeu de vivre.* Paris: Presses Universitaires de France.

McNamara, Patrick, Andresen, Jensine and Gellard, Judit (2003) "Relation of Religiosity and Scores on Fluency Tests to Subjective Reports of Health in Older Individuals", *The International Journal for the Psychology of Religion* 13(4): 259-271.

Pargament, Kenneth (1997) *Psychology of Religion and Coping*. New York: Guilford Press.

Plante, Thomas G. and Sherman, Allen C. (eds.) (2001) *Faith and Health: Psychological Perspectives*. New York: Guilford.

Stark, Rodney (1996) *The Rise of Christianity: A Sociologist Reconsiders History*. Princeton: Princeton University Press.

Theissen, Gerd (1996) *Histoire sociale du christianisme primitif* (Le Monde de la Bible 33). Geneva: Labor et Fides.

–. (1999) *A Theory of Primitive Christian Religion*. London: SCM (trans. John Bowden).

Weber, Max (1920/1978) *Gesammelte Aufsätze zur Religionssoziologie I: 7. photomechanisch gedruckte Auflage*. Tübingen: Mohr.

Silvia MANCINI

Salvation Goods and the Canonization Logic: On Two Popular Cults of Southern Italy

1. Introduction

If the comparative history of religions, anthropology and sociology of religion are interlinked, we cannot take for granted the nature of their mutual relationships. My intention is to show first at what level it is possible to compare the problematics of the comparative history of religions and anthropology, as I understand and practice them, with those that certain representatives of the sociology of religion develop starting from the Weberian notion of "salvation goods" – a notion that re-emerges in contemporary debate. Then, locating myself, as a historian of religions, in relation to this sociological notion, I will present (in the second and third parts) the results of a field study conducted in South Italy between July and August 2004, bearing on the canonical cult of San Pio da Petrelcina and the extra-canonical cult of Alberto de Serradarce.

In the study of these forms of popular devotion, it is indeed always important to take into account certain factors traditionally privileged by sociologists. These relate, notably, to the existence of social and cultural conflicts that underpin the opposition between official religious concepts and the religious forms considered minor; these relate also to the socio-economic interests connected with the salvation goods conveyed by such forms of devotion. It nevertheless remains the responsibility of the historian of religions to integrate these forms in a specific thinking. This must include the *efficacy proper to the symbolic measures* marshaled by the religious practices concerned, and the *nature of the issues* carried by this very efficacy. Among these issues appears in particular the question of "salvation goods", whose status has rarely been the subject, in social sciences, of such thought. The latter is, in contrast, an integral part of the history of religions, always torn between historical or sociological "reductionism", and recognition of the autonomy or specificity of the mythico-ritual lan- guage active in the magico-religious life of societies.

In proceeding with the study of the two ethnographic cases mentioned above, I shall therefore attempt to show how, in the cul- tural regions where the cults of Padre Pio and Glorioso Alberto have flourished, this "mythico-ritual" logic appears as a true cultural tech- nique in service of a specific vital economy, whose object is a particular "salvation good". My concern will then be to compare the two cults, which have experienced different historical destinies. Finally, I shall examine the socio-cultural reasons for this difference.

2. The notion of "salvation goods": What pertinence in history of religions?

In the study of institutions, practices and representations commonly approached in the West through the category of "religion", sociology, besides the fact that it operates according to a class perspective (thus the sociology of domination, of Marxist inspiration), or according to the theory of rational choice, of Neo-liberal inspiration, has long had the tendency to reduce all this domain of the "religious" to extra- religious factors, identified alternately with economic, political, or social issues, whose actors would be more or less conscious. In fact, everything happens as if sociology were incapable of approaching the magico-religious as an autonomous field, without misrepresenting it in some manner. The task of the social sciences of religions would then consist in reducing the apparent irrationality of magico-religious productions to a fundamental rationality which, in these productions, would appear as "masked". The history of religions since the 1920s has shown itself much more interested, on the other hand, in the non-conscious "reasons" at work in mythico-ritual life, in other words, in a form of rationality underlying behaviors judged "irrational" at first. That is why this history has not hesitated to turn toward sciences such as psychology, psychiatry, and psychoanalysis, just as to certain philo-sophies of consciousness like phenomenology and existentialism. They have found themselves thus summoned with a view to clarifying the mode of functioning of mythico-ritual life in what it has that is most specific and most original.

How do historians of religions issuing from this same tradition re-act to the sociological notion of "salvation goods" (Weber 1922)? All at once confronted with it, and accustomed to working on different cultures and epochs, they can react in two ways.

The first, inevitable, consists in previously raising the following question: Is this notion pertinent to understanding civilizations not based on the market and its underlying economic logic, but rather on the principle of bartering and reciprocity? The question is all the more pertinent as in history of religions and anthropology we are often dealing with holistically oriented societies. In the latter – as all the anthropologists have emphasized – the same symbolic logic subtends and organizes social relationships, economic forms, power structures, mythical conceptions, ritual practices, and modalities of relationship with the natural and the supernatural in a coherent system – the whole, understood as an indissociable unity. Now, to think of the forms of production and circulation that are clearly material, on the one hand, and the transactions and exchanges with the extra-human world, on the other, as two distinct and independent spheres, would amount to postulating as universal the existence of two institutions that preside, in our own case, over these types of transactions (as it happens, the economy and religion). This would also amount, in fact, to "natural-izing" the notions of "market" and "salvation" implicit in our concept of the economy and religion – the first, integral with a mercantile civilization; the second, indissociable from the individual plan of sal-vation that Judeo-Christianity conveys. Thus, not only do the market and human salvation look like the two *identity markers* that differentiate and distinguish us Westerners from all other cultures; but also, they incarnate the two complementary *practical modalities* that organize, in our case, the relationships that people maintain as much with commodities of use as with these commodities of exchange with the extra-human world (associated, in the biblical tradition, with concepts of creation, incarnation and salvation).

For a historian of compared religions, this first manner of taking a position in relation to the notion of "salvation goods" denotes a certain reservation toward its operative use. However, a second manner can provide a wider view of the possibility of a fruitful dialogue between the comparative history of religions and the sociology of religion. One could express it by asking the question in these terms: if this notion (even understood on an immanent level) proves, because of its "economist" and ethnocentrist implications, irrelevant for understanding cultures and subcultures less touched by Western modernity, must we by the same token renounce examining the *practical logic*, *benefits* and *factual efficacy* of certain symbolic behaviors of a mythico-ritual nature that these cultures and sub-cultures produce?

To look at it closely, we perceive that an examination related to the logic underlying mythico-ritual behaviors and to their function, benefits and "pragmatico-factual" efficacy (as if these behaviors were subject to a specific economy), has always accompanied the approach of the social sciences of religions. That is why nothing prevents the historian of religions from considering myth and rite as *forms* and *instruments* of production (Bourdieu 1974, Dumont 1983, Godelier 1984, Lanternari 1959, Meillassoux 1960, Polyani 1944), without thereby succumbing to what is ordinarily qualified as "economicist/sociological reductionism". Indeed, as Karl Marx already noted in *Introduction to a Critique of Political Economy* – and as subsequently Max Weber and Pierre Bourdieu would sustain – myth and rite can be considered as *forms* and *instruments* of production, in the sense that they constitute precise social modalities meant for the production and consumption of certain immanent human goods. At this point, the economic metaphor that is here inspired from

Marxist categories reveals itself as pertinent as it is stimulating. This parallelism between economy and mythico-ritual activity appears all the less forced if, instead of considering the economy in terms of the production, distribution and marketing of material or symbolic goods that are already present and complete, we understand the economy *as the implementation of particular techniques* which, by either constraining nature or assisting it, result in factual practical effects, in the resolution of vital human problems. What problems are we dealing with? To answer, I propose to pursue to the very end the parallelism between economic activity and mythico-ritual activity.

On a first level, we can see in mythology and ritual *forms of production* of vital commodities, to the extent that, in the words of Marx, "All production is appropriation of nature by the individual within and through a definite form of society." However, they are also *means of production*, in the sense that they employ a particular technique, which, like any technique, enables people to "subdue, control, and fashion the forces of nature" (Marx 1859: 150). As Bronislaw Malinowski, Claude Meillassoux, Maurice Godelier and so many others have already mentioned, mythology and ritual are indissociable from the processes of production of material goods. In fact, on the one hand, in pre-modern societies their origin myths establish and legitimate all productive activity; and on the other hand, ritual activity appears as an indissociable complement of the profane activities aimed at the production of the material goods that enable survival.

On a second level, we can consider the mythico-ritual instrument as a technique whose efficacy, like any technique, is measured in relationship to the goals attained and the problems resolved. Ernesto De Martino calls it a "technique of dis-historicization" (De Martino, 1953, 1958, 1958, 1977), which acts as much in myth as in rite. Dis-historicization is a cultural operation that consists in "acting as if" man was not the author of his own productions. If, in myth, the responsibility for the creation of goods and institutions, both material and symbolic, is attributed to the action of an extra-human entity, we can say in return that in rite it is indeed man who acts. Nevertheless, he acts here according to a modality of action, stereotyped, frozen and outside time, which makes this action something de-realized, devoid of historical impact – a dis-historicized action. The mythico-ritual logic or technique, which characterizes the mode of functioning of religious consciousness, is defined in brief as a characteristic form of negation, because in fact, in this consciousness man denies himself as a fully-fledged historical agent. We could say that, paradoxically, it is by "denying" the historicity of his activity that he manages, by experiencing the myths and rites, to give meaning to his existence. Much more, established by this detour in a rule of protected existence, and thus endowed with an amplified capacity for action, he especially manages to confront and sometimes practically to resolve the contradictions and concrete problems with which he finds himself faced. Therein indeed resides the strategic efficacy of this measure.

What is, more precisely, the vital problem that this strategy permits resolving? In many strands of the history of religions, researchers have sought the reasons for this detour of consciousness. Some have attempted to explain it (thus, religious phenomenology) through an irreducible demand of *homo religiosus*, or by advancing arguments drawn from psychology, psychopathology, or psychoanalysis. In my view, we must here retain one thing, namely, that the mythico-ritual detour would comprise a *practical functional strategy* that permits safeguarding the fundamental "good" which is the psychological unity of the subject. As De Martino has rightly observed, this unity, presupposed at the base of all cultural and social activity, constitutes the *sine qua non* condition of human action in the world – a psychological unity that the mythico-ritual measure is supposed to protect, defend and reinforce in exchange for a strategic fiction. By acting *as if...*, and *as if he* were not acting, man takes shelter from events, and the mythico-ritual technique allows him, de facto, to take action upon the latter. Recourse to this measure would then resemble, as Ernesto De Martino wrote, a true "pedagogy" of the psychological unity of the subject (De Martino, 1948).

These reasons, in my view, therefore permit a comparison of magico-religious life with an *economy* based on the production and conservation of basic "salvation goods". It is not a matter of identifying these goods with ultimate salvation, health and wealth, but with everything underlying them – in brief, with the creative psychological energy continually open to challenge from the crushing power of the negativity that confronts peoples and cultures; and this, notably, where conditions of extreme poverty and psychological, social, cultural and material precariousness make existential stability problematic indeed. That is how the analogy between economy and religion can be more than just a *metaphor*.

At this point, a parallel between the problematics of comparative history of religions, on the one hand, and those of sociology of religion, on the other, proves possible on condition of seeing in mythico-ritual life a form of economy employing a specific technique (the technique of dis-historicization). However, the sociology of domination also offers the historian of religions many subjects of consideration in dealing with certain subcultures of South Italy, the bearers of practices and concepts which still today lend themselves to an interpretation founded on the hegemony/subalternity opposition. This model was provided by Antonio Gramsci in the context of his class approach to popular cultures and their forms of religiosity (Gramsci, 1950; Cirese, 1976).

Now, in this context my approach is precisely to verify two positions. On the one hand, the first is expressed through the Gramscian structure, which invites us to approach subaltern popular cultures in terms of relationships of competition and conflict between the popular and the hegemonic cultural forms. On the other hand, the second is the position explained above, which consists in considering recourse to mythico-ritual technique as a form of economy responding to vital needs. For this purpose, two cases will serve me as examples. They were the subject of two field missions both accomplished in the summer of 2004, the one at San Giovanni Rotondo, in Apulia, and the other in Serradarce, in Campania.

This two-week-long ethnographic fieldwork, led according to the methods of participatory observation of interviewing and filming resulted notably in the production of a twenty-two-minute film. When compared with films made in the 1960s in the same areas, that of 2004 permits measuring the extent of the development of the mentioned cults.

3. The canonical cult of Padre Pio
and the market of the sacred at San Giovanni Rotondo

Padre Pio de Petralcina, deceased in 1968 and canonized by Pope John Paul II in 2001, is probably the last of the great thaumaturgists of the twentieth century. He has been the subject of outstanding interest on the part of countless numbers of the Catholic faithful come from not only the rural milieux of the Apulia region where the Capuchin convent in which he lived is located, but also the Italian lower middle and middle classes – on the part, also, of emigrants among whom the man's fame had spread through the testimony of close friends and relatives remained in Italy. In the summer of 1918, in the chapel of his convent, having entered into prayer before his wooden crucifix, Padre Pio received stigmata that continued to bleed in an uninterrupted fashion during fifty years. From the 1920s to the end of the 1960s, he was the object of uncommon devotion. A crowd of visitors awaited him every morning at five o'clock for the celebration of Mass. They went there to receive Confession from him, or simply to meet him, to shake his hand, or to ask him to intercede with Christ for the benefit of a loved one. This human tide finally created some embarrassment for the Church, which tried to salvage the phenomenon and to lead this miracle-working cult back into its fold. The "miracles" attributed to Padre Pio, recognized after official ecclesiastical enquiry or simply witnessed by the beneficiaries, cannot be counted. What especially struck the faithful was his multiple "charismas", his gifts as a "sensitive", as they used to be called (like clairaudience, remote viewing, inedia, precognition, telepathy, prophecy; the gift of fragrance, miracle-working, bilocation, or again the ability to take upon himself some of the mental and physical states of his faithful) (Mancini 2004).

This is nevertheless not the place to paint an in-depth portrait of the character himself, who has not lacked biographers. Let us instead examine the modalities according to which, still currently, his faithful pay their respects to him and address him with a view to obtaining graces. What appears pertinent from the start is the very nature of the salvation goods concerned here. Now, noteworthy on this point is that from the time when the Church officially took over the matter, going so far as finally to proceed with canonizing the monk, the cult of Padre Pio found itself influenced in a direction rather different from the spontaneous forms that had characterized it during the course of three decades (from the 1940s to the end of the 1960s).

These changes consist essentially of an increased retrospective "moralization" of the character's image. The official discourses of the Vatican, as well as those of many Catholic associations proliferated around this devotion – like prayer groups, medical volunteering, helping the disabled, etc. – favor the Christian qualities of prayer, neighborly love, fraternity, mercy, and spirit of sacrifice. However, what about the magico-thaumaturgic dimension, so apparent in the practices adopted by Padre Pio, such as auricular confession, manual contact, the laying on of hands of the faithful, or again the direct sight, during church services or private interviews, of the blood and suffering body of the monk? Now, this aspect does indeed seem to have been relegated to the background today. The decline, in the contemporary cult, of his image as a healer goes together with the emergence of other modalities to access the benefits with which this exemplary figure is considered very generous. Let us highlight one aspect of these new modalities. In the past, the relationship of the believers to Padre Pio, and his relationship to his faithful, included the physical body, which in both cases functioned as the visible place marked as much by the suffering experienced as by deliverance from the latter. Faith itself used to demand the administration of tangible "proof" that could be seen and experienced in the miracle that followed the request for intervention. A few words, a touch, some prayers said – these calmed the pains. This faith remained, in brief, indissociable from an audience of eyewitnesses of the pain undergone as much by Padre Pio as by his visitors. The monk, notwithstanding, had in his mission explicitly pursued the task of alleviating the physical and moral pain of humanity. Thanks to major funds donated by the faithful, he had constructed next to the convent the most modern hospital in South Italy, the renowned Casa del Sollievo della Sofferenza, a gigantic building endowed with the most sophisticated medical equipment and top-level medical teams. Dominating from mid-village, this Casa, visible from miles away, contrasts with the surrounding rural landscape. Let us also emphasize the impression of hyper-modernity made by the presence of these avant-garde medical structures and hospital, of a new church (the work of Enzo Piano, currently the most fashionable Italian architect), by the existence of a local radio station, a magazine published by the Capuchins *(La Voce di Padre Pio)*, a website, and finally a visible reorientation of the cult based more and more (at least exteriorly) on a more interiorized, moralized and sublimated faith.

Several elements observed in the field, however, belie this impression. If an indisputable metamorphosis of the relationship to the healing saint has occurred by virtue of the official discourse that makes him the incarnation of the spirit of love and mercy already personified by Francis of Assisi, it nonetheless remains that, in the current cult of Padre Pio, something endures that neither the ecclesiastical powers of Rome, nor the bishop of Manfredonia, manages to contain. This concerns the spontaneous behavior of the faithful who continue to enter into relationship with the saint by using as mediating instruments not only their faith, but also their bodies and all the senses that are part of them. The triggering of such non-verbal behaviors is patent when one visits the places where Padre Pio lived. One realizes, in fact, the important place held by what Frazer called "contact magic" (in other words, the material and moral benefits due to contiguity with an object having been in relationship with the extra-human dimension). The major concern, here, is to impress upon one's body the memory of the holy place visited and to impregnate one's senses with it (hearing, sight, smell, touch). That is why one will stop in the room where he lived, linger at the crucifix before which he used to pray and received the stigmata, touch the display cases showing his personal possessions, or retrace his habitual walks in the convent corridors or the sacristy. By this ritualized itineration of the daily existence of the healing saint, a sort of exemplary model of the victory over suffering and misfortune, the faithful complete a certain work. This consists of reabsorbing, in the paradigmatic stability of this living myth, all the negativity that burdens their existence and their bodies, which through this act are relieved of pains.

The work of conservation accomplished by the Capuchins of the convent has produced a rather surprising result. The display cases show the mittens that Padre Pio wore during the day to hide the bandaged wounds of his hands. They show his cassocks, his bloodstained linen, his confessional, his breviary, etc. People parade silently before these relics, touch what they can while out of view of the guards, and do not spare the offerings that they are invited to leave in boxes hung on the walls of the mystical course. However, an unusual practice also strikes the visitor. As soon as they can elude the guard's eyes, visitors slip the photo of a loved one (newborn baby, sick grandmother, adolescent in crisis) into the cracks of the glass panes of the shrines and display windows. These photos secretly thrown inside the space containing the relics, to impregnate them with the power of thaumaturgy, are often accompanied by words of prayer, supplications, and expressions of gratitude. Photos and letters are regularly collected.

Certainly, such forms of popular piety are hardly appropriate in what has become a high place of official Catholicism; nevertheless, we must not believe that the Capuchins of the convent follow the directives of Rome literally. In reality, they act as relays between these directives and popular piety. To this actual state of facts, two examples would suffice as testimony. On the one hand, the institution of the blessing of objects, including cars; on the other hand, the perpetuation, by the well-known Padre Modestino, of the practice of auricular confession and the private interview. On the plaza facing the convent, at a determined corner and at particular times, one can observe the line of cars waiting to be blessed. Situated between the place housing the crucifix that served as a model for Padre Pio's stigmata and the super-modern hospital, the place where "large scale" objects (such as automobiles) are blessed thus represents something like an extension to near-infinity of the healing principle and magical protection against all sorts of accidents to which people and objects are exposed, including traffic accidents.

Is there any need to say how much the commercial business of the Capuchins is booming, recently placed by the Roman curia under the financial control of the bishop of Manfredonia? To this success contributes one special asset. This concerns Padre Modestino, whose name has just been mentioned. An octogenarian who originates from the same village as Padre Pio, a sort of avatar, in a minor tone, of Padre Pio himself, this monk continues today to maintain certain customs. Thus, he receives daily a considerable number of consultants. They are hoping for counsel, advice, and words of encouragement, which might contain a cryptic message about a critical situation, a difficult doubt, or a dark conjuncture they are experiencing. There are rumors that he is endowed with some of the charismas of his co-religionary (gift of vision and premonition, notably). On this point, I obviously cannot comment.[1]

The Vatican has made Padre Pio's cult a supposed means to revive in consciences concern for salvation of the soul; as for the faithful, they ask the new saint for signs capable of indicating to them the way to relieve body and mind. Let us finally note that the activities of the

---

1   What is certain, in any case, is that my visit to Padre Modestino, on the 30th of July 2004, ended with three gifts. He gave me a book, of which he is the author and which he autographed for me; about thirty blessed medals and holy pictures of Padre Pio, which he took out of a drawer containing plastic bags full of thousands of identical items; and an illuminating piece of advice, which leaves no doubt as to the magico-apotropaic scope of the cult of the new saint. When he learned that I was a university lecturer, Padre Modestino advised me not to be too strict with my students during examinations, otherwise they might be tempted to curse me and say bad things about me – which would expose me, obviously, to dangers. To protect myself from what looks all too much like the evil eye, all I had to do therefore was to be lenient….

Capuchins are historically situated within the sphere of influence of the already very old oracular practice active in a Roman-period sanctuary located not far from the convent, a sanctuary whose titular was the son of Asclepius. Padre Modestino, presented as a wise and inspired monk, fulfils the function there, precisely, of a junction between, on the one hand, the official Christian model, and on the other hand, a model still rather conforming to the expectations of the pilgrims in search of both miracles and punctual, immanent relief of their ills.

4. The extra-canonical cult of Alberto of Serradarce

Elsewhere in South Italy, we find again this inspired and thaumaturgic mantic dimension, characteristic nevertheless of many other popular cults. Indeed, since antiquity these regions have undergone the most diverse cultural influences (Greeks, Romans, Carthaginians, Normans, and Arabs). Onto these influences that of Catholicism was then grafted, whence the apparition of hybrid forms of cult. The historico-religious archeology of this area attests not only to the heritage of ecstatic cults spread throughout Greater Greece, of which Italy was one of the cultural provinces, but also to the possession cults having flourished in popular Islam and more generally in the Mediterranean area (De Martino, 1958). The involvement, for various cultural uses, of altered states or dissociated from consciousness (states nevertheless perfectly mastered by the population through centuries of practice) therefore appears here as a cultural constant (De Martino, 1961; Mancini, 2004). The second cult, extra-liturgical, now introduced, is localized at Serradarce, a hamlet of the village of Campagna situated in the province of Salerno. The protective saint of Campagna is Saint Antonio, a twelfth-century monk whose name is connected with a tradition that attributes to him the gift of delivering the possessed from the Devil. In the church dedicated to him, a chapel still houses a column to which, according to the tradition, the possessed were held tied for several days, until the time when a mysterious sound of bells would announce the miracle of their liberation by the saint. The Church having, especially after the Second Vatican Council, discouraged the practices of exorcism, the possessed of the region turned elsewhere, indeed toward extra-canonical exorcist cults like that of Serradarce (Risso, 1972, 1976; Luna, Scafoglio, 2002).

Everything began in 1959, following events that have as a protagonist a woman, Giuseppina Gonella, born in 1912. Possessed by the devil in 1949, she had been exorcised in the church of Saint Antonio. In addition, she was a former initiate of the practices of witchcraft; she had learned how to compose love philters or to dissolve their effects, prepare potions meant to harm or to protect from the dangers of magical nuisances called, in the South, *fatture* (a *fattura* can be of love, death or illness). Onto this scene emerged, in 1959, an event that would change Giuseppina's fate. On 26 October, Alberto Gonella, her nephew, twenty-one years old – a seminary student – was, during the course of farm work, accidentally killed because of a clumsy maneuver by one of his uncles who was driving a truck. Terrible quarrels then exploded in the family, linked to this tragic demise. Death threats were uttered by the father of Alberto against his brother responsible for the accident. Three days after these facts, Giuseppina, while present in Alberto's bedroom, began to feel sharp pains in her legs. Her relatives put her to bed where she remained lying for twenty-four hours, as though dead. Then she began to speak in Alberto's voice, to make predictions, and to give precise and detailed information (that Giuseppina was not supposed to know) about the relatives and guests at the funeral. The family was persuaded that Giuseppina was possessed by the nephew's spirit. The meetings with the spirit of the deceased became increasingly frequent, and the woman medium managed to organize around her a true "Alberto cult" that soon magnetized hundreds of people.

Starting in summer 1963, every day except Sundays, at the very hour of Alberto's death and for almost twenty years, Giuseppina found herself possessed by the spirit of the deceased, soon qualified as "blessed". Pilgrims come from the surrounding areas and even other regions of South Italy converged on Serradarce, and crowded into Alberto's home-sanctuary, in anticipation of seeing, while packed in the room, hallways and stairs, the possession of Giuseppina. In fact, using techniques of autohypnosis (deglutition, rhythmic breathing, etc.) she finished by entering a trance. At that exact moment, she was seen to assume a second personality, to the point of expressing herself in perfect Italian, although she was supposed to know only dialect. She proceeded to exorcize the faithful. She spoke in the first person, as if she were Alberto, who by this procedure recalled the circumstances of his own death, qualified as "martyrdom", prayed, and recalled his powers of alleviating the sufferings of the penitent souls in Purgatory – but he also mentioned, in his discourse, his power to free the recipients from curses and *fatture*. Giuseppina-Alberto undertook to orchestrate a dialogue with the people present. Bringing the emotional tension in the room to fever pitch, she blessed the objects and clothing brought by the relatives of those who had been unable to attend the cult. Then, in the "room of secrets" next to the main room, Giuseppina received the postulants in small groups and proceeded with exorcisms. She not only used *fatture*, but also diagnosed diabolical possession and cast out the Demon.

As early as 1968, a new temple was built with the donations made in favor of the blessed Alberto. It contains an *ex voto* of silver, images of the saint, precious gifts, wedding dresses given in gratitude, photos of the recipients of Alberto's miracles, and even the truck-relic of martyrdom. Thirty years after the first studies made during my field trip in this magico-therapeutic community, the situation at Serradarce has greatly changed. A hired killer assassinated Giuseppina in 1970. The sorcerers of Salerno, tired of seeing her monopolize the free market of exorcism, gave the commission. Was she not in fact draining away a constantly increasing flood of people who wanted assurance and protection from the misfortunes that burdened their daily lives?

Following this drama, the family decided to give the temple and the collection of relics to the Church of Rome, in the hope that this generous act would accelerate the process of Alberto's canonization.

However, this did not happen. The only consequence of the donation was that the temple was transformed into a church placed under the jurisdiction of the bishop of Salerno, where Catholics of the neo-catechumenal movement (a sort of evangelical variant of contemporary Catholicism) still meet, under the guidance of an American priest. The group of Alberto's followers, organized around the surviving members of his family, was relegated to tiny premises, transformed into a chapel dedicated to the one who no one doubts will soon be proclaimed a "saint". His followers are today joined in an Association, "Associazione di volontario Gruppo di Preghiera 'Alberto'", which continues to promote the canonization of the blessed one by gathering documents and witness statements – duly composed in writing by the beneficiaries – and tangible proofs of the many miracles accomplished by the "martyr". Directed by a niece of Alberto's, this Association continues to coordinate the initiatives connected with the cult (for example, the pilgrimage and the procession that take place at the anniversary of the saint's death; the making of DVDs, the dissemination of recordings of songs celebrating Alberto, etc.). In the course of the interview that I carried out in August 2004, the niece of Alberto and her daughter complained of the ingratitude of the Church, accused of having taken over the collection of the relics of the "saint" and the family home transformed into a temple. However, they did not hesitate, since I had introduced myself as of Roman origin, to ask me to exert some pressure on the Curia with a view to accelerating the examination of the file on canonization.

5. Perspectives

The adoption of the notion of "salvation goods" as a working tool, a notion often employed today in studies of contemporary religiosity, appears to us indeed capable of clarifying the logic that underlies the popular cults of Padre Pio and Alberto de Serradarce. In fact, our comparative enquiry produces two results that concern as much *the nature of the salvation goods* at issue in these two cults (goods invested, at least at a first stage, with a common nature), as the *institutional destiny* reserved for them (a very different destiny in both cases).

1) The notion of "salvation goods", understood as the final product of the application of a particular technical modality – the magico-religious modality – to produce human cultural goods, has enabled us to reread the ethnographic facts, presented above, through the structure of what I have qualified as the "technique of mythico-ritual dis-historicization". This is a technique put in service of the production and management of the particular "salvation goods". Here this technique takes the form of a particular cultural economy of controlling and guarding this fundamental vital "good", which is psychological unity exposed to critical states during periods of bereavement, illness, serious trouble and other conditions recurring in these underdeveloped socio-economic strata.

Thus, just as in the case of Padre Pio (for whom certain traumatic events connected with the First World War, and his own state of precarious health, prepared the ground for his charismas), the emergence of Alberto's personality, in the case of Giuseppina, enabled her to channel in another direction the family's emotional tensions resulting from the tragedy, of the "miraculous revelation" variety. Herself possessed, Giuseppina not only managed to "save herself" on her own and to save her family; in addition, she transformed into a great exorcist for others, delivered thanks to her and to Alberto, her double, from states of psychological, physical and existential alienation that, in these parts of Italy, take the form of a chronic feeling of subjection and powerlessness. In these regions and for centuries, such critical states have been counteracted by the implementation of specific institutional techniques of expression, objectivation and correction. These techniques consist, on the one hand, of the implementation of a repertory of mythic images (drawn from pre-Christian folklore or chosen from the symbols of official Catholicism, as in the case of Padre Pio); on the other hand, of ritual actions using dissociated psychological states for corrective ends (states of possession based on personality doubling; ecstatic states; auto-hypnotic practices, etc.). Such actions offer simultaneously the possibility of expressing states of psychological lability and of surmounting them through the ritual discipline to which they are subject.

2) The application of the notion of "salvation goods" to the ethnographical materials discussed above has allowed us to observe *in vitro* another interesting datum. The latter is a dynamic differing little from what has probably often happened in the context of other popular cults of healing saints. In this case, saints that alone, at the end of the process, receive ecclesiastical approval – saints who protect the vital goods that are health, love, good luck and, especially, psychological and existential stability. However, because of the very modalities of the communication that he maintains with his faithful, Alberto will be able to overcome the resistance of the ecclesiastical organs in charge of his canonization only with difficulty. In effect, the purpose of the demurrer of the Church is not essentially based, in this specific case, on the too ostensibly immanent nature of the salvation goods that the faithful request from Alberto. We have seen that the goods requested from Padre Pio are similar, and indeed elements of convergence exist between the two cults. These are, for example, the magico-thaumaturgic dimension; the centrality of the body and the senses in the devotional practices addressed to the two saints; the employment of ecstatic states, as much in the case of Giuseppina as in that of Padre Pio, states understood as the privileged way to access normally inaccessible information; the phenomenon of multiple personalities observed in both Giuseppina and Padre Pio; the oracular dimension underlying their discourses, etc.

Yet, four more factors may hinder the fulfillment of the hopes of the followers of Alberto for his canonization. First is the fact that Giuseppina's state of possession is that of a medium – through which Alberto is manifested – that by nature constitutes a detrimental element to any undertaking whose purpose is to integrate this cult into core Catholicism. In fact, the only form of possession recognized by the Church is demonic possession (object of exorcism). Second,

Giuseppina is a woman who, in her past, practiced sorcery. It is conceivable that, in this case, this biographical element can render even more difficult, from the standpoint of the church authorities, the recognition of a true resolution of continuity between extra-canonical practices and official Catholicism. Third, Alberto, who expresses himself through the voice and body of Giuseppina, is himself a mediator between God, the Madonna, and humanity. In his case, therefore, and unlike Padre Pio invested directly by the Lord, the multiple degrees of mediation between God and humanity contrasts with the Church line, today committed to spreading a model of Catholicism more inspired by inner faith, directly connecting the believer to God. Fourth, finally, in Alberto's case, it is the faithful, the bearers of a devotional practice not enshrined by the Church, who claim from the central religious authority the legitimation and recognition of their healing and exorcist saint. In Padre Pio's case, on the other hand, the Church itself has strategically taken over the worship of this monk-thaumaturgist by absorbing it into its institutional devotional forms.

That said, in the two cults we see at play the same tensions and the same competing interests, opposing subaltern religious forms and official religious forms. This competition is permanent, in truth, in a country where the internal socio-cultural divides always remain so present, as much between the North and the South, as between the cities and rural areas. Certainly, to consider such factors is to shed light on the nature of these cults. However, they give only a partial view of it, which must be completed by a specific examination bearing on the *technique of dis-historicization*. This indeed confers meaning on the critical times of individual and collective existence, and it does so by the mediation of mythology. Equally, this technique introduces into this same existence, and in a recurrent manner, the appropriate corrective element, and it does so by the practice of ritual.*

---

*   Translated by Christine Rhone

References

Bourdieu, Pierre (1971) "Genèse et structure du champs religieux", *Revue française de sociologie* 12.

Cirese, Alberto Mario (1976) "Concezioni del mondo, filosofia spontanea, folklore", in *Intellettuali, folklore e istinto di classe*. Turin: Einaudi, pp. 65-104.

Dumont, Louis (1983) *Essai sur l'individualisme* (see especially the "Introduction" and chapter 1). Paris: Seuil.

De Martino, Ernesto (1948/1999) *Il Mondo magico* (French translation: *Le monde magique)*. Paris: Sanofi-Synthélabo.

–. (1977) *La Fine del mondo*. Turin, Einaudi,

–. (1958/1975) *Morte e pianto rituale*. Turin: Boringhieri.

–. (1957) "Storicismo e irrazionalismo nella storia delle religioni", in *Studi e Materiali di Storia delle Religioni*, vol. 28, fasc. 1: 89-107.

–. (1969/1999) *La Terre du remords*. Paris: Sanofi-Synthélabo.

Godelier, Maurice (1984) *L'Idéel et le matériel: Pensée, économies, sociétés*. Paris: Fayard.

Gramsci, Antonio (1950) "Osservazioni sul folklore", in *Letteratura e vita nazionale*. Turin: Einaudi, pp. 215-221.

Lanternari, Vittorio (1959/1978) *La Grande festa*. Bari: Dedalo.

Luna, Simona and Scafoglio, Domenico (2002) *La Possessione diabolica*. Cava de' Tirreni: Avagliano.

Mancini, Silvia (2004) "Mimétisme et rite: de la lamentation funéraire à la phénoménologie de Padre Pio", in *Revue de l'Histoire des Religions*, fasc. 3 (July-Sept.). Paris: P.U.F., pp. 327-353.

Marx, Karl (1954) "Introduction to a Critique of Political Economy" (1859), in *The German Ideology: Part One*, Karl Marx and Frederick Engels, ed. C. J. Arthur. London: Laurence and Wishart.

Meillassoux, Claude (1960) "Essai d'interprétation du phénomène économique dans les sociétés traditionnelles d'autosubsistance", in *Cahiers d'études africaines*, 4.

Polanyi, Karl (1944/1983) *La Grande transformation*. Paris: Gallimard.

Risso, Michele (1973) "Miseria, magia e psicoterapia: Una comunità magico-terapeutica nell'Italia del sud", in *Materiali per lo studio delle tradizioni popolari*, Rome, Bulzoni, pp. 329-352 (reprinted in : *Mondo magico: Possessione e società dei consumi nell'Italia meridionale*, in Diego Carpitella, ed., *Foklore come analisi differenziale di cultura*. Rome: Bulzoni, 1976, pp. 145-162).

Rossi, Annabella (1986) *Le Feste dei poveri*. Palermo: Sellerio.

Weber, Max (1995) "Les voies de salut et leur influence sur la conduite de vie", in Max Weber (1922) *Economie et société*. Paris: Plon, vol. 2, pp. 294-346.

Enzo PACE

Salvation Goods, the Gift Economy and Charismatic Concern

1. Introduction

In this article, I want to demonstrate the following thesis: salvation goods are governed not only by the exchange economy, but also by the gift economy. They have less to do with the logic of social action aimed at profitable returns and more to do with the non-utilitarian aspects of behaviour. I will attempt to show, first of all, that salvation goods possess features which cast serious doubts on the hypothesis that they are basically governed by market forces. There are two reasons for this. First, they may be self-produced by individuals – this is the autopoietic dimension of religion (Kilani, 1997) – independent of the religious institutions that exist in any given society. Second, these goods are acquired and produced as free gifts, generally outside the logic of the exchange economy (Bourdieu, 1971; Guizzardi, 1979). The empirical terrain which seems best suited for testing the above is that which, for the sake of brevity, we shall call charismatic interaction. By this I mean a type of social action in which the basic relations between leader and followers are founded, as Max Weber has taught us, on the non-economics of religious experience.

It therefore follows that the regime of salvation goods will change if a religious organization intervenes in the administration (or in the process of domestication or routinization of charisma) of the goods. The religious institution constitutes an organized belief system that seeks to transform the spontaneity of the gift into a product for the market for religious goods. Hence, the idea of drawing a distinction between free salvation goods, on the one hand, and religious goods for the market, on the other. The former appear particularly resistant to any attempts by an institutionalized belief system to reduce their complexity. The latter, on the other hand, are produced and placed on the market by an institution which consciously deals with the problem of how to reproduce itself over time and in society. It often happens that the religious autopoiesis of salvation goods produced by "spontaneous" movements in a given socio-religious context is perceived by a religious institution as an interesting new niche in the market. As such, the niche has to be occupied to achieve greater control of a socio-religious environment which is increasingly varied and where there is a real risk of losing "customers". From this point of view, what is taking place in Latin America is noteworthy. The growth of charismatic and Pentecostal movements and churches is eroding the Catholic Church's traditional monopoly. The latter's valorization of the charismatic and Pentecostal experience, which had spread within the Church with no help from it, is an empirical statement of a phenomenon that has been illustrated in numerous excellent studies in the past decade (Antoniazzi et al., 1996; Aubrée, 2000; Bastian, 2001, 2004; Corten, 1996, 1997; Freston, 1995; Machado, 1996; Mafra, 2002; Martin, 1990; Oro et al., 2003).

2. Salvation goods and the gift economy

From this perspective, the idea of the religious marketplace is rather like Bentham's Panopticon: it prevents us escaping linguistically from the economic metaphor and conceals the connection between the sacred and the gift, of which religions – even the more rationalized ones – are custodians. To clarify this, we must first make a preliminary distinction. At least three categories of religious commodities can be distinguished, according to criteria which measures in abstract terms the symbolic (exchange) value of the commodities concerned.

First, *supply-side commodities* produced by a religious "firm" which, whether in monopoly or competitive conditions, attempts to consolidate its own brand in time and obtain a greater share of the market *(marketoriented-religious commodities)*. Within this category of goods fall identity markers, goods that socio-religious actors use to distinguish themselves from other subjects, according to the contingency formula: "I am different from you", so I must display types of behaviour which convey a sense of belonging. In monopoly situations, for example, in countries with a large Catholic majority, such as Ireland or Italy, it may no longer be enough to rely on the Sunday Mass to affirm the code of authority (the true or false of believing as defined, in this case, by the ecclesiastical hierarchy) and for the individual believer to identify fully with the institutional aims of the Catholic Church. In Italy, the percentage of "Sunday Mass consumers" has been a steady 30-35% of the population over the past thirty years in a situation of true religious monopoly; the vast majority of Italians still define themselves as Catholic. This situation presents the Italian Catholic Church with the problem of how to reach potential consumers or those who have been discouraged. These may be of various types: there are those who are critical of the products traditionally on offer, or lukewarm or only partially interested (think of the parents who never set foot in church, but who trustingly send their children to Catechism classes every Saturday), or they may be openly in search of an alternative product, though their quest is not perceived as contrasting with their own historical and cultural Catholic identity. The Church finds itself bound to introduce a new line of products when its monopoly is threatened by the presence of rival or alternative belief systems. It is not so much a question of inventing new goods able to keep the present clientele or attract new customers. Rather, it is a matter of marketing a special product called collective identity. In other words, a commodity which spreads the belief that there exists a collective consciousness, a founding myth of national identity (according to the contingency formula "we are the way we are, and cannot be otherwise"), a symbolic code that evokes the idea of unity in a society which, in reality, is deeply divided. All this despite the fact that at the end of Sunday Mass, the person to whom you turn to exchange the sign of peace may have views which are diametrically opposed to yours on many crucial points concerning life and politics.

Second, *demand-side commodities* produced by multifaceted, unpredictable and somewhat anarchical producers of symbols, which are not necessarily controlled by the supply side. To use the terminology of the system theory, they are commodities which exceed the belief system's capacity to transform them into effective means of communication, since by definition the socio-religious environment with which the system interacts is the realm of contingency (Iannaccone, 1990). This notion is similar to the concept of optional beliefs which Durkheim mentions (Durkheim 1898). A good example of this category of salvation goods is provided by what is normally labelled "popular religion". Goods of this type are to be found in many of the great world religions, including Christianity and Islam (especially in the cults of saints and Sufi), Judaism (at least in the Hassidic variant), not to mention Buddhism, Hinduism and Shintoism. Such goods constitute a powerful stream of symbols which flow like an underground river in the channels carved out by the human civilization of the great world religions. They have, in fact, continued to carry within the religious systems those magic-sacral aspects forming part of previous systems, which had either been violently put down or replaced peacefully. Thus, the simulacra of ancient beliefs survive and still continue to circulate in the great world religions, despite the many attempts to stop their spread, reduce their effects or simply destroy them. What we conventionally call popular religiosity, therefore, is the excess meaning which the official belief systems are unable to lead back into the regularity of belief. In this way, popular religiosity keeps open a space which might otherwise be reduced within the functions and principles of official or orthodox belief systems (Deconchy, 1971). Popular religiosity thus gives space to fresh ritual practices, which are often deliberately separate and distinct from those of official rites, presided over by clerical authorities. For example, Giuriati and Lanzi-Arzenton (1992) observed the development of the shrine in present-day Bosnia-Herzegovina at

Medjugorjie, where some claim to be able to communicate with the Madonna, and noted the process of differentiation of ritual practices. This has also been noted in other similar shrines and in other religious settings, for example, at the Shinto shrine of Kamakura in Japan. On the one hand, there is the Church with the official system and its well-defined confines, easily identified by the authority which governs the times and gestures of rituals; on the other, we have the ongoing spontaneous invention of unconventional symbols, forms and paths of worship which are either tolerated or considered marginal by the local ecclesiastical authorities.

This is because the so-called sacred is neither given nor fixed, but is created and has to be re-created. Given the need to undertake a journey (i.e. the pilgrimage), for instance, and enter an altered state of mind, it might seem justifiable to assume that without these items the sacred does not exist. Given that the invention of a set of extra-liturgical practices (termed thus to distinguish them from official liturgies under official control) has all the features of improvisation and sometimes even of latent conflict with the dominant institution of salvation, these goods are *demand-side* ones. They also share many of the characteristics of charismatic interactions. It is as if the devotee had relations with a kind of "non-present presence" with whom he wished to make contact, in a certain sense. These extra-liturgical practices generate a complexity which lies outside a belief system defined by its symbolic boundaries, a complexity that can be reduced by the system itself but only to a certain extent. From this viewpoint, there are systems capable of tolerating such external complexity to a greater or lesser degree. They may be placed along an imaginary scale of tolerance/intolerance, or to use Luhmann's (1977) terminology, inflation/deflation of the multiplicity of socio-religious forms present in the environment.

Finally, *largely gratuitous commodities*, i.e. gift commodities which cannot be reduced to the logic of symbolic exchange since they contain added value. The gratuitous nature of the gift enables one to imagine "another world"; it is a form of communication which has nothing to do with the law of marginal utility normally governing the great systems of religious belief. They are based on the expectation of possible future returns, resulting partially from existing facts and partially from future events, of varying degrees of certainty – as Max Weber teaches us in *The Protestant Ethic and the Spirit of Capitalism.*

If we adopt the framework dear to rational choice theorists, salvation commodities are only those produced by the supply side (the organizations of the eternal on Earth, the works of God or the parties of God which abound in the great world religions). But by so doing, "religion" as an object is impoverished, since by definition the rational choice theory precludes the possibility of understanding at least two facets of the religion. The first is the spontaneous production of salvation commodities, including those achieved through the experimental search for personal patents, leading to the discovery of transcendental spiritual techniques (mystical and ecstatic experiences, trances, visions, revelations, etc.), as Moshe Idel (2000) has shown with great acumen. The second is the gratuitous aspect which forms a structural part of many salvation commodities. Examples of this include the foundation and recognition of charisma, its intrinsically non-economic nature, linked to the fact that in the relationship between the charismatic leader and the community no exchange takes place, but rather a radical change of perspective as to the meanings to be attributed to the world and towards the order of belief held before the bursting onto the socio-religious scene of the charisma. Moreover, charisma has a dark side which brings it closer to the sphere of the sacred rather than the religious. This dark side is irreducible and cannot be brought into line by any religious organisation.

Rational choice theorists talk of the supply and demand of goods, and so the price of a salvation commodity in religious terms is the marginal utility of that commodity for all religious *consumers*. By contrast, the added value of the gift in the religious field lies precisely in its having nothing to do with the utility which that particular salvation commodity might have for individuals, considered singly. Because of its gratuitous nature, it is removed from the standardization typical of religious supply. In fact, the difference between founding charisma and constructed belief systems derives from the fact that, in the first case, the non-economic nature of communicative action prevails, whereas in the second the need for rational action (in terms of a means to an end) tends to impose itself. In charismatic relations, what counts is having an extraordinary experience, communicating the unthinkable and the unutterable, and making religion together, to paraphrase Alfred Schütz's making music together (Schütz, 1996). The difference, for instance, between Sunday church-going in the Christian environment, on the one hand, and making a pilgrimage to a non-conventional shrine, on the other, has to do with the distinction between an ordinary and an extraordinary experience. In the former, the subjects act in a codified context, above all from the socio-linguistic viewpoint. As a rule, in fact, liturgies trace the linguistic and symbolic confines within which collective rites are performed and individual behaviour is limited to pre-fixed and predictable formulae, in order to reduce cognitive and symbolic dissonance. In the latter, especially when the experience is what Turner (1969) calls *liminal*, i.e. when the individual feels that he or she is actually crossing the threshold which separates the ordinary from the extraordinary, the salvation commodities which he or she feels are received are gratuitous in character, a personal gift which is not necessarily governed by the principle of symbolic exchange. It is quite different from saying: "I go to Mass; I feel at peace with my conscience and I am offered symbols which bear my Church's seal of approval." By contrast, the experience of liminality, crossing the threshold of the sacred, is more in the order of an unexpected gift which "fascinates me and helps me see the world as a fascinating place again". Moreover, national and international research has shown that the sense of belonging to a religious institution may be experienced with varying degrees of intensity (Davie, 2002; Campiche et al., 2004; Garelli et al., 2003; Inglehart and Norris, 2004; Lambert, 2004), right down to those who belong without believing. In this case, what is the salvation commodity that relates to those who continue to see and define themselves as part of a religion, but have little or no faith? It is a symbolic commodity governed by the flexibility of the supply and demand of identity, which changes in time and varies with variations in the recognition or disdain of the other. To cite one example, in Italy many non-practising Catholics (and perhaps even non-believers) have felt the need not so much to return to churchgoing as to declare themselves Catholic in the face of the imagined threat from Islam. Clearly, what is at stake – i.e. the object of the symbolic exchange between these individuals and the Church as an institution – is not so much believing as belonging. This, however, is not religiously-oriented belonging but a matter of reassuring oneself that one is part of a cultural tradition which is different from that of the supposed Enemy. The Enemy has now crossed the border and lives within "our" society; the threat no longer comes from the invading unknown soldier but from the people who live next door. As both Inglehart and Norris (2004) affirm, where identity is insecure, religion is also highly likely to be seen again as the "anchor" of salvation as regards identity.

The existence of salvation gifts or goods, outside the narrow confines of the cost-benefit analysis, also reminds us of one aspect which both Durkheim and Weber were wont to point out: the connection between disorder and order in the production of the sacred and later of religion (or religious belief systems). This connection is more evident in charismatic interaction (rather than the charismatic action to which Weber refers) between the charismatic leader's virtuosity in improvising and the community of his followers. Charisma creates a mobile frontier between the leader and the group that follow him, since it is through his charisma that the followers experience *limen*, the crossing of the threshold perceived as meta-utilitarian solidarity, which is neither mechanical, nor organic. Charisma in this sense is an exercise of the virtue of improvisation. It is a higher gift, unexpected and often unutterable. These types of experience are often the subject of an act of reflection, which is conventionally known as liturgical practice. In fact, in their initial stages, they are *autopoietic* forms aimed at reducing the permanent tension between the charismatic leader and his community along the mobile frontier of meanings. When later we pass from the foundation and recognition of the cha-risma to that of preserving his memory, as Danièle Hervieu-Léger (1993) put it, in the notion of *lignée croyante*, liturgies together with their performance may be seen as socio-religious procedures to determine the legitimate borders of word and memory. They reduce the variability of the socio-religious environment which has suddenly been left unprotected by the virtuoso improviser. How can the improvisation continue without the virtuoso? Therefore, the rituals and liturgical practices which stem from some form of charismatic action are structurally exposed to the risk of contingency. In other words, they constitute an area where meanings are negotiated with greater freedom (and improvisation) than in other liturgical practices organized on the basis of restricted symbolic codes. Restricted codes usually discipline bodies, words and memories as the charisma gradually becomes institutionalized and the organizational model weakens with the growing functional distance between specialists in liturgical management and the so-called layman. In contrast to the warm, emotional performances of charismatic groups, liturgies derived from restricted codes are generally cold. We could perhaps distinguish between *pre-cooked liturgies* (offering the religious equivalent of fast food) and *raw liturgies* (offering *slow food* to be consumed hot on the premises), with greater opportunities for improvisation.

3. Charismatic liturgies and salvation goods

On the basis of these considerations, we will attempt to verify whether a sociological approach to liturgy, an approach which has been little used since the pioneering work of François Isambert (1979) and Jean Rémy and Liliane Voyé (1978) of a charismatic type might enable us to discover how salvation gifts or goods work. Their forms are more independent than those produced through the exchange economy and it may be possible to juxtapose the one with the other, without, however, nullifying the one in the other. In the complex interplay of imposed order and more or less spontaneous disorder, charisma seems to constitute an excess, preventing us from reducing what is produced in the liturgical area to religiously standardized goods.

To verify this thesis, we will use two case studies. They by no means provide concrete proof, so our conclusions cannot be generalized. Rather, they serve to pave the way for broader-based research. Our examples are taken from a series of participatory observations of the liturgy of the Universal Church of the Kingdom of God (Igreja Universal do Reino de Deus) which I carried out during two lengthy stays in Brazil, in Rio de Janeiro, São Paulo and Rio Grande do Sul and two previous studies of the Catholic Neo-Pentecostal movement in Italy (Diotallevi, 1999; Pace, 1983). From the methodological viewpoint, the choice falls on those liturgical performances which bear the hallmark of the charismatic experience. We compare the two types of liturgy to see whether it is in fact true that such an experience, once established within a belief system, finds it hard to adjust to a reduction of its complexity by an institution claiming to control the authenticity of all salvation goods that it does not produce directly, but which in theory come within its competence. The institution knows about these salvation goods and is therefore concerned about them at times. There is a kind of sequence which goes from free salvation goods to a charismatic situation and then to organized forms of religion, and which constitutes the framework for our case-studies. It should be made clear once and for all that the word "sacred" is a linguistic tool which serves to classify the socio-religious phenomena that form part of the sequence described above. To use the terminology of the classical tradition, the central dimension of the sacred is the production of a charismatic rituality which organized religions attempt to bring to order. All the distinctions introduced by the conventional sociology and anthropology of religion (such as that between the sacred and the profane or magic-sacral and secular religion) are still valid, provided we accept that they are linguistic short-cuts to understanding the irreducible relationship between system and environment in the sphere of beliefs of a religious nature. The two cases we investigated, the Universal Church of the Kingdom of God and the Catholic Neo-Pentecostal movement in Italy, are apparently very dissimilar. They represent two different stages in the institutionalization of charismatic experience. Yet, there are some interesting analogies. The hinterland or environment, to use the terminology of systems theory, in which they both sprang up, is one of Catholic religious monopoly. At the same time, however, this environment has been shaken by the profound changes and new conflicts that conventionally date back to the Second Vatican Council (1962), which began a process of internal reform, with often unexpected results. From the sociological viewpoint, an internal event in a complex organization such as the Catholic Church may be read as an increase in external complexity. An indicator of that new complexity which the Catholic Church was unable to dominate and reduce may be traced back to the emergence of religious free-riders or outsiders, bringing about new religious movements within or even outside the Church itself. Indeed, the initiators and founders of the United Church and the Neo-Pentecostal movement, respectively, are socio-religious actors who have distanced themselves from church religion and gone for charismatic experience, with a greater (in the case of the former) and lesser (in that of the latter) degree of freedom. From the very beginning of these new experiences, in fact, their leaders have tried out liturgical and ritual models which are unconventional, i.e. different from those traditionally followed by the Catholic Church. Their aim was to shift the well-established symbolic boundaries of the belief system, challenge institutional resistance and cross a threshold which casts doubts on the type of church, the hierarchical model of the monopoly of truth according to the contingency formula: *the Spirit blows where it will.*

These are the similarities between the two movements, but what interests us most are the differences. Their study enables us to see what happens in the long term in the process of institutionalization of charismatic experience in the two cases in question. The difference is contained within a paradox: where free salvation goods, such as those of a charismatic experience, are administered by an organization that uses them to hallmark its own social identity in the religious marketplace (as in the case of the United Church), the tendency to transform those goods into products for the religious market is far greater than in the second case, that of the Neo-Pentecostal renewal within the Catholic Church. This movement, in fact, has been steadily "brought back to the fold" and its innovative force gradually blunted. Nevertheless, despite this institutionalization, it still manages to keep a certain degree of autonomy as far as liturgical expression is concerned, thus marking out its own spiritual specialization and competence. The most suitable context for a comparison is liturgy, that complex collective movement which develops within a defined time and space and has all the features of an extraordinary order – at the same time both planned and unpredictable – of body gestures and postures, prayers and chants, repetitive rituals and unplanned events. In short, it is a performance in which not all that happens is completely controllable or under control; even the repetition of gestures may suddenly be interrupted to give way to manifestations of charisma, subjective drives which exist in the environment, which are liberated by the liturgical procedure, and which cannot always be traced back to the pre-established outline. On the other hand, charisma is structurally anti-liturgical, in that it is based on action which goes against the conventionalities of public worship (*leiturgia* in its original Greek sense) which a belief system has laid down. And the charismatic *interaction* between the leader and his followers is originally non-economic because it contrasts with the salvation goods economy administered by the official liturgy, which a belief system has created and imposed on its environment. For example, Jesus' disciples and Jesus himself were continually asked by the rabbis of the time whether whatever they were doing complied with the observance of the Torah. The famous passage from Luke (6: 1-2) is eloquent on this point:

> And it came to pass on the second Sabbath after the first, that he went through the corn fields; and his disciples plucked the ears of corn, and did eat, rubbing them in their hands. And certain of the Pharisees said unto them, "Why do ye that which is not lawful to do on the Sabbath days?"

Is not this act by Jesus and his disciples a risky one? The price they have to pay in social terms is high: they will be cast out of the community of the pure, no longer considered practising Jews (a kind of civil death). Jesus and his disciples, therefore, have nothing to gain by keeping alive a (charismatic) religious experience which openly challenges the codified rules of conduct which the official liturgies undertake to demonstrate in public worship. This is why, in the two case studies in question, we concentrate on the liturgies they organize.

4. The structure of the liturgical performance in the IURD

We will consider salvation commodities of the third type (gifts) by observing the structure of a liturgical performance at a charismatic meeting of the Universal Church of the Kingdom of God in Brazil (IURD). This will then be compared with what used to take place in the early days of the Catholic Pentecostal movement in Italy.

The guidelines for the performance of the standard liturgy of the Universal Church of the Kingdom of God contains a point-by-point account of the complex rites which are usually performed in large halls (with a seating capacity of 4'000-5'000, often former cinemas). The procedure is as follows:

1. People arrive in dribs and drabs, receive on entry the laying on of hands from two lines of young helpers, who also make sure no "weirdoes" get in; they sit down in comfortable seats facing a stage with a backdrop of mountains, rivers and freshwater springs, above which is written the name of Christ; on the stage, there is a microphone, an electric organ, a lectern with an open book (perhaps the Bible) which is, however, never used during the liturgical performance.

2. After a series of songs and chants, there is a brief sermon by the officiator (generally a relatively young person, of good appearance, wearing a shirt and tie, who moves confidently about the stage, capturing the congregation's attention with his direct and effective style of communication); he officiates throughout the entire liturgy.

3. This is followed by a communal prayer which starts calmly and grows in intensity (increasingly up-tempo invocations for a manifestation of the power of Christ), backed up by the unrelenting voice and convulsive gestures of the officiator.

4. The lengthy period of excitement is followed by a phase of emotional discharge in which members of the congregation in various parts of the hall go into trances or become possessed; the numerous aides throughout the room immediately go to their help, laying on hands and driving away the "demons"; by so doing, they demonstrate the triumph of Christ in the struggle against Satan which manifested itself "right there, at that very moment"; this phase may last a long time, depending on the number of intervention carried out by the aides on people in altered states of consciousness (trance and possession); the manifestations of trance alternate with intense prayers recited aloud individually asking for grace (of various types: healing, success, family reconciliation, blessing for a forthcoming wedding or birth) and indicating by means of photographs of dear ones or their possessions those for whom divine protection is invoked.

5. Once this liturgical action – "the struggle between Christ and Satan" – is over, the ritual continues with the entrance of "Christ's workers" from side doors; these girls carry large trays and distribute a small piece of bread and a plastic beaker of water to all those present; what follows is very reminiscent of the Eucharist, but with two important differences: first, the water is the sign of the purification which has taken place in the room thanks to Christ's victory over Satan; and second, having drunk their water, the congregation are invited by the officiator to crush the plastic cup – the symbol of Satan's head – in their hands and then underfoot. This gesture unleashes a collective burst of laughter and a contagious sense of contentment among the entire congregation. The joyful singing which follows (with very loud musical accompaniment) emphasizes the level of emotional intensity achieved during the "live" victorious battle against Satan.

6. Once calm has returned (after more than an hour and a half of collective excitement), the congregation sits down again, happy, smiling and relaxed (at least this is the impression they give) as if taking a well-earned rest after a fruitful emotional effort. The officiator gives his longer, second sermon, which revolves around two basic points: the importance of the extraordinary event which has taken place and which all have experienced (directly or indirectly) concerning the power of Christ to save, and the beneficial effect which this event has on the lives of the people. At this point, the officiator sometimes invites members of the public to come "spontaneously" up onto the stage and testify to the changes which have taken place in their private or family lives, at work, or in business after their "conversion" to the message of Christ which the Universal Church states is within the reach of every human being. Variations on this theme sometimes include the need to make a voluntary contribution – a percentage of one's income – to the life of the Church, a gesture of loyalty and faith which is encouraged by calling other witnesses who show the amount of money they have donated or plan to donate. At election times, candidates recognized by the Church are given publicity (I had occasion to witness this personally when President Cardoso was re-elected; one of the candidates in the campaign in Rio de Janeiro bore the unlikely name of Pastor Divino!).

7. The lengthy sermon concludes with a song of thanksgiving and as the music fades, the congregation drift slowly towards the exit.

5. The structure of the liturgical performance in the Catholic Neo-Pentecostal movement

At this point, a comparison should be made between the foregoing liturgical complexities and the rituals of the Catholic Neo-Pentecostal movement in Italy at its origins in 1971-72. Before the latter was gradually normalized and made compatible with the official belief system (a change demonstrated partially by the altered wording from Renewal of the Spirit to Renewal in the Spirit), the amount of room for improvisation conceded to the individual participants was far greater than in the Universal Church. Control and management of "charismatic" phenomena are more evident in the Universal Church. At least at the outset, the liturgy of Renewal – held in parish halls or private homes, not in churches or chapels – rose in a crescendo which was supposed to climax in a state of communal ecstasy ("speaking in tongues"), preceded by praying, singing and manifestations of altered states of consciousness (the manifestation of charisma). Close observation of the ritual reveals that also in this case control of language gradually slackened as the finale approached: the ecstatic moment of "speaking in tongues" (glossolalia). This liturgical performance typical of the initial stages of the movement effectively illustrates the passage of the charismatic rite from the liturgical deregulation phase to a second phase incorporated in the varied offer of liturgical goods under the control of an institutional authority. As for other movements which arose in the 1970s within world-wide Catholicism, the liturgy constituted a kind of rite of passage, an initiation process which enabled people to experience something which initially clashed with the Catholic-form (Schmitt) as it had taken shape over the years since the Counter-reformation. The traditional division between the clergy and laymen was overridden not only in the functional or sacral sense, but also more significantly in the management of the liturgy. In the new movements such as Renewal the principle of spiritual parity was put into effect, freely reinterpreting the collective spirit of original Christianity. It is noteworthy that the first charismatic experience of the Renewal movement was the reduction to a minimum of the organizational apparatus of the ritual act. In the end, the rite became a collective trance session with preparatory readings, prayers and chants in a crescendo of emotional intensity. The final goal to be achieved, the long-awaited event, was the "descent of the Holy Spirit", which constituted the climax of the collective trance. Everything else was important but not essential. Indeed, the very essence was the cancellation of the division between the defined and the undefined (the main systemic function of the communicative code we call religion), the perception that the division between these two spheres had vanished.

One thing that emerged clearly, and which continues to hold true for the current Catholic Neo-Pentecostal movement in Italy, was the effort to maintain the experience of the *limen*, crossing with ease the threshold which marks the liturgical border between known and unknown words, and between a more or less structured code of liturgical communication and another characterized by individual recitation, following the virtuosi of improvisation capable of creating a sound (glossolalia) which disarticulates the common meaning attributed to conventional liturgical words. Continuing our comparison of the two cases in question, let us look at the gradual "tidying up" of the initial liturgical practice of Renewal and the way it was brought back within a more orthodox scheme of things. The evolution of the movement was marked by a progressive but somewhat laborious process of recognition by the bishops and the ecclesiastical authorities in general. Eventually, the movement's initial innovative thrust, which conjured up for its activists the image of a Church of the Spirit, mystical and community based, was removed. The initial absence of the traditional division between clergy and laymen (hence the diffidence of the ecclesiastical authorities) was also reinstated. Thus, Renewal has become one of the many possible options which the Catholic Church offers today, and it may be freely chosen without provoking the conflicts and tensions of the past. Nevertheless, there remain some traces of the original experience without which the Neo-Pentecostal element on offer would cease to exist.

These two case studies should be taken for what they are. One day it might be possible to carry out a comparative study of Neo-Pentecostal liturgies (including all the local variants: Asiatic, African, Latin American and European) to explore their differences with regard to relations between salvation gift/goods and salvation exchange/goods as they are presented to and perceived by participants in charismatic events.

For sociologists, the interest in such a study would lie precisely in the fact that the subject of the investigation is the interplay between exchange goods and gift commodities, a distinction which is not always absolutely clear. Moreover, the charismatic experience assumes the existence of a mobile border between a system of codified (liturgical) signs and the variability of the socio-religious environment. In abstract terms, the latter is represented by the unpredictable skills of improvisation of the individuals who may invent new ritual gestures, words and cadences. The unexpected element means that a system of signs must continually attempt to transform the excess of meaning which manifests itself in the environment into internal complexity. The most crucial point for the relationship between system and environment (in terms of liturgy) is the highly gratuitous nature of the salvation goods which come into circulation freely and through the independent initiative of single individuals and which cannot always be reinvested in the symbolic capital accumulated by the (codified liturgical) system. The most disruptive gratuity is what Victor Turner called *communitas*: the experience of collective fusion which would be impossible to express otherwise. *Communitas* does not always or easily adapt itself to the system, but tends to be unregulated and non-economic.

6. Conclusion

The two cases we have briefly examined present quite a good illustration of the tension between profit and gratuity in the economy of salvation goods produced in liturgical practices. In the Universal Church of the Kingdom of God, this gratuity manifests itself but is closely controlled and comes back as proof of the originality of the product which the Church itself is capable of offering. As regards the Renewal movement, there was obvious tension in the early days between the virtues of improvisation stimulated by the private liturgies practised by the movement, on the one hand, and the traditional ritual, as administered by the Catholic Church at its Sunday services, on the other. After institutional recognition and control of the liturgy by the clergy and theologians, the amount of freedom for the layman to appropriate the symbolic capital (to use Bourdieu's words) of the liturgical signs appears, in the light of the present situation, to have been reduced to a routine and left devoid of most of their communicative power *(communitas)* set in motion by the charismatic events.

In these two case studies, we may observe the dialectic between the supply side and the demand side in the production of salvation goods. The Catholic Neo-Pentecostal movement may be considered a successful case of reduction of complexity. The excess meaning which it gave rise to more or less spontaneously in the initial stages (since it easily overcame the traditional division between Protestantism and Catholicism) constituted an increase in complexity outside the Catholic belief system. Transferring this complexity from the outside to within the system itself enabled the system to boost its capacity to function as a *complexio oppositorum*; it adapted to the difference stemming from the external socio-religious environment by changing it into a difference compatible with the authority principle which governs a traditional pyramid-like organization such as the Catholic Church. Unable to sustain the presence of different sects within it, the Church transforms the sect into an order, whence it can be reduced to come within the contingency formula: "charisma for the greater glory of the Church". The process of reduction does not entirely suppress the charismatic dimension spontaneously produced by the movement. Rather, it confines itself to making it compatible with the law of religious supply and demand within the system. It is no longer regarded as avant-garde, but as one service among many provided by the Church and it holds a position on a scale of influence alongside other movements within the Church. Those who wish to do so may undergo a charismatic experience with Renewal, just as they may embark upon a Neo-Catechumenal experience. Some may be convinced they are inventing a new way of attending church; others are persuaded they are perfectly in line with the official Church. In such cases, as Weber has taught us, institutionalization turns invention into routine and improvisation into institutional mediation. The institutionalization of Catholic Neo-Pentecostal Renewal confines the experience to a specialized sub-system within the macro system of Catholic belief. This, in the end, compresses the space for the free production of (demand-side) salvation goods, since charismatic improvisation is taken away from the supply-side and brought back to being a marginal variation in the Catholic portfolio. In the case of the United Church, on the other hand, the gratuitous nature of the gift (i.e. the charisma) appears to be defined by the liturgical framework, within symbolic confines and the practices of specialists in the sacred (the bishops and the officiators of the rites). At the same time, however, it cannot be completely reduced because it allows for individual improvisation in the liturgy, as regards both the meanings attributed to liturgical interaction and the gestures and emotions entailed. The United Church has, thus, developed greater flexibility in terms of the market, since it can offer salvation goods which seem to be made-to-measure, on a just-in-time basis (*a post-Fordist religion?*).

Generally speaking, wherever religious organizations are founded on charisma, competition with the Catholic Church for the control of the market for religious goods becomes acute. The latter tends to lose the monopoly position it enjoyed until recently, while the former appear to be flexible models of religious supply that leave ample margin for creativity on the demand side.

References

Antoniazzi, Alberto, Mariz, Cecilia, Sarti, Ingrid, Filho, B. José, Sanchis, Pierre, Fernandes, R. Cesar and Gomes, Wilson (1996) *Nem anjos nem demônios.* Petropolis: Vozes.
Aubrée, Marion (2000) "Dynamiques comparées de l'Eglise Universelle du Royaume de Dieu au Brésil et à l'étranger", in J.-P.

Bastian and F. Rousselet (eds) *La globalisation du religieux*, pp. 113-124. Paris: L'Harmattan.

Bastian, Jean-Pierre (2001) "Pentecostalism, Market Logic and Religious Transnationalism in Costa Rica", in A. Corten and R. Marshall-Fratani (eds) *Between Babel and Pentecost*, pp. 163-180. Bloomington: Indiana University Press.

–. (2004) *Emotion et tradition: La recomposition des protestantismes en Europe latine*. Geneva: Labor et Fides.

Bourdieu, Pierre (1971) "Genèse et structure du champ religieux", *Revue française de sociologie* 3: 295-334.

Campiche, Roland (2004) *Les deux visages de la religion*. Geneva: Labor et Fides.

Corten, André (1996) *Os pobres e o Espirito Santo: O pentecostalismo no Brasil*. Petropolis: Vozes.

–. (1997) "Miracles et obéissance: le discours de la guérison divine à l'Eglise Universelle", *Social Compass* 2: 283-303.

Davie, Grace (2002) *Europe: An Exceptional Case*. London: Darton, Longman and Todd.

Deconchy, Jean-Pierre (1971) *L'orthodoxie religieuse*. Paris: Les Editions Ouvrières.

Diotallevi, Luca (1999) *Religione: Chiesa e modernizzazione*. Rome: Borla.

Durkheim, Emile (1898) "De la définition des phénomènes religieux", *L'Année Sociologique* 1: 1-28.

Freston, Paul (1995) "Pentecostalism in Brazil: A Brief History", *Religion* 25: 119-133.

Garelli, Franco, Guizzardi, Gustavo and Pace, Enzo eds (2003) *Un singolare pluralismo*. Bologna: Il Mulino.

Giuriati, Paolo and Lanzi-Arzenton, Gioia (1992) *Il senso del cammino*. Padova: CRSR Edizioni.

Guizzardi, Gustavo (1979) *La religione della crisi*. Milan: Edizioni di Comunità. Hervieu-Léger, Danièle (1993) *La religion pour mémoire*. Paris: Cerf.

Iannaccone, Laurence (1990) "Religious Practice: A Human Capital", *Journal for the Scientific Study of Religion* 29: 297-314.

Idel, Moshe (2000) *Mistici messianici*. Milan: Adelphi.

Inglehart, Ronald and Norris, Pippa (2004) *Secular and Sacred*. Cambridge: Cambridge University Press.

Isambert, François (1979) *Rite et efficacité symbolique*. Paris: Cerf.

Kilani, Mondher (1997) *L'invenzione dell'altro*. Bari: Dedalo.

Lambert, Yves (2004) "A Turning Point in Religious Evolution in Europe", *Journal of Contemporary Religion* 1: 29-45.

Luhmann, Niklas (1977) *Funktion der Religion*. Frankfurt: Suhrkamp.

Machado, Maria das Dores Campos (1996) *Carismaticos e pentecostais*. São Paulo: ANPOCS.

Mafra, Clara C. (2002) *Na posse da Palava*. Lisbon: Impresa de Ciências Sociais.

Martin, David (1990) *Tongues of Fire*. Oxford: Blackwell.

Oro, Ari Pedro, Corten, André and Dozon, Jean-Pierre, eds (2003) *Igreja Universal do Reino de Deus*. São Paulo: Paulinas.

Pace, Enzo (1983) *Asceti e mistici in una società secolarizzata*. Venice: Marsilio.

Rémy, Jean and Voyé, Liliane (1978) *Produire ou reproduire?* Brussels: Vie Ouvrière.

Schütz, A. (1996) *Fragments towards a Phenomenology of Music*, in A. Schütz (ed.) *Collected Works*. Dordrecht: Kluwer.

Turner, Victor (1969) *The Ritual Process*. Chicago: Aldine Publishing Company.

Jean-Pierre BASTIAN

The New Religious Economy of Latin America

1. Introduction

Latin America is experiencing rapid religious change, characterized by the diversification of denominational affiliations and increasing pluralization. Pentecostal organizations nevertheless dominate the new non-Roman Catholic religious landscape; divided into dozens of small competing organizations, some of them number several hundred thousand followers at the national and international scale. This new reality merits analysis in terms of market theory, because it is possible to advance as a hypothesis that in Latin America the dynamics of religious pluralization is determined by a "market situation" (Berger 1969:138). This concerns an overall development of Latin American societies in which "it is no longer the modernizing or repressive State that is the central character of each country, but the world of commercial firms, in other words, social actors responding to the logic of economics" (Touraine, 1992:17). Economic rationality informs religious business strategies that stimulate the development, distribution and consumption of new symbolic products in a system of generalized competition of religious agencies and authorities (Silveira Campos, 1997; Chesnut 2003). From this follows a decline of the Catholic monopoly and the transformation of practices and beliefs. This leads to an examination of the current religious pluralization from the perspective of new theories of the "religious market". To what point do they support a pertinent model and what are their limits? This important question has for the present time little impact on the sociological literature dealing with religious change in the region. The current changes can be explained by economic theory. This approach, necessary but not sufficient, must nevertheless conjoin with the field theory of Bourdieu. To that purpose, I intend first to examine micro-economic theory applied to religious facts in the Latin American region, then the manner in which the Pentecostalisms take part in the logic of performance. Here we will be dealing with locating three characteristics of the new Latin American religious economy: demo-nopolization, hybridity, and the media visibility of practices and beliefs. Finally, in order not to reduce the analysis to market logic alone, I will discuss the relation to the political context, which induces an understanding of religious developments in terms of field.

2. A ground in ferment

The sociological theories having recourse to the application of micro-economics to the analysis of the religious fact stress the connection between religious demonopolization and the vitality of practices. In systems of a single religion or strongly backed by the status of a state religion, practices would tend to lose vitality. They would be more intense in societies deregulated on the religious plane (Finke and Stark 1992: 18) or, as Iannaconne says (1992: 124), "where religion is less regulated ... competition among religious firms is more pronounced". This hypothesis is problematic in Latin America. Until the mid-twentieth century, Catholicism remained the dominant and hegemonic religion in the whole region, enjoying privileges reinforced by con-cordats constantly renewed by all the Latin American countries except Mexico. The liberal constitutions of the preceding century had cer-tainly opened the region to freedom of religion. Various religious movements, principally Protestant, spiritualistic, Mormon, and theosophist, had tried to gain a foothold but had achieved only very limited results in terms of recruitment. Their religious and social mar-ginalization was just as obvious one hundred years after their first attempts at expansion. This was due as much to the situation of monopoly that benefited Catholicism as to the dynamism of the Catholic actors. Latin American Catholicism benefited from a rent of monopoly, but religious practices did not necessarily decline. Nor have they ever been homogenous. On the contrary, "baroque" Catholicism has always revealed itself extremely flexible and able to differentiate its offers in function of specific social problems. It has shown, and continues to show, sustained vitality through not only the intensity of so-called popular practices but also the successful mobilization of the middle classes through Catholic action movements. Moreover, the reiterated concordats served to reinforce a national Catholicism on the offensive, which took the form of the consecrations of various countries to the Sacred Heart of Jesus in a context where anti-Communism and the nation's affirmation of Catholic identity went hand in hand. Catholic resistance to the attempts at secularization was so intense that it even gave rise to civil wars such as the Cristero Wars in Mexico (1926-1929) or the period of violence in Colombia (1948-1952). The dynamic monopoly of Catholicism explains a good share of the failure of historical Protestantism and Kardecist Spiritism in the region, confined to sectors of emerging middle classes. In the 1960s, Catholicism continued on the same trajectory of mobilization of the masses through devotional practices adapted to various social demands. The institutional monopoly implied neither the lack of diversification of offers nor the uniformization of symbolic products. There existed an array of rites and representations connected to specific social actors. The faithful could choose their devotion from a wide range associated with a pantheon of patron saints and Marian images in competition according to their supposed efficacy. The principle of costs and benefits dear to the theory of rational choice was active there, insofar as the faithful pursued the most effective devotions and discontinued the others. Popular cults like that of Nino Fidencio in northern Mexico or that of Maria Lionza in Venezuela, created by anonymous actors as early as the 1930s, constrained the Catholic clergy to co-opt them in order to respond to a innovating social demand. Thus, new Catholic forms of worship were on the rise, while others were in decline. In other terms, the institutional monopoly did not imply devitalization of the religious. This does not contradict the theory of rational choice, to the extent that competition is operating concealed among "Catholic products" in function of their performance, but it challenges the idea according to which the monopolistic situation would, as though necessarily, engender the reduction of practices and the decline of religion. The Pentecostalisms did not come to redynamize an amorphous religious field or create a market situation. Rather, they amplified a pre-existing religious diversity upon which they were grafted. Nevertheless, the question remains: what happened so that, over the past fifty years, the region switched from the situation of a dynamic religious monopoly in a system of multiple offers of services and goods to a competitive religious upsurge?

A set of macro-social factors led to this swing: the anomie of the peasant masses immigrated to the outskirts of the megalopolises, the globalization of markets starting in the 1960s with the circulation of capital, workers and ideas, and the growing role of the media, especially of television in the spread of new religious practices. The microeconomic theory of competition as the revitalization of religious practices does not explain the Catholic dynamism preceding the current deregulation if it does not consider the possible connection between the monopoly and the diversification of offers. The Latin American religious ground did not go from a state of apathy to one of ferment, but from a differentiated ferment within a monopolistic situation to a pluralization in ferment. It was on a dynamic religious ground in the core of the Catholic universe that Pentecostalisms began to proliferate exponentially in the region during the 1950s and 1960s. With these Pentecostalisms, Latin America went from an *ad intra* religious competition, internal to Catholicism, to an *ad extra* competition induced by the pluralization of non-Roman Catholic religious organizations. The new religious economy that ensues from it conjoins with the one that preceded it. It is to be explored in the light of microeconomic theory.

3. The transformation of symbolic offers in market logic

In a classical view, to set agencies and religious firms in competition struggling for the accumulation and distribution of symbolic goods likely to meet the interest and demand of ever-greater sectors of the population is to characterize market logic (Berger, 1969; Bourdieu, 1971a; Iannaconne 1992). However, a tension exists between the economic model of rational choice and the model of the religious field advanced by Bourdieu. The latter specifically rejects the utilitarian finality of rational choice. Nevertheless, can we not connect both models in hopes of simultaneously explaining the commercial deployment of the religious in the region and objective relationships within field logic where the search for hegemony drives the dynamics? The behavior of the actors reflects the development of a practice of performance on both the subjective and the institutional planes. The cost-benefit principle is at work there. At the same time, in a region where religious secularization remains weak, the production of new symbolic goods is an issue in the displacement of power relationships between the Catholic Church, which held a historical monopoly, and the new Pentecostal incomers. This is precisely because the separation between religion and politics remains a legal fiction. In practice, the religious actors are co-opted by the political actors, and conversely, the religious actors are backed by politics in order to reinforce their positions in the religious field. The connection of these two theoretical models provides us with an instrument that can explain the logics of interaction among the religious actors in the region.

The Charismatic Catholic Renewal, Evangelical Pentecostalism and the Pentecostal millenarianism of endogenous construction are deployed in competition. The Pentecostal cathedrals, newly built in all the great cities of the region, match the Catholic cathedrals as markers of the pluralized symbolic space. Catholic television programs of charismatic tone strive to rival Pentecostal television networks, which for some time have held the advantage of the initiative. The acceleration of exchanges and religious transnationalization thus stimulate the cult of performance in both. It is true that, in the beginning, the situation of the differentiated Catholic monopoly gave impetus to religious innovation, but not to this culture of performance, whose main criterion is the number of members. The search for results stems from the fact that the new Evangelical Pentecostal entrants suffered from a lack of status, unlike followers of historical types of Protestantism or Kardecism, who benefited from the support of political liberalism. For the Pentecostals, the law of numbers has become an accessible criterion of success. Thus, business logic set in motion the global spread of Pentecostalism, which has the merit of adapting very well to the principles of transnationality (Colonomos 2001:250). The Pentecostalisms have become business firms, developing strategies to commercialize and distribute symbolic goods multilaterally. The Catholic Church was impelled to do the same, cultivating its transnational networks already long in place in a procedure of competitive mobilization and adopting new so-called charismatic practices borrowed from its competitors. For the latter, the multilaterality of exchanges induced a transformation of the type of product offered. This developed in a context of accelerated urbanization, which is one of the causes of the intensification of cultural hybridization. In a few decades, Latin America has in fact shifted from societies dispersed in thousands of rural communities with their traditional local cultures to an urban framework with populations characterized by a high level of illiteracy (Garcia-Canclini, 1990: 135-136). Within this framework is deployed a heterogeneous symbolic offer renewed by the constant interaction of the local with national and international communication networks.

The eclecticism of Pentecostal practices and beliefs manifests in its triple Evangelical, Catholic and millenarian deployment. We are dealing here with a process of hybridization that is not syncretism. The latter term, in a culturalist approach to the religious, reflects the idea of the purity of religious traditions and a normative classification of types of conduct and elements of imaginaries. On the other hand, the notion of hybridity indicates rather the juxtaposition of different registers of borrowings, including the contents of beliefs, the forms of transmission and communication, recourse to both the most archaic and the most modern mediations, and the eclectic and pragmatic use of the models joined to market logic. Furthermore, in Latin America, the notion of hybridity accounts for the modalities by which various social sectors appropriate the multi-temporal heterogeneity of the heritages and religious influences specific to the region. Indeed the Pentecostal hybridity responds to a demand for connection of the religious to the diversity of existing traditions, while demonstrating the ability to absorb new practices and discourse likely to attract increasing attention. As Corten has noted (1999: 171), "the Pentecostal discourse sucks in symbolic particles in a transnational circulation". In hybridity is decided not only the adaptation to a market, but also the creation of a religious demand that the hybrid product seeks to anticipate by stimulating. Latin American Pentecostalism until the 1960s reproduced the North American religious model in a system of "truth" close to the original Evangelical Protestant model. However, since that period a hybrid endogenous religiosity has been developing in a system of "performance", making eclectic use of elements issuing from diverse local, national and transnational sources in order to offer a novel and attractive product.

This is expressed, for example, in the rapid changes in the forms of praising. While at first Pentecostal Evangelical hymnology was of Anglo-Saxon origin, much attention has been focused since the 1980s on incorporating kinds of music and rhythm from different national musical traditions (salsa, salsa-gospel, and so on), transforming the very shape of the religious service. Solemn services and preachers with a rigid role have been replaced by pastor-presenters and overhead projectors that show the words to the hymns on the walls of the place of worship in the manner of a Japanese "karaoke". Thus, the services have in fact become shows featuring an electric orchestra and little groups of singers. The "ministers of musical praise" determine the success of the service-shows, whose implementation they enable in the logic of performance. The "nativization" of hymnology favors the emergence of dynamic forms of worship, connected or not to the Pentecostal expressions of North American origin. On the register of an emotional piety on the look-out for new service gimmicks through rhythm, songs, hand-clapping, and controlled swaying, a communion is created which is indeed that of the "discourse of praise" (Corten, 1995: 137ff.), rooted in Latin American musical culture and popular modes of communication. This musical boom is carried out in an entrepreneurial sense, that is, through an Evangelical singing industry whose main actors, professional Latin American singers, have converted to Pentecostalism (Yuri, Rabito, José Luis Guerra, and so forth) and retrained for this type of production. In this way, an audiovisual commercial circuit (videos, CDs) has been created from inside the most dynamic Pentecostal churches, evidence of the appropriation of market strategies by religious actors. The Catholic Church is not left out, since it has produced its own singers, of whom the best known is a young Brazilian priest from Sao Paulo, Father Marcello Rossi. Likewise, the design of the houses of worship echoes the aesthetics of the television world. Not only have many Pentecostal churches of recent creation taken over old cinemas, but the interior of the buildings, the prominence of the electronic equipment, the presence of a sound engineer, and the use of electrical musical instruments are testimony to the appropriation of modern performance technologies and the symbols of mass audiovisual culture.

Visible all over the region are pastors, charismatic priest-presenters, and religious singers who have combined the profane musical styles in religious musical entertainments that fill the stadiums. Real firms to commercialize religious products have thus emerged, which incorporate marketing techniques, strategies for media promotion, stage preparation for the performances, and public relations. Mass audiovisual culture has formed a factor to legitimize the cosmovisions proper to each particular religious trend, giving it a code of communication that lends credibility to the values and interpretations of the world that have currency starting from other discursive codes.

This appears clearly in one of the principal Pentecostal practices, exorcism, that allows detecting both the hybridity of the phenomenon and the commercial logic that informs the practices. The religious trance and possession that are the manifestations of exorcism belong to the register of popular religious mentalities. They contribute to reinforce the image of intercessor in the case of the religious director, agent of revealed knowledge, because the unction that sanctions liberation from demons functions through him. The pastor/intercessor is assumed into the shamanic continuity of the one who has the power to recognize the spirits, speak to them and expulse them; he shares the ability to communicate with the numinous and distributes strength, freedom and healing. The reformulation of the practices is expressed, in Brazil as in the rest of the region, by a growing mercantilization of the services through the "sale of religious objects, the 'donation' (in exchange for money) of blessed objects (soaps, handkerchiefs, oils, wedding rings, palm branches, keys, etc.) and the sale of prayers" and blessings (Oro, 1992: 426). This is also expressed by a constant renewal in the choice of objects that are intended to circulate in the transnational networks, just like the words they represent. As Corten points out (1999: 170), "the phrase 'Jesus is the solution' has become common to the Pentecostal churches". It eclipses the term "salvation" in theological discourse and makes the miracle an opinion that is no longer an inner personal belief, but an element of the imaginary "produced like a public opinion".

Thus, since the 1990s, the practice of exorcism has been enriched by that of "spiritual war" which has become predominant in Latin American Pentecostal discourse. The latter innovation is an example of the current logic of networking, which, as Colonomos observes (1995: 126), implies "a transnational detour", most of the time North American. This notion comes largely from the practice of Latin American Pentecostal preachers, in particular the Argentinian Carlos Annacondia (Wynarczyk, 1993). It was observed and systematized by certain contemporary North American Pentecostal actors who brought it up to date at the end of the 1980s (Murphy, 1994). In turn, it has been adopted, reformulated and realized within a Latin American mental and physical context. Pentecostal star-presenters, such as the Costa Rican Rony Chaves (1992), have made themselves the national specialists of this popular theology of the "spiritual war" resumed during "international conferences of God's word". According to their terms, this matter is a "battle to wage against Satan, the demons and the occult practices" connected with them, developing "a war strategy to clean up the occupied territories". This geopolitical dimension of the mobilization of the powers of the invisible characterizes a discourse that no longer addresses just the individual, but the nation-State, which must therefore be liberated in a national and international strategy. Around such concepts conferences, "intercessor" associations, and television programs are arranged, which comprise diverse and various transnational trajectories, even if they often imply a North American relay. Such activities and ideas, which can be perceived as "American" and "Protestant" (Martin, 1990), are above all transnational, because one of the traits of transnationality is the favorable context that it provides for cultural borrowings of every type. In this sense, a great many forms of Latin American Pentecostalism are not "emotional Protestantism" (Willaime, 1999:5), but hybrid religious movements borrowing countless elements from the endogenous popular cultures which, reformulating the original Pentecostalism, represent a redefinition of the original Protestant modes of belief and practices in function of the market. As Willaime has stated (1999: 10, n. 12), "Pentecostalism has too many ambivalent characteristics, and its capacity to flow into various indigenous cultures is so strong that future developments may occur in rather different directions". Diffusion by capillarity fortifies these centrifugal tendencies. The recourse to popular culture and the direct appeal to language and the myths of popular religion, in particular to demonology, have transformed the original Pentecostalism into a Latin American religious movement recognizable by the masses, the reason for its success.

Nevertheless, the Pentecostal dynamics is not due to its inclusion in the archaic religious universe, but to its capacity to bridge archaism and hypermodernity in a floating universe of references. The fluidity of the practices and beliefs is reflected in the weak roots of affiliations, the faithful transiting from one religious expression to another, ultimately recognizing themselves in all of them. It is true that the Pentecostal churches define the lines of demarcation between them through sartorial, ritual and organizational markers. However, all of them integrate at least three common practices: glossolalia, thaumaturgy and exorcism. This renders the boundaries porous and means that the "Pentecostalization" of practices and beliefs covers a wide spectrum that goes from Pentecostalized Evangelical movements to Catholic Pentecostalism, including a thick layer of endogenous Pentecostalized millenarianisms.

The delocalization of beliefs and practices operates in particular through recourse to the media, which facilitates immediate networking in an open religious market. The management of the religious by the media, and especially by the television image, is probably the central factor of the current market logic and the major expression of the hybridity that permits, as Gruzinski (1994: 211) has noted in the context of Mexican commercial television, "a return in force of the pervasive miraculous image of baroque times".

4. Media and networking

One of the characteristics of Latin American Pentecostalisms is the juxtaposition of discourse drawing from traditional religious registers and recourse to the most performing media. The transmission of the image certainly operates there through relations of kinship and proximity, but also and equally through modern means of communication. It is easy to locate to what point the commercial culture of the "mass media" has penetrated the Latin American Evangelical environment. In October 1999, the Ibero-American Christian Confederation of Communicators and Mass Means of Communication (COICOM) assembled in congress in Lima, Peru, claimed to include "more than 1000 radio channels, 200 television stations, 500 newspapers and 5000 Evangelical Ibero-American journalists and communicators" (Agencia Latinoamericana de Comunicación, Lima, 7-10-1999). As early as the 1940s, pioneering Evangelical radio emerged in the region and especially, from the 1980s, religious television channels have considerably increased the visibility of these movements. Apart from the channels connected with the *Trinity Broadcasting Network* of Miami, one finds television empires of which the best known is the Brazilian TVRecord bought in 1989 by Edir Macedo, founder of the Universal Church of the Kingdom of God. This firm transformed into *Rede Record* which today controls 17 television-broadcasting stations, thus becoming the second Brazilian television network in number of stations (Corten, 1999: 179). This is a transnational structure of images and sound complemented by North American relays of the "*700 Club*" style broadcast on national channels. These initiatives have even provoked identical Catholic responses with the establishment of an important Catholic telecommunications network. As an attentive observer has written (Piedra Solano, 1994: 89), this concerns "an electronic church, a church of the airwaves that is entering into competition with the formal church". Furthermore, is it not surprising that many Pentecostals regularly watch the religious broadcasts on television and listen to the religious programs on the radio, and that a media audience should be created independently of specific religious affiliations? Evidence of this appeared in a recent survey carried out in Costa Rica (Bastian et al: 2000). To the question "which religious character plays the most important role in your life?", Costa Rican Evangelists, two-thirds of them Pentecostal, named someone belonging to the media world, in the person of a charismatic Costa Rican priest who appears on channel 40 (Telefides) of Catholic television, Father Maynor Calvo, who received 16.3% of the votes. Another great communicator, Pentecostal this time, follows him from far behind; this is "Hermano Pablo" (8.5%), the director of an Evangelical radio station broadcasting a mini-program from El Salvador called "A Message to Conscience" in 27 countries. Those coming after them are all Latino or North American televangelists (Yiye Avila, 3.4%; Billy Graham, 3.1%; Benny Hinn, 2.3%; Luis Palau, 1.8%), and also Costa Rican (the charismatic Catholic preacher Salvador Gómez, 2.6%). Even if Jesus Christ occupies a comfortable position with 10.6% of the votes, the Pope, media figure par excellence, ranks rather well (7.5%) in an environment that in principle should be hostile to him. On the other hand, Archbishop Roman Arrieta, the Catholic primate of the country, is practically absent with 0.5% of the votes, just like the Virgin of Los Angeles (0.8%), who is the Patroness of Costa Rica, or Martin Luther (1%). This confirms the distance of these movements from both baroque Catholicism and historical Protestantism, but even further situates the religious actors in an active field of competition in the media market.

The media coverage of religious references has led to changes in the formation of services with the increasing theatricalization of the conduct of the preachers, the appearance of religious presenters on radio and television, the display of religious music concerts in public places and the appropriation of a transnational religious culture. The products of the Universal Church of the Kingdom of God (Silveira Campos, 1997: 421-433) circulate in Latin America as well as in the United States, Europe and Africa. The same applies to the media novelties of the international Pentecostal world. Thus the phenomenon of "holy laughter" of the "Toronto Blessing", which appeared in 1994 in a community close to the airport of this Canadian city, reoccurred barely a few months later in Latin America. Likewise, the notion of a "spiritual war" propagated by the North American Pentecostal Evangelist Benny Hinn has spread from its beginnings in 1990 to all of Latin America and the evangelizing methods of the preacher Jonggi Cho, creator of the macro-church Yoido in Seoul, are now common throughout the region. Finally, the theology of prosperity which has become the predominant discourse in middle class Pentecostalisms can be read as that of the sacralization of the market by social sectors that are experiencing its insecurity and flexibility. However, it belongs to the traditional religious register of the mediation connecting sacrifice, symbolic effectiveness, and the promise of salvation. In this register, the TV channel Enlace, whose owner is the pastor Gonzalez Ortiz in San José, Costa Rica, offers for twenty dollars "healing, economic prosperity, success in business and salvation of the soul". He estimates thus receiving 860,000 dollars of donations per year. Founded in 1988, TV Enlace reaches the faithful in 55 countries, having created other similar channels affiliated and connected since 1996 by renting a Mexican communications satellite (Servicio de noticias ALC 3-03-2005). TV Record, bought in 1991 for some 55 million dollars by Bishop Edir Macedo, founder of the Universal Church of the Kingdom of God in Brazil, offers similar products.

Globalization involves phenomena of mimicry and simultaneity in behaviors that the national Evangelists immediately adopt under pressure to innovate in the competitive commercial culture of the religious show. The national Evangelists conduct their activities in this constant exchange between the national and international in a permanent concern to promote media coverage of the message. The media image of the successful Evangelist further implies trips and campaigns abroad. That is why all the principal Latin American Pentecostal pastors try to cultivate a transnational image. They create religious branches of their movements at the continental scale on the principle of franchising, and they take part in the process of religious globalization. Until toward the end of the 1980s, North American preachers predominated on the television religious market. Since the 1990s, Latin Americans have been in the process of forging a spectacular breakthrough in a globalizing media world. At the same time, the image of the religious entrepreneur has been developing, an "executive" with a particularly full agenda and with an aura expanding in function of the audience that he draws "urbi et orbi". The image of the successful Pentecostal pastor exercises a powerful attraction to the youth of the underprivileged social classes. For the latter, the career of pastor (with perhaps those of football player and singer) is one of the few professions attainable from inside the so-called informal economy, in other words, the underground economy that escapes tax regulation. It has the advantage of demanding a very small investment in studies, bypassing the modes of government-controlled regulation of credentials that give access to social recognition, and allowing a rapid social ascent according to the level of the results and the gains achieved.

The process of networking, recourse to the media and the executive image of the directors with the best performances explain the recent spectacular breakthrough of the Pentecostal movements in particular among the middle classes and even the upper middle class. Pentecostalism is there acquiring a cultural legitimacy that it had been hitherto denied. Although long denigrated by the dominant social sectors, it is in the process of coming out of the religious ghetto and the culture of the social fringe thanks to media transnationalization. It is doing this by integrating into its practices both the culture of the miraculous image which is becoming that of the television screen (that one touches to receive a blessing or before which one leaves objects with a view to a "*limpia*") and the media resources that provide a gain in the technical quality and "commerciability" to the message. The Pentecostals draw a double profit from it and increased competitiveness in a bitterly disputed market. It becomes a religious product acceptable for middle social sectors particularly receptive to contemporary modes of consumption. The Pentecostal mega-churches surrounded by vast parking areas that have sprung up in all the large towns of the region correspond to the more widespread consumption of standardized products. One of the most recent is that of the so-called "theology of prosperity", which is none other than the logic of *do ut des* restated within the framework of the discourse of performance. It attracts precisely the middle classes of precarious social status subject to the risks of economic conjuncture. They find in this symbolic product both the confirmation of their relative economic success and access to the traditional discourse of the retributive religion in which Catholicism also flourishes through the mediation of the patron saint.

The innovative use of the means of mass communication combined with the promotion of renewed symbolic products and an intense community life has furthered a transnational expansion by capillarity. The latter reveals itself more dynamic than the previous international expansion regulated by missionary societies or North American mother churches. The reason is that it creates hundreds of relational and organizational networks whose relays are the evangelizing crusades, aid and development agencies, alliances, conferences, confraternities of pastors, associations of businessmen or Christian athletes, missions and – last but not least – the radio and television networks. Thus, during the course of the 1980s a global religious economy emerged from a market-oriented production (Beyer, 1990). The novelty resides in the fact that the Pentecostal discourse was transformed. As Corten remarks (1999: 171), it "is constructed not primarily to transmit a truth in the image of the effect produced by a prophetic discourse, but to assure success for itself". The "narrative machine that produces success" is characterized by an increasing diversification of the religious actors. This leads one to speak of the religious deregulation of Latin America by the market (Bastian, 1997) inasmuch as the Catholic Church, for the first time in its history in the region, is no longer managing to control the religiosity of the masses. Market logic underpins the deregulation in progress.

5. Beyond the market: the field

Market theory has the virtue of making us attend to the dynamics of differentiation at work in Latin America. It enables accounting for the strategies of the individual actors in terms of cost-benefit and that of the collective actors comprising the religious organizations and the directors in terms of profit and productivity. For any religious organization to survive in a dynamics of sharp competition, it must be able to innovate by offering an effective product. Any survival includes the accumulation of a capital of confidence and credibility that must be expressed in an efficient management of the resources and infrastructures necessary to any organization. This engages the religious actors to seek a profitable relationship to the sacred through the establishment of the mediations necessary for the expansion of their movements. Economic theory permits explaining the fact that religious organizations are increasingly behaving like "entrepreneurs", using various resources and the most modern mediations to "sell" their product. The latter has been transformed. The facts thus explained are just as much the transformation of the forms of praise and the production of innovative products as the standardization of the offer and the recourse to the most modern techniques of communication. In this sense, the religious actors have become businesspersons and managers. The experience of the sacred is deployed in a market of salvation goods, an ordinary economy of the sacred established on rationality and usefulness, efficiency and performance.

Market theory, however, has only a relative explanatory value and cannot reduce the motive of the action to the single motivation of productivity or the principle of rational choice. It does not explain in particular the interaction of different religious organizations with the State and their struggles for hegemony whose finality is the definition of the legitimate religious in the region. Because, in their strategy of commercial growth, the religious actors thus enter into what is advisedly called a field of religious forces whose regulation is not reduced to market law. Logics of power exist, conjoined to those of the market. The field theory of Bourdieu (1971 a, b) permits clarifying the interactions and constitutive relationships of religious pluralization. The connection to the political reveals most clearly the issues induced by field dynamics.

At the local level, the *Iglesia de la luz del mundo* born in the outskirts of the city of Guadalajara in Mexico as early as the 1930s is a good example of the connection of a religious organization to the political on the basis of the exponential growth of its faithful. It powerfully supported the revolutionary party in power that in exchange granted it substantial property and tax concessions (De La Torre, 1995). The Chilean context illustrates such logic on the national level[1]. Until the 1970s, the oldest Pentecostalism of Latin America (1910) was ignored by the State as well as by the Catholic Church. Starting in 1974, however, the enormous success of the clientelist

---

1   The actors lay claim to the term "evangélico" in reference to themselves and not that of Protestant. The following data come from the Servicio de Noticias ALC: (alc+@amauta.rcp.net.pe) 24/09/1997 ; 30/09/1997 ; 18/06/1999 ; 12/08/1999 ; 07/10/1999 ; 13/01/2000 ; 27/01/2000 ; 13/03/2000 ; 21/03/2000 ; 22/05/2000 ; 02/06/2000 ; 18/09/2000 ; 19/10/2001 ; 26/11/2001 ; 15/12/2001 ; 04/07/2002 ; 18/09/2002.

mobilization achieved by the Pentecostal Methodist Church of Chile (about half a million members including the Pentecostal Evangelical Church closely related to it) drove the latter and the dictatorial State of Pinochet to enter into negotiations. For its recognition by the State, this Church, allied with the other Pentecostal churches that represent about 80% of the Evangelicals[2], lent its support to the regime. An expression of this was the building of a Pentecostal cathedral in the center of Santiago, on Jotabeche Street, which was a counterpart to the Catholic cathedral of Santiago insofar as, in 1975, it was the venue for a *Te Deum*. This event was on the anniversary of Chilean independence with the presence of the dictator and his ministers, that is to say, with State recognition. Even though the Catholic Church was opposed to the dictatorship, this action was in competition with the previous ecumenical *Te Deum* carried out in parallel since 1968 in the Roman Catholic cathedral. With the fall of the dictatorship in 1990, the new Christian Democrat political directors under the presidency of Andres Aylwin attempted to impose a return to the single *Te Deum*. This action would thus bring Pentecostalism back to its just measure in a religious order regulated by the Catholic monopoly supported by the State through a statute of public law according to the constitution of 1980 (Precht Pizarro, 2001: 150). It was in vain. The Committee of Evangelical Organizations (COE), umbrella organization of the Evangelical churches, opposed it and maintained the Evangelical *Te Deum*. Why did the State not manage to disengage from this type of co-optation established by the dictatorship? It is because in the meanwhile, from 1960 to 2000, the Evangelicals had gone from 5.6% of the population in 1960 to 12.4% in 1992 to 15.1% in 2002[3]. Even if they do not constitute a homogenous mass and a univocal electoral block, they represent a reserve of about 1.7 million converts and sympathizers in a position to translate politically their denominational

---

2   Servicio de Noticias ALC (alc+@amauta.rcp.net.pe) 26/11/2001
3   Lalive d'Epinay 1975: 62-63; Servicio de Noticias ALC
     (alc+@amauta.rcp.net.pe), 28/03/2003. The Catholics went from 76.8% of the
     population in 1992 to 69.96% in 2002.

choices with a view to defending their religious interests. The strength of Chilean Pentecostalism is to have succeeded in moving over the long term from secrecy to the public arena. In order to do this, market logic has been at work. It alone is insufficient to explain the strategy of the actors, which in any case is not reducible to simple individual or business profit. The search for performance does not exhaust the reasons for the action. Beyond the organizational success emerge social issues which are issues of class and recognition in a dual society (Touraine, 1988) characterized by social and racial differences. Issued from economically and racially dominated social sectors, the Pentecostal actors had the purpose rather to transform the economic religious capital into the capital of social recognition. This could only have been accomplished through negotiation with the political field. Since then, these same religious actors have managed to have the Chilean constitution changed. They have succeeded in that, for the first time in the country's history, the constitution guarantees the same rights and duties to the minority religious actors as it does to the Catholic Church in terms of religious teachings in the schools, chaplaincy in the armies and prisons, chaplaincy of the presidency of the republic, and so forth. The case of Chile highlights that, beyond market logic, motivations are at work directed toward turning the stigmatized and marginalized second-class popular social actors into legitimate social actors and thus giving them access to a dignity that the situation of the former religious monopoly denied them. Market logic is, overall, only one of the explanatory dimensions of the religious transformation of the region. The economism underlying all market theory is worthy of restoring in an approach in terms of field, bringing into play the socio-political context that explains the finality of the action of the Pentecostal actors in competition, whose ultimate motive is less the market than social recognition and the search for citizenship.*

---

*   Translated by Christine Rhone

References

Bastian, J.-P. (1997) "La dérégulation religieuse de l'Amérique latine", *Problèmes d'Amérique latine, La documentation française* 24: 3-16.

Bastian, J.-P. et al. (2000) *Religiöser Wandel in Costa Rica. Eine Sozialwissenschaftliche Interpretation.* Mainz: Matthias Grünewald Verlag.

Berger, P. (1969) *The Sacred Canopy: Elements of a Sociological Theory of Religion.* New York: Doubleday.

Beyer, P. (1990) *Religion and Globalization.* London: Sage.

Bourdieu, P. (1971a) "Genèse et structure du champ religieux", *Revue française de sociologie XII*: 295-334.

–. (1971b) "Une interprétation de la religion selon Max Weber", *Archives européennes de sociologie* XII: 3-21.

Castells, M. (1999) *La société en réseaux.* Paris: Fayard.

Chaves, R. (1992) *Tercera conferencia internacional de la palabra de Dios en Costa Rica. El Espíritu Santo señor de la Iglesia.* San José: Ministerio Avance Misionero Mundial.

Chesnut, R. A. (2003) *Competitive Spirits: Latin America's New Religious Economy.* New York: Oxford University Press.

Colonomos, A. et al. (1995) *Sociologie des réseaux transnationaux.* Paris: L'Harmattan.

Colonomos, A. (2001) "Entre Europe et Amérique latine: les performances des réseaux à l'épreuve des civilités institutionnelles", in Bastian, J.-P. et al. (2001) *La modernité religieuse en perspective comparée, Europe latine-Amérique latine.* Paris: Karthala, pp. 241-256.

Corten, A. (1995) *Le pentecôtisme au Brésil. Emotion du pauvre et romantisme théologique.* Paris: Karthala.

–. (1999) "Pentecôtisme et néo-pentecôtisme au Brésil", *Archives des Sciences Sociales des Religions* 105 (January-May): 163-183.

De La Torre, R. (1995) *Los hijos de la luz. Discurso, identidad y poder en la Luz del mundo.* Mexico: Iteso.

Demerath, N. J et al. (1998) *Sacred Companies: Organizational Aspects of Religion and Religious Aspects of Organizations.* New York: Oxford University Press.

García-Canclini, N. (1990) *Culturas híbridas. Estrategias para entrar y salir de la modernidad.* Mexico: Grijalbo.

Gogin Sias, G. (1997a), *Presencia religiosa en las radios limeñas.* Lima: Universidad de Lima.

– . (1997b) "La apropriación de la cultura masiva en construccion de la doctrina religiosa. El caso de la Hermandad de Cordero de Dios 'Alfa y Omega'". Universidad de Lima: Faculdad de Ciencias de la Communicación.

Gogin Sias, G. and Vela Pérez, R. (1997c) "Mediaciones comunicacionales en el rito y la cultura religiosa. El caso de la Iglesia pentecostal Dios es Amor". Universidad de Lima: Faculdad de Ciencias de la Communicación.

Gruzinski, S. (1994) *La guerra de las imágenes. De Cristobal Colón a "Blade Runner" (1492-2019).* México: F.C.E.

Finke, R. and R. Stark (1992) *The Churching of America, 1776-1990.* New Brunswick, NJ: Rutgers University Press.

Iannaconne, L. (1992) "Religious Market and the Economics of Religions", *Social Compass* 39 (1): 123-131.

Lalive d'Epinay, C. (1975) *Religion, dynamique sociale et dépendence. Les mouvements protestants en Argentine et au Chili.* Paris: Mouton.

Lehmann, D. (1996) *Struggle for the Spirit: Religious Transformation and Popular Culture in Brazil and Latin America.* Cambridge: Polity Press.

Martin, D. (1990) *Tongues of Fire: The Explosion of Protestantism in Latin America.* Cambridge: Blackwell.

Murphy, E. (1994) *Manual de guerra espiritual.* Miami: Editorial Caribe.

Oro, A. P. (1992) "Religions pentecôtistes et moyens de communication de masse au Brésil", *Social Compass* 39/3: 423-434.

Pédron-Colombani, S. (1998) *Le pentecôtisme au Guatémala. Conversion et identité.* Paris: CNRS Editions.

Piedra Solano, A. (1994) "El protestantismo costarricense entre la ilusión y la realidad", *Senderos* 11/2: 77-96.

Precht Pizarro, J. (2001) *Derecho eclesiastico del Estado de Chile.* Santiago: Andros Impresores.

Sánchez Paredes, J. (1998) "Pentecostalismo católico, religión y sociedad en el Peru", *El pentecostalismo en América Latina entre tradición y globalización.* A. Pollak et Y. Salas (ed.). Quito: Abya Yala, 148-169.

Servicio de noticias ALC "Costa Rica: aumentan cuestionamientos a TV Enlace", 3-05-2005, http/www.alcnoticias.org.

Silveira Campos, L. (1997) *Teatro, templo e mercado. Organiçao e marketing de um empreendimento neopentecostal.* Petropolis: Editora Vozes.

− . (1999) "Pentecostalismo urbano e meios modernos de comunicaçao no Brasil", *Ibero-Amerikanisches Arkiv* 25/1-2: 115-144.

Touraine, A. (1988) *La parole et le sang. Politique et société en Amérique latine.* Paris: Odile Jacob.

− . (1992) "Mutations de l'Amérique latine", *Espaces latino-américains* 90 (June): 13-25.

Vazquez, M. and M. F. Marquardt (1993) *Globalizing the Sacred: Religion across America.* New Brunswick, NJ: Rutgers University Press.

Willaime, J-P., (1999) "Le pentecôtisme: contours et paradoxes d'un protestantisme émotionnel", *Archives des Sciences Sociales des Religions*, January-March: 5-28.

Wynarczyk, H. (1993) "Carlos Annacondia. Un estudio de caso en neopentecostalismo", *Nuevos movimientos religiosos y ciencias socials.* A. Frigerio (ed.), Buenos Aires: Centro editor de América Latina S.A.: 80-97.

Terry REY

Worthiness as Spiritual Capital:
Theorizing Little Haiti's Religious Market

1. The refugee Pentecostal

At 27 years of age, with his fourth son just born and his mistress preg-
nant with another of his children, Ronald Pierre-Louis's financial
burden was about to destroy him. The measly US$100 that he earned
each month as a servant in the home of a wealthy Port-au-Prince
entrepreneur was not going to cut it, not that it ever did. So, Ronald
did what thousands of his compatriots have done over the last 30
years: he got on a boat in the hopes of reaching Miami. To do so, he
borrowed US$1000 from a loan shark at 40% annual interest, and put
his two-room shantytown home up as collateral. That is what it cost to
put his life at tremendous risk with 100 other likewise desperate Haitians who boarded a rickety wooden sailboat with him one day in the
summer of 1999. After two days at sea Ronald had depleted his avo-
cado and soda stash, and he was sick, dehydrated, and filthy.
Fortunately, early the following day the boat anchored just off a
Bahamian island, and several canoes and rowboats approached
Ronald's vessel to ferry its passengers to shore. He was alive and
barely well, but not yet in Miami.

Quickly blending into the large community of Haitians in the
Bahamas, Ronald landed steady work cleaning up construction sites.
He was in transit, so to speak, thought without passport, visa, or con-
necting ticket. But he prayed much, worked hard, and persevered.
Then, late one night in May 2000, he boarded a small shallow-hulled
speedboat with 20 other passengers bound for "the promised land."

The trip was but a couple hours, and when they were within 100 yards of Florida, the boat's captain told his passengers to jump in and wade for shore. Once reaching dry land, Ronald scrambled for some nearby bushes and hid there for about an hour. All of the others were arrested almost immediately, and Ronald thought he, too, was done for when a police officer shined his flashlight into his hiding place. But instead of arresting Ronald, the officer instructed him in Spanish to wait a while longer for a taxi that would slowly pass on a nearby road. The taxi soon arrived, and its Haitian driver brought Ronald to a storefront Baptist church tucked away in an industrial park in Little Haiti, as if by miracle. The night-watchman was waiting for Ronald, welcomed him, and told him that he could sleep in the pews.

A few weeks later Ronald managed to track down a cousin he'd not seen in over ten years, Emile, who had arrived in Little Haiti several years prior in similar circumstances to his own. For a nominal boarder's fee he was taken into the efficiency apartment that Emile shared with his wife and three young children. Motivated to pay off his loan shark and send money to his family in Haiti, Ronald landed two full time minimum-wage jobs in Miami, one stocking shelves in a local Haitian grocery store, and the other toweling off cars at an automated car-wash.

Ronald's new lodging arrangements allowed him to leave the Baptist church for a different church with greater resonance with his Pentecostal worldview and dispositions, or his Pentecostal "habitus," to use a key Bourdieuian term to which I return below. Though grateful to the congregation that received him and allowed him to gain a foothold in the US, Ronald was spiritually unsatisfied in a church where no one got possessed by the Holy Spirit, no one spoke in tongues, and no one engaged in faith healing, which were the hallmarks of his church in Haiti, *l'Armée Céleste*. To Ronald, the lack of "heat" in this particular Baptist church meant that his prayers were likely not as effective there. It was thus time to find a new church, and there were many in Little Haiti from which to choose. But what, really, were his choices? Once he made them, could we soundly label his choices as "rational"? How, furthermore, were they defined and limited, and what could a sociologist expect and/or say about his search and negotiation thereof?

2. Habitus, needs, and/or choice

Haitian refugees like Ronald began arriving in South Florida in significant numbers in the early 1970s and by the end of that decade numbered around 50,000, most of them residing in Miami, a modern American city just 700 miles from Haiti. Today there are over half a million Haitians living in Florida, more than in any other state in the US. Many of them arrived as refugees and started their new lives in Little Haiti, where almost invariably they received material assistance from the neighborhood's churches' social programs, and spiritual assistance in the form of Sacraments administered by a Catholic priest, healing hands laid upon them by a Protestant pastor, or divination performed by a Vodou priestess. In the language of economic theory of religion, such variegated assistance might be understood as forms of "capital" that local churches "market" to the potential "consumers" (newly arriving Haitian immigrants), with both the church leaders (CEOs) and the consumers acting in the religious market "so as to maximalize their net benefit" (Iannoccone, 1992: 124).

The enthusiasm with which the sociology of religion has embraced the "market theory of religion," most identified with Rodney Stark and his collaborators (e.g. Stark and Finke, 2000), is not at all universal, and its critics make some very important points. The analytical power of such a paradigm is certainly enticing, but religion is not as rational as the leading "rational choicers" would have us believe, one's religious practice being far more determined by tradition, socialization, and mysticism than by calculating rationality. That being said, economic theory of religion is not, I think, as "beyond redemption" as Steve Bruce (2002: 182), its leading critic, argues; nor is it merely "the malign influence of a small clique of US sociologists of religion" (Bruce, 1999: 1). To be sure, as articulated thus far, it does have certain limitations; but these limitations, rather than suggesting its dismissal, should be approached as invitations to correct, adapt, or extend its obvious theoretical promise. In this paper, I seek to do so by taking seriously both economic theory of religion and some of the valid criticisms thereof made by Bruce and Roland Robertson (1992), with an eye toward infusing it with Pierre Bourdieu's key concept of "habitus" and grounding it in Max Weber's discussion of religious needs.

The leading proponents of rational choice theory of religion seem at pains to avoid citing Bourdieu, despite their adopting economic terminology in the study of an extra-economic social field in ways that strongly evoke him; e.g., "capital," "market," "interest," "consumer," "profit," etc.; and despite the fact that, like them, Bourdieu sees competition as integral to the nature of religion (Rey, 2004). Rational choice theorists would be very ill-advised, as they seem to realize, to cite such a "consecrated" thinker as Bourdieu too extensively, however, because Bourdieu is quite opposed to the radical subjectivity and freedom of individual choice upon which their "new paradigm" is predicated. In one sense, in fact, Bourdieu developed his pivotal notion of habitus to destroy the kinds of subjectivist assumptions underlying rational choice theory: "Thus, against the scholastic illusion which tends to see every action as springing from an intentional aim, and against the socially most powerful theories of the day which, like neomarginalist economics, accept that philosophy of action without the slightest questioning, the theory of habitus has the primordial function of stressing that the principle of our actions is more often practical sense than rational calculation" (Bourdieu, 2000: 63-64). Put otherwise, "most actions are objectively economic without being subjectively economic, without being the product of rational economic calculation" (Bourdieu, 1990: 90-91). Robertson (1992: 151) helpfully suggests how Bourdieu's theory of practice, despite a structuralist rigidity that many scholars have assailed, can help counter the "complete absence of constraint on consumers" in rational choice theory of religion. Such a Bourdieuian adjustment guides inquiry into how "choices are formed by circumstances" (1992: 155), being neither freely individualist and subjective nor the unalloyed products of circumstance and social structure, though for Bourdieu the latter are resoundingly dominant over the former in the production of religious practice.

As pertains to his theory of religion, meanwhile, Bourdieu's critics are as numerous as Stark's, and they are generally in agreement that Bourdieu's model of the religious field over-emphasizes institutions to such a degree that individual agency is, for all intents and purposes, effaced (e.g. Hervieu-Léger, 2000). Taken together, the criticisms of either rational choice theory of religion or Bourdieuan theory of religion are to be welcomed by anyone who, like me, is uncomfortable with their perceptively *a priori* dismissal of both the sacred and the believer's engagement thereof. Part of the problem with rational choice theory of religion is, as Bruce (1999: 44) observes, that its users seldom concern themselves with "personal biography" and therefore wind up demonstrating "an excessive distance from their subject matter" that does not, ultimately, allow them truly "to understand the people whose behavior they are explaining." Similarly, I have been quite struck by the lack of qualitative ethnographic data in market interpretations of religion, and so I include some measure of each personal biography and qualitative ethnography in this chapter.

3. Little Haiti's religioscape

It is easy to think of Little Haiti as a religious marketplace. Nearly 100 churches grace its 500 square blocks; botanicas retailing Vodouist ritual paraphernalia abound; murals of Catholic saints adorn grocery stores; and on any given Sunday scattered throngs of well dressed, Bible-toting Christians shuffle about neighborhood's streets. Across Biscayne Bay from glitzy Miami Beach, and just north of the city's downtown skyscrapers, Little Haiti is one of the poorest inner-city neighborhoods in the US. Just 20 years ago there were merely a dozen or so Haitian churches in the neighborhood (Vaughan, 1983). In the interim this number has multiplied nearly tenfold, while the city's Haitian population has "only" tripled since then. To illustrate, on NE Miami Ave., just two blocks north of Notre Dame d'Haiti Catholic Church, one of the most significant "ethnic parishes" in US history, are aligned four other Haitian churches. Clustered within three blocks, they are all freestanding and hence not of the storefront variety: Grace United Methodist Church; *l'Eglise de St. Paul et les Martyrs d'Haiti*; *l'Eglise du Christ de North Miami*, and the First Haitian Free United Methodist Church. Fanning out a few blocks in any direction, one finds numerous other churches, most of them storefronts, an approach to physical church establishment that Haitians in the US have inherited from African Americans.

South Florida received a massive influx of Haitian refugees in 1979/1980. Local churches scrambled to create Haitian ministries and support programs, while some pastors among the new refugees managed to open their own churches, some of them soon becoming formidable competitors in the Little Haiti religious marketplace. "When something called the Haitian Church of the Open Door puts up a sign and has someone who speaks Creole, where's the Haitian going to go?" Father Thomas Wenski, erstwhile Catholic Bishop of Miami, raised this rhetorical question when a local reporter asked him in 1983 to explain the recent appearance of several Protestant storefront churches in Little Haiti. An astute ecclesiologist, Wenski offered two other reasons for the spread of independent churches: 1) Until 1983 the only Catholic church in Little Haiti was the Miami Cathedral of St. Mary, whose "English signs and wood panelled rooms scared away many Haitians"; and 2) "These congregations, because they are smaller, tend to offer that sense of community that attracts many of these people who are new to the country" (cited in Vaughan, 1983). Both of these reasons ultimately are rooted in the widely accepted notion that religion plays a key orientating role in the immigrant experience in urban America, offering a space where, and a means whereby, a sense of homeland cultural identity is rediscovered or maintained.

Raymond Williams (1988:29) explains the strength of immigrant religion in terms of identity maintenance and ethnic solidarity: "Immigrants are religious – by all counts more religious than they were before they left – because religion is one of the important identity markers that helps them preserve individual self-awareness and cohesion in a group." I have found the case of Haitian religion in Miami to be consistent with Williams' findings, though two other factors must be taken into account here: 1) that Haitians attend church more frequently than any other immigrant group in the United States (Stepick and Portes, 1986); and 2) that Haitian religious leaders have been quite adept at adopting ecclesiological and homeletical approaches typical of urban African-American churches.

Since the 1979/1980 wave of Haitian refugees arrived in Miami, Little Haiti has witnessed an astonishing proliferation of churches: from approximately 12 in 1983 to nearly 100 in 2000! Of the 84 churches that I have located in Little Haiti,[1] independent storefronts of either Baptist (15) or Pentecostal (51) persuasion predominate, as reflected in the following sampling of their names: *Eglise Baptiste de la Rénaissance*; *Eglise Missionaire Trompette de Sion, Inc.*; *Eglise Evangélique Maranatha*; *Eglise Baptiste de la Régénération*; *Eglise de Dieu du Temps de la Fin*; and *Eglise de Dieu l'Arche de Déliverance*.

The typical trajectory of Haitian storefronts in Miami is as follows: A pastor arrives from Haiti and establishes a church either in a private home, a restaurant, school gymnasium, or the like, and attracts an initial following by word-of-mouth or by radio advertisement. Once

---

1   There are certainly more churches in Little Haiti than I was able to find, as many congregations meet in private spaces that are unmarked, while others change location occasionally. Thus, while I have located 84 churches in the neighborhood, there are easily more than 100. I mapped the neighborhood's religioscape in 2000 with the help of Emmanuel Eugène, an anthropologist and a local Haitian pastor, and with the support of funding from the Pew Charitable Trusts. My gratitude is theirs.

enough funds are secured, the congregation rents a small building and seeks to gain members. This is a critical phase in any congregation's life, and numerous churches in Little Haiti have folded at this stage. Fundraising becomes crucial toward making the next step in the Haitian storefront trajectory, which is the purchase of a building. Generally, churches that rent their space count fewer than 75 members, whereas the most successful Protestant churches in Little Haiti all own the buildings that they occupy and count roughly ten times the number of members than congregations that rent their space. The actual construction of a church edifice is something to which few Haitian congregations aspire, however, because many of them deem that the required funds for such a project would be better spent helping sister congregations in Haiti, or on health fares for the poor of Little Haiti. Although much of the trajectory that I have just described may be fruitfully *explained* (though not *described*)[2] by market theory, such a self-imposed limit on congregational growth, however, clearly cannot. It makes perfect sense to Little Haiti's priests and pastors, in any case, as part of the biblical mandate and mystical intuition that inspired them to pastoral ministry in the first place.

4. A tale of two churches

To further illustrate the nature and trajectory of storefront Christianity in Little Haiti; to identify forms of "spiritual capital" (Verter 2003) that they produce and offer to their congregants; and to provide context for Ronald Pierre-Louis's own quest to find a new church, I consider ethnographically and historically two of the neighborhood's

---

2   I am thinking here of Wayne Proudfoot's (1987) compelling discussion of the difference between descriptive reductionism and explanatory reductionism in the study of religion, the former being a *faux pas* and the latter a sound analytical move.

storefront churches: *Eglise de Dieu Santifiée Haïtienne* (EDSH), founded in 1968, and *Mission Evangélique du Christianisme* (MEC), founded in 1993. Being the oldest Haitian church in Miami, the former typifies in several ways the city's abundant Haitian-American storefronts: for instance, its membership is fewer than 100 and shows no signs of increasing; it is independent and transnational; and it is decidedly Pentecostal. MEC, meanwhile, counts thousands of members in numerous congregations found in four different countries; its Miami membership is over 300; and it is not Pentecostal. MEC also represents a unique phenomenon in Haitian Christianity in being indigenously Haitian; i.e., its mother church in Haiti has never relied on affiliation with any foreign missionary group, and much of the Mission's understanding of Christian practice derives from the mystical experiences and healing ministry of its Haitian founder, Missionary Salomon Sévère Joseph (1891-1973). Both EDHS and MEC are also significant for our purposes because Ronald Pierre-Louis has attended services at each church in his search for a spiritual home in a strange land.

4.1 *Eglise de Dieu Sanctifiée Haïtienne, Inc.*

Before the 1979/1980 exodus, a few Haitians had already settled just to the north of downtown Miami in a neighborhood then known as Lemon City. One of them, Rev. Pascal Duclair, had enjoyed a long career as a pastor of *Eglise de Dieu de la Prophétie* in his hometown of Les Cayes prior to immigrating to Miami in 1968. Upon his arrival, one of the first things that Duclair did was to open a Pentecostal storefront church on NW 14th Ave., where his small Haitian flock would recreate the lively worship and healing services that drew hundreds to his church in Haiti. By 1973, Duclair's *Eglise de Dieu Sanctifiée Haïtienne* (EDSH) had raised enough funds to purchase a small abandoned commercial building in Lemon City on NW 2nd Ave. Duclair and his nascent congregation could not then have known that this would soon become the very heart of Little Haiti when some

10,000 refugees arrived in South Florida from Haiti in 1979/1980. From then on, Lemon City would be known as Little Haiti.

In response to the overwhelming needs of the swelling and impoverished Haitian immigrant community, many of whom were Pentecostals in need of a whole litany of miracles, EDSH began holding Friday night healing services called "The Cry of Midnight" (*"le Cri de Minuit"*). Word soon spread of all kinds of miracles happening at EDSH, especially healing the sick and exorcising *move zespri* (evil spirits), two forms of spiritual capital that continue to hold much currency for EDSH and its members, however few they may be. Such healing miracles continue to be the church's mainstay, as, for example, on one evening in 2004, a family who had just arrived from Haiti brought their young-adult daughter to The Cry of Midnight. She had not spoken a word since arriving in Miami some three months prior. After much prayer and laying on of hands, a Vodou spirit allegedly responsible for her muteness was exorcised, and the young women began to speak again.

Usually attended by about 30 women, ten men, and a few children, the Sunday worship service at EDSH routinely opens with a benediction, followed by several minutes of spontaneous communal prayer. Everyone prays softly aloud, mostly in Creole, though as the fervor builds most become entranced and speak in tongues. After a reading from Psalms, more hymns follow, led by an elder and projected through a speaker so loud that it can be heard blocks away (the church door is kept open for this reason, and at least a couple of EDSH members were initially drawn to the church by its hymns wafting outside and down the ghetto streets). Following the hymn is another period of very moving spontaneous communal prayer, during which the gifts (charisms) and sometimes messages *(komisyon)* from the Holy Spirit are received. Next is a reading from the Gospels, and then the sermon, which always includes prayerful solicitation of funds for EDSH's mother congregation in Haiti, reflection on the causes of Haiti's many and grave social ills, and calls for regular prayers for peace and unity in Haiti. EDSH sermons iterate the typically Pentecostal conviction that prayer has the power to bring God into the hearts of any and all malefactors who are blameworthy for Haiti's poverty and suffering. Therein lies the truest hope for the Haitian people, both at home and it the "diaspora," and the main reason, along with the praise of God and renewal in the Holy Sprit with all its accompanying ecstasy, for which Duclair founded EDSH in the first place, and for which most of its members make this congregation their spiritual home, something that Ronald Pierre-Louis would eventually do as well.

Being the oldest Haitian church in Miami, EDSH has been quite an influential congregation, if not for its size then as a model healing sanctuary, and as a *"pépinière"* ("tree nursery") seeding Miami with faith in Jesus Christ and the gifts of the Holy Spirit. Several other Little Haiti and North Miami Churches have been founded by former EDSH members, including Miami's largest storefront, *Eglise Baptise Emmanuel* (est. in 1974), whose founder, Rev. Wilner Maxy, had his conversion experience at EDSH a couple of years prior. Healing and spreading the Christian faith are thus the raisons-d'être of EDSH, over and above the growth of its own membership.

4.2 Mission Evangélique du Christianisme

In such a competitive religious market as Little Haiti, congregations must distinguish themselves in order to appeal to newly-arrived immigrants like Ronald Pierre-Louis, or to longer-standing residents who somehow become dissatisfied with their churches. If EDSH's claim to uniqueness among Little Haiti's Protestant storefront churches lies in its age, its healing prowess, and it's spawning other churches, then that of the *Mission Evangélique du Christianisme* lies in its absolute Haitian-ness, or, as its leaders explain with pride, in its being "the only truly indigenous form of Haitian Christianity."[3] Indeed, whereas all other Protestant Christian churches in Haiti and in the Haitian diaspora are either parts of mainstream mission churches, offshoots of mission churches, or inspired by and/or modeled on North American

---

3   Rev Fandor Saint-Felix, interview with Terry Rey, March 21, 2004, Miami.

churches (Brodwin, 2003: 86), MEC's origins lie in the mystical experiences and healing ministry of its remarkable Haitian founder, the
Missionary Salomon Sévère Joseph.

Born near the town of Aquin on the rural southern coast of Haiti in
1891, Salomon Sévère Joseph was raised Catholic and excelled in
school, eventually pursuing studies in law.[4] In 1930 he began to have
tremendous mystical experiences, namely having visions and hearing
voices, which inspired him to begin a healing ministry. The tree be-
neath which Joseph received some of these initial visions is deeply
revered by MEC members, and is the site on which the first MEC
church was constructed in 1934. Talk of miracles spread, and peasants
from the surrounding hills soon brought to Joseph loved ones who
were possessed by evil spirits, who were blind, and who were impo-
tent or barren. He implored the afflicted to renounce Vodou, to repent,
and to have absolute faith in God. And he healed them.

Joseph's visions eventually compelled him to read the Bible, which
led him to the arresting conclusion that Catholicism was not true
Christianity. Thus convinced, he abandoned his native church and
began incorporating the burning of Catholic icons and other ritual
paraphernalia in his ministry, a move that led to the first in a series of
arrests and, to MEC memory, to his persecution.

Over the ensuing decades, Joseph was credited with having performed countless miracles, usually in the form of healing sick humans
and animals. Some attest that he even raised the dead. People from
throughout Haiti flocked to his church, and Joseph's mission flourished, even after his death in 1973. Eventually MEC would become
not merely a transnational church but a well-organized international
network of congregations, all inspired by Joseph's ministry and
achieved without affiliation with any non-Haitian church. Besides its
numerous congregations in Haiti and the several congregations located

---

4   Details about the life of Joseph here summarized are entirely derived from
    Valéry 2000 and from insights provided to me by members of the MEC church
    in Miami.

in the United States, MEC also has branches in Canada, France, St. Martin, and French Guyana.

Reasons for MEC's remarkable success are of course varied and complex, though the Mission's adoption in Miami of African-American style homiletics is key among them, especially in its ministry to second generation Haitian youth, who recently have been gravitating toward African-American churches, in part because they are much more comfortable with English than Haitian Creole. English prayers, sermons, and hymns at MEC are thus forms of spiritual capital that appeal to second generation Haitian youth, who might otherwise seek them elsewhere. However, this is one of the things that Ronald Pierre-Louis, who knows very little English, did not like about MEC during his several attendances there – that and the fact that "it does not heat up enough there," a reference to the absence of the kind of religious ecstasy that abounds at EDSH and in his homeland church, *l'Armée Céleste*.

Finally, the Mission's stress on being originally Haitian and having never relied on any larger church association or foreign mission quite effectively appeals to Haitian pride, and its leaders advertise this widely, both through traditional forms of evangelization and through the distribution of its biennial magazine. Several congregants indeed have explained to me that MEC's uniquely Haitian origins were what most attracted them to its pews, and we might soundly call their joining, at least in part, a "rational choice" intent on "maximalizing" their pride in being Haitian in a country that has often quite strongly denigrated their people.

Founded in 1993, the Miami MEC congregation today counts about 300 members, many from the region in Haiti of Joseph's healing ministry. During Sunday worship services, generally women, their heads covered in veils, sit on the left side and men, in suits and ties, on the right side of the church, each in about 20 rows of pews separated by an aisle leading to the pulpit, which sits atop a low stage. Communal prayers at MEC services are spontaneous and moving, though seldom, if ever, do people receive the gift of tongues; such forms of ecstasy are actually discouraged by MEC pastors, who are clear that their church is not Pentecostal in any way. Still, communal prayers are very worshipful and sweeping, and many people sway joyfully with their hands in the air. The content, in Haitian Creole, is usually simple and almost mantra-like: *"Jezi sove ... Jezi sove ... Jezi sove ... Se li mem ki mèt mwen ... "* ("Jesus saves ... Jesus saves ... Jesus saves ... It is he who is my lord").

MEC takes music very seriously, and, in point of fact, one member of its Paris congregation, Missoule Guirand, released a CD of original MEC hymns in 2003. The choir has electric guitars, a bass guitar, drum set, trombone, organ, and large Peavey amplifies. They are very loud, such that it is impossible to hear one's neighbor speak in the pews during hymns, which are often followed by thunderous rounds of applause. MEC features a wider variety of musical styles than most Haitian Protestant churches, and some hymns are even played to the driving rhythms of *kompa*, contemporary dance music that is hugely popular in nightclubs and on the radio in Haiti and its diaspora. This is particularly appealing to young MEC members, though Ronald Pierre-Louis feels that such "brothel music" has no place in a church.

5. Conclusion

For all of the developments in the social-scientific study of religion since his classic *The Sociology of Religion* first appeared in German 1922, few contributions approach the interpretive acumen of Weber's theory of religion. Weber's focus on religious needs and their material influences and on "salvation goods" presages both the predominant theoretical discussions on immigrant religion today and the chief concerns of contemporary market theories of religion. It is thus curious, as Jörg Stolz (2006: 18) rightly points out, that in applying their paradigm to religion "rational choicers have not yet fully taken into account the work of Max Weber, who is, after all, the most important classic author discussing religious goods." By integrating into rational choice theory of religion Weber's original model of salvation goods, Stoltz helps mitigate the rather disturbing tendency of rational choice theory to portray religious persons as little self-interested capitalists driven to religious practice solely by rational calculations of maximizing profits. "But is choice really possible in religion" asks Rex Adhar (2006: 59)? "To the extent that the individual is 'embedded' or 'situated', ... her faith may reflect little real 'choice' on her part."

One notion that is most fundamental to Weber's theory of religion, and most relevant to the interpretation of immigrant religion in US, is that the "disprivileged" of any given society are pushed to religious practice by a "hunger for a worthiness that has not fallen their lot, the world being what it is" (Weber, 1964: 106).[5] Weber's needs model of religion posits that the material conditions of one's existence create the needs that determine the kind of religion that s/he inherits or adopts. Bourdieu compellingly refines this line of theorization with his notion of religious habitus, "the principal generator of all thoughts, perceptions and actions consistent with the norms of a religious representation of the natural and supernatural worlds" (Bourdieu, 1971: 319). Bourdieu's suggestion that one's religious habitus (as *both* the "matrix of perception" through which one makes sense of religious things *and* the locus of dispositions that manifest as religious belief and practice) is thoroughly conditioned by agents' socioeconomic and cultural background is most helpful for understanding Ronald Pierre-Louis's ultimately joining EDSH instead of MEC. To be sure, Ronald demonstrated the same kind of "hunger for worthiness" that most Haitian refugees experience upon arrival in the US, a country whose Center for Disease Control in 1984 formally listed Haitians, evidently by virtue of something so scientifically verifiable as their ethnicity, as

---

5   Lest one argue that worthiness described here by Weber is precisely the kind of "compensator" or "reward" that rational choice theorists perceivably identify as the virtual essence of religion, it should be remembered that Weber (1963: 107) also identified worthiness, or at least the legitimation of their right thereto, as the motivating force (actually, the *sole* motivating force) behind the religious practice of those who hardly require of religion compensation for material want, namely "the privileged."

"at risk" for carrying AIDS, along with homosexual males, hemo-
philiacs, and heroin addicts! Worthiness thus ranks paramount among
all forms of spiritual capital that are marketed in Little Haiti. And
although Ronald found a healthy offering of this at MEC during his
several visits there, his Pentecostal habitus ultimately disposed him to
gravitate toward EDSH, a church with more "heat," as he puts it,
though one not without its own considerable stock in worthiness, it
being the oldest Haitian church in Miami.

Ronald was thus "embedded" in his language, class, ethnicity, and
race, just as he was "situated" by his religious habitus in ways that in
fact greatly limited his religious possibilities. His is a case in point of
what Bruce (2002: 182) means in saying that "religious behavior is
shaped by social norms that prevent maximizing opportunities: class,
race, ethnicity, nationality, and language all limit choice. But religion
itself limits choice. To the extent that people are successfully socialized into a particular religion they are not able to see other religions as
utility-maximizing opportunities." Worthiness and heat, in the end,
were what brought the refugee Pentecostal, more through "practical
sense" than "rational calculation," to the pews of *Eglise de Dieu
Sanctifiée Haïtienne*. He really didn't have much of a choice.

References

Adhar, Rex (2006) "The Idea of 'Religious Markets'", *International
   Journal of Law in Context* 2(1): 49-65.
Bourdieu, Pierre (1971) "Genèse et structure du champ religieux."
   Revue française de sociologie 12, 2 : 295-334.
–. (1990) *In Other Words*. London: Polity Press.
–. (2000) *Pascalian Meditations*. Trans. Richard Nice. Stanford, CA:
   Stanford University Press.

Brodwin, Paul (2003) "Pentecostalism in Translation: Religion and the Production of Community in the Haitian Diaspora", *American Ethnologist* 30 (1): 85-101.

Bruce, Steve (2002) "The Poverty of Economism or the Social Limits on Maximizing" in Ted G. Jelen (ed.), *Sacred Markets, Sacred Canopies: Essays on Religious Markets and Religious Pluralism*, pp. 167-185. Lanham, MD: Rowan and Littlefield

–. (1999) *Religion and Choice: A Critique of Rational Choice Theory*. Oxford: Oxford University Press.

Hervieu-Léger, Danièle (2000). *Religion as a Chain of Memory*. New Brunswick, NJ: Rutgers University Press.

Iannaccone, Laurence R. (1992) "Religious Markets and the Economics of Religion", *Social Compass* 39(1): 123-131.

Proudfoot, Wayne (1985) *Religious Experience*. Berkeley and Los Angeles: University of California Press.

Rey, Terry (2004) "Marketing the Goods of Salvation: Bourdieu on Religion", *Religion* 34(4): 331-343.

Robertson, Roland (1992) "The Economization of Religion? Reflections on the Promise and limitations of the Economic Approach", *Social Compass* 39(1): 147-157.

Stark, Rodney and Finke, Roger (2000) *Acts of Faith: Explaining the Human Side of Religion*. Berkeley and Los Angeles: University of California Press.

Stepick, Alex and Alejandro Portes (1986) "Flight into Despair: A Profile of Recent Haitian Refugees in South Florida." *International Migration Review* 20(2): 329-350.

Stolz, Jörg (2006) "Salvation Goods and Religious Markets: Integrating Rational Choice and Weberian Perspectives", *Social Compass* 53(1): 13-32.

Valéry, Jude (2000) *Manifestation du Saint Esprit dans le ministère du Rév. Salomon Severe Joseph (1891-1973)*. Port-au-Prince: Fardin.

Vaughan, Chris (1983) "Churches Vie for the Soul of Little Haiti." *The Miami Herald*, April 16.

Verter, Bradford (2003) "Spiritual Capital: Theorizing Religion with Bourdieu against Bourdieu". *Sociological Theory* 21, 2: 150-174.

Weber, Max (1963) *The Sociology of Religion*. Trans. Talcott Parsons. Boston: Beacon.

Williams, Raymond Brady (1988) *Religions of Immigrants from India and Pakistan: New Threads in the American Tapestry*. Berkeley and Los Angeles: University of California Press.

Véronique ALTGLAS

Indian Gurus and the Quest for Self-perfection Among the Educated Middle-Classes

1. Introduction[1]

One of the most fascinating religious markets is probably to be found in India. For centuries, a lively mosaic of religious schools, the *sampradayas,* coexisted alongside brahmanical orthodoxy. Those traditional communities were based on the teaching of a guru, who relatively freely reinterpreted Hindu doctrines and philosophy for his own purposes. Thus this fragmented and effervescent religious milieu represented a fertile field for religious innovations, schisms and heterodoxies, alliances to the temporal powers and rivalries between gurus who travelled in the country to disseminate their teachings, challenge each other in argument, and win disciples. The plurality and competitiveness of this lively ancient religious market seemed to predict the success of contemporary forms of Hinduism in western societies since the 1960s. Indeed, among the profusion of exotic and extremely diverse practices and beliefs on the contemporary religious market, Hindu-based items seem to be quite serious competitors. Indeed, one can hardly fail to be struck by the spread of yoga classes, *tantra* workshop, ayurvedic medicine, and the success of Indian gurus. Several have indeed travelled all around the world, and created transnational organisations which disseminate their teachings in Europe, North America and elsewhere. Why are beliefs and practices related to

---

1   I would like to thank Suzanne Hasselle-Newcombe for reading and commenting this paper; our discussion incitated me to refine some of its ideas and rethink its content.

Hinduism so attractive to westerners? How do gurus succeed in presenting religious practices and beliefs that seem utterly foreign to their audience?

On the basis of two case-studies, Siddha Yoga and Sivananda Centres, studied in France and England[2], this paper will firstly provide an analysis of the ways in which Indian gurus have adapted their salvation goods to their new audience as they came to the West; then emphasis will be placed on disciples' religious expectations. The analysis of salvation goods in neo-Hinduism raises question about the social groups that may be particularly attracted by these Indian religious movements and on the way gurus' teachings may reflect these socially conditioned religious needs. In this regard, we hope to contribute to an analysis of the affinities of social groups with religious choices, in line with Max Weber's and Pierre Bourdieu's pathbreaking work on salvation goods. Whereas Weber analysed the religious attitudes of different social classes, Bourdieu stated that religious organisations respond to "a particular category of needs proper to determinate social groups by determinate type of practice or discourse" (Weber, 1996; Bourdieu, 1987: 119-136). Nevertheless, in their analysis of the religious market, both, in different ways, argue that religious choices are connected with the expectations of specific social groups.

---

2   Participant observation was conducted for two years in France and England and entailed the collection of eighty interviews with members of Siddha Yoga and Sivananda Centres. Unlike Rajneesh or Hare Krishna, there were little research on Siddha Yoga and Sivananda Centres, although their development has been as important as many other neo-Hindu movements. Indeed, they spread all over the world and attract, in France or in England, hundreds of disciples and sympathizers. In addition, this analysis is contextualized by taking into account previous research on Sri Chinmoy and Sahaja Yoga in France, as well as yoga classes, Tantra workshops, etc.

2. The religious offer of neo-Hindu movements

Siddha Yoga, Sivananda Centres, as well as several other neo-Hindu movements grew tremendously fast during the counter-culture in the late 1960s and 1970s, first in North America, then in Europe and other parts of the world. Of course, their success has been relative. They are still minority movements, each of which in France or England for example probably inspires only a few thousands of disciples. Yet they established themselves durably and proved to be continuously attractive for newcomers. It is probably worthwhile at this point to outline some aspects of their religious teachings, particularly their adaptive strategies and patterns of transmission. But I shall start by offering a brief outline of the two case-studies discussed in this article.

2.1 Two case-studies: Siddha Yoga and Sivananda Centres

On behalf of his master, Nityananda, Muktananda (1908) claimed to have the mission of disseminating his teaching and going to the West. A few months after Nityananda's death in 1961, Muktananda started his own ashram, in Ganeshpuri near Bombay, and welcomed westerners. The seeds of Siddha Yoga's expansion were already planted: local centres of the "path of the perfect ones" began to be established in the seventies in the West by disciples who had come back from India. Moreover, some of Muktananda's disciples were famous and influential in the counter-culture milieu: they supported his tours in the United States and Europe, and introduced him to alternative and spiritual circles, especially Transpersonal Psychology and the Personal Growth training called *est*. Muktananda made his first world tour in 1970; at the end of the second one in 1974, Siddha Yoga seemed to be firmly established at an international level, with more than 150 centres and 3 ashrams, which are administered from the United States by a Foundation, the Siddha Yoga Dham Foundation, created in New York in 1974. In 1982, when Muktananda died, Siddha Yoga represented allegedly 300 centres in 52 countries, which were said to attract 300'000 disciples, a third of which are American. Some disciples, whether residents only or swamis (monks), live permanently in the two main Siddha Yoga ashrams, in Ganeshpuri and in the Catskills mountains, in the United States (New York state). Nevertheless community life experiments in France and England have been unsuccessful, and disciples gather regularly in local centres to chant and meditate together. In both countries, Siddha Yoga has a thousand disciples although it may attract many more sympathizers. It is currently a woman, Gurumayi (1955-), who is the spiritual leader of the movement and is known to be the guru of many American celebrities. Siddha Yoga implies a strong devotional relationship between the disciple and the guru, who bestows the awakening of divine energy, called *kundalini-shakti*. This experience called *shaktipat* or "spiritual awakening", as well as meditation, chanting and *seva* (selfless service) are regularly practised in ashrams and centres, and are supposed to lead to Self-realization, that is to say, the awareness of God within. Indeed, "nothing exists that is not Shiva": the monist belief in a divine and universal consciousness is one of the core principles of Siddha Yoga teachings.

Sivananda Centres' teachings place more emphasis on yoga practice. Sivananda (1887-1963) established his ashram in 1932 in Rishikesh in India, and founded the *Divine Life Society* whose aim is to disseminate yoga, presented as a means of individual and social progress. Sivananda quickly became a renowned guru in India, as he endlessly participated in conferences and religious tours. He also created in 1948 the Yoga Vedanta Forest University in which he trained several students. As a guru who never went out of Asia and preceded the counter-culture's fascination for the East, Sivananda was remarkably successful in extending his influence in the world, thanks to his Indian and western disciples. Vishnu-Devananda (1927-1993), yoga professor in Sivananda's ashram, was one of them. Claiming that his master had asked him to spread yoga in the West, he left India for the first time in his life in 1957, and with the support and help of his first followers, he opened his first ashram in Quebec, in 1959. In the name of his guru, Vishnu-Devananda never stopped travelling, organizing yoga courses and demonstrations, training yoga teachers and initiating swamis enabling them to establish and run centres in their own countries. By 1975, most centres and ashrams that exist today had already been created: eight ashrams and more than nineteen Sivananda centres are located mainly in American and European cities, as well as in India. The Centres' and ashram's spiritual and material life is managed by an Executive board, composed of swamis whom Vishnu-Devananda had appointed before his death. In the absence of a guru, discipline and respect of the swamis' authority are core-values. These centres shelter few permanent members living in a religious community within the ashram: *swamis*, *brahmacharyas* (aspirants) and lay members called "staff" or "residents". However, hundreds of students attend yoga classes, meditation sessions, as well as various workshops on vegetarian cooking, *ayurveda*, etc., each week. The Sivananda Yoga centres also developed a Teaching Training Course and trained more than ten thousands yoga teachers, which represents a very efficient means of disseminating the practice of yoga. As a result, their teaching of yoga is one of the most widespread in the world. Unsurprisingly, the practice of yoga (postures, breathing) is at the core of the *sadhana* (spiritual path) which also includes vegetarian food based on ayurvedic principles, meditation and chants, contemplation of the masters' writings, and voluntarily work (housework, cooking, yoga teachings in the ashrams and centres).

2.2 Exoteric religious teachings

What should be stated at the outset is that the adaptation of neo-Hinduism to western societies has often entailed a de-ethnicization and a simplification of the religious message. Sivananda's discourse on India's timeless wisdom and religious supremacy is clearly identity-affirming, but 20th century gurus whose aim was to target a non-Indian audience and establish themselves in Western countries have often delivered a universalistic message removed from its Hindu roots. As inheritors of Vivekananda's "practical Vedanta" (Vivekananda, 1985: 100)[3], but also of traditional *bhakti*, the "easy" (A.-M. Esnoul, 1952: 661-667)[4] path based on devotion, gurus have given precedence to a fundamental exotericism. Siddha Yoga and Sivananda Centres offer an updated, modernized and "mainstream" Hinduism for all (Burger, 2006:81-95).[5] "Only (Siddha Yoga's) language comes from India; the meaning, the essence of rituals is not Indian and besides they do not belong to any other country" (Muktananda, 1981: 39)[6] asserted Muktananda, whereas his disciples praised the modernized approach of his successor, Gurumayi:

> Whereas non-Indian Siddha Yoga students of the seventies often experienced their involvement in yogic practices as a choice that took them out of the mainstream of their culture, Siddha Yoga under Gurumayi has tended to be increasingly mainstream in character. Her style as a teacher – her ability to blend tradition and modernity, keeping alive classical forms while recognizing the contemporary issues that colour the spiritual lives of her students, makes her accessible to many who would have been uncomfortable in *Bhagawan* Nityananda's environs, or had difficulty in relating to the Hindi-speaking Muktananda (Douglas et al., 1997: 151).

---

3   In the eyes of Vivekananda, the first Indian religious figure to successfully introduce Hinduism on the international scene during the world parliament of religion in Chicago in 1893, the conversion of westerners represented a means by which national Indian pride and identity could be valorised, and the role of India in World redefined, as a spiritual guide for a materialistic West. "Heroic workers are wanted to go abroad and help to disseminate the great truth of *Vedanta*. The world wants it; without it the world is destroyed (...) We must go out ; we must conquer the world with our spirituality and philosophy. There is no alternative, we must do it or die. The only condition of national life, of awakened and vigorous national life, is the conquest of the world by Indian thought".

4   *Bhakti* is the Hindu path of salvation which has been defined as "easy religion", because of its emphasis on devotion and its opposition to ritualism and the intellectual approach of religion. It is also a path accessible to women and lower castes which doesn't require ascetic renunciation.

5   The exoteric teachings of Siddha Yoga and Sivananda Centres contrast sharply with Pattabhi Jois' elitist yoga and harsh discipline.

6   My translation.

Sivananda insisted too on the fact that his Vedanta-oriented teaching was accessible to all, irrespective of social class, religion, nationality, gender, etc. It is worth noting that this religious exoterism is also expressed in his books by a remarkable didactic approach, presenting yoga, meditation and rules of the salvation path in the form of handbooks or lists of simple and concise principles. In addition to simplicity, these exportable and trans-cultural religious teachings give precedence to practices over doctrines and rituals, which incidentally do not attract the attention of disciples, as we shall see. Vishnu-Devananda's teaching is focused on the diffusion of hatha yoga, summarised in five principal points "in an effort to simplify and clarify the complex philosophies and teachings of Yoga": 1. proper exercise, which means the practice of hatha yoga (the benefits of hatha yoga's countless postures are allegedly compiled in 12 basic postures); 2. proper breathing (it refers to *pranayama* techniques that are also part of hatha yoga); 3. proper relaxation; 4. proper diet ; 5. positive thinking and meditation.[7] Standardization and adaptation are well underscored by the introduction of relaxation in the main principles of Vishnu-Devananda, as well as "positive thinking": the expression is obviously reminiscent of personal growth and, strikingly, it has sometimes been equated with *Vedanta* in presentations of the "five points" offered by the movement.

Vishnu-Devananda teachings throw light on the emphasis placed on the practical aspects rather than on the philosophical contents of the message. Siddha Yoga also teaches essentially practices, especially chants of mantra and meditation, but also hatha-yoga and contemplation of the guru's words of wisdom. These practical teachings are not only presented as a means to reach the divine and all-pervading absolute, but also as tools enabling control of the mind, the attainment of well-being and self-fulfillment, and the development of one's own potential, etc. The emphasis on the efficiency, power and "positive effects" of religious practices reveal a rationalization of the salvation path. Indeed, Vishnu-Devananda described yoga as a "sci-

---

7   International Sivananda Vedanta Yoga Centres, *The five points of yoga*, (online), (2006-04-02). http://www.sivananda.org/teachings/.

entific method"(Vishnu-Devananda, 1995: 23), the effects of which
are objectively verifiable, where Muktananda claimed that Siddha
Yoga has all the virtues of therapy"(Muktananda, 1981: 93). It is well
worth noting that Muktananda's success in the West is partly the outcome of his participation in Transpersonal Psychology conferences in
the 1970s, and of his presentations during the *Erhard Seminar
Trainings* (est), the famous American personal growth training that
inspired him to create his own initiation programme, the "intensive".

2.3 Practical religions, inner-wordly ends and capitalism

One of the striking features of the exoteric teachings of Siddha Yoga
and Sivananda Centres is the emphasis on praxis, rather than on doctrines and philosophy, for very inner-worldly ends. According to
Muktananda, meditation enables one to be more efficient in all kind of
activities; he recommended disciples to "meditate, even just to fulfil
your desire for temporal objects" (Muktananda, 1995: 15, 32, 34).[8]
According to him, the kundalini, the cosmic energy he awakened
within his disciples, "makes a writer a better writer, a politician a better politician, a businessman a better businessman, a mother a better
mother. All talents, all skills lie in it, and when the kundalini is
awakened these abilities are evident in our daily lives. The kundalini
improves everything that needs improvement; when we have imper-
fections, it strengthens us and gives us balance" (Muktananda,
1986:72)[9] Muktananda's teachings are therefore not only for an ascetic

---

8   My translation.
9   My translation. In this respect, one can hardly avoid noticing *How to become
     rich, by... Swami Sivananda*, which states that *moksha* (liberation) is only one of
     the four *Purusharthas* (goals of life), whereas the three others relate to this
     world and represent the first step before renunciation. Although Sivananda
     warns the reader against the "impermanence of worldly happiness and the
     supreme felicity of desirelessness", this book is about "the development of
     certain virtues which will enable one to increase his earning capacity and to
     become a self-made man ... Some suggestions to start business, the role of

elite wishing to renounce the world. Even if the core of Siddha Yoga (as well as the Sivananda Centres) is represented by the gurus and a small number of disciples who choose a monastic life in the ashram, "Yoga, mediation, renunciation are precisely for those who live in this world", affirmed Muktananda (Muktananda, 1990: 243).[10] The organization of daily yoga classes for the public in Sivananda Centres seems to reflect the same inner-worldly emphasis.

The ways in which these two neo-Hindu movements encourage a pragmatic and inner-worldly engagement with their teachings is underscored by the particular activities they organise, the aim of which is to disseminate the teachings as well as to satisfy a large number of individualistic, even consumerist, disciples. Siddha Yoga ashrams are open during holidays to non-residents who can undergo short but intense spiritual training (Hervieu-Léger, 2001: 147-153) there, allowing them to revitalize their day-to-day solitary practices. These "retreats" provide a multitude of activities handled by the swamis: chanting, meditation and hatha yoga, introduction to the gurus' messages, etc. They are also the occasion to receive the guru's grace and participate in the initiation "programme" called "intensive". The "intensive" lasts two days, during which the guru awakens participants' kundalini, delivers a message, answers questions, leads chants and meditation. Similarly, Sivananda Centres' "holiday camps" allow disciples to rejuvenate in the confined environment of the ashram and to maintain discipline, which includes two classes of asanas and pranayama every day, meditation every morning and evening, and daily voluntary work. But the movement also organises training for hatha yoga teachers: the "Teacher Training Course" (TTC), open to all aspirants, whatever their level of practice – nevertheless rigour, motivation and respect for the daily routine are expected from everyone. In the course of one month, disciples explore postures and breathing techniques, mantra chants and meditation, and discover Indian myths and philosophies. At the end of the TTC, the new professors receive a "diploma"

---

agriculture and industry in the business-life and the ways of making best use of money are also explained".

10   My translation.

allowing them to teach yoga. Nevertheless, for many participants the TTC is principally a way of improving their own yoga practice and of encouraging personal discipline. Finally, in addition to these short-term stays in the ashram, Siddha Yoga and Sivananda Centres provide "trainings" and "workshops" which introduce disciples to various practices and life principles they will be able to adapt and apply in their daily life. As an example, workshops organised in the Spring of 2006 at the Sivananda Centre in London tackle different issues such as: energy, willpower and success, relaxation, break with bad habits, develop concentration, how yoga helps to channel mental energy, increase willpower, focus on the positive, have a healthy lifestyle, detach and let go, control stress[11]... The description of the "course" organised in May 2005 by the French Siddha Yoga local centre reso-nates with Sivananda Centre' activities:

> It invites each participant to take responsibility for his life joyfully. Its gives tangible tools for acquiring determination, strength, clarity of the mind, which enable him to make choices in his daily life reflecting the greatness and the beauty that are within him. [12]

These religious "how-tos" and reference to "tools" can't help but reveal the strategic selling of spiritual services and the instrumentali-sation of an inner-worldly religion to enlarge the audience. Other movements such as Transcendental Meditation went even further as they developed management courses and seminars in order to target specific professionals. For Vijay Prashad, this outlines the close asso-ciation between capitalism and "New Age orientalism" in which Indian gurus participate. His analysis of several gurus' discourse (esp. Rajneesh and Maharishi Mahesh Yogi) regarding economics and poli-tics emphasizes their explicit support for capitalism and their insistence on individual responsibility for the material conditions of life. This affinity with capitalism can also be seen in gurus'

11   Sivananda Yoga Vedanta Centre, *Workshops*, (online), (2006-04-14). http://www.sivananda.co.uk/workshops_yoga_london.html

12   My translation. Siddha Yoga France. *Cours sur le message 2004/2005*. (online), (2005-04-10). http://www.siddhayogafrance.org/cours-bruxelles.htm

evolutionist interpretation of reincarnation. Not only are Human beings responsible for their own fate, because of actions in previous lives, but contemporary gurus also tend to interpret reincarnation as an opportunity, and therefore a personal responsibility, to improve oneself and act on one's own future. "You are responsible for your well-being or otherwise, through your own *Karma* or action", stated Sivananda, "the Law of *Karma* gives liberty and freedom to an individual to grow to his full perfection" (Prashad, 2000: 62).[13]

3. The disciples' quest for self-perfection

3.1 NRMs, social protest and downward mobility

Turning now to the disciples of Siddha Yoga and Sivananda Centres, how do these religious messages meet their expectations? Salvation goods can be sociologically interpreted as the implicit expression of the temporal interests of their addressees (Bourdieu, 1987: 124); according to Weber, they can offer a "theodicy of good fortune", which legitimates the conditions of existence of the privileged, or the promises from a religion of salvation oriented towards the deprived (Weber, 1996). The vast majority of Siddha Yoga and Sivananda Centres' disciples are from the urban middle classes; a majority have been to university, a third of whom have a Master degree.[14] More than half of disciples of both movements, in France and England, work in liberal professions and management, while others are often self-employed, mainly in artistic activities or in the field of alternative

---

13   See also: Sivananda, *What becomes of the soul after death.* (online). (2005-09-03). http://www.dlshq.org/download/afterdeath.htm.

14   These descriptions are based on the social characteristics of the 80 people interviewed in both movements, in France and England. Strikingly, characteristics proved to be identical in both groups, and in both countries.

therapies; farmers, manual workers are absent.[15] This might be a general tendency of disciples in neo-Hindu movements: my previous research on two other neo-Hindu movements in France, Sri Chinmoy and Sahaja Yoga, uncovered a significant number of educated middle-class disciples in arts and skilled professions.

Strikingly, the religiosity of the 1960s – to which Asian-based religions contributed greatly – and the counter-culture have been analysed as an outcome of the liberalizing effect of education and the crisis of the middle bourgeoisie. White middle-class adolescents and young adults had benefited from the prosperous economic conditions and the democratisation of education of the 1960s and 1970s in the United States and Western Europe. But this educated class expanded beyond the needs of the economic system, and became to a certain extent ill-adjusted. Thus the counter-cultural quest for new lifestyles and values and the exploration of alternative religions have been interpreted as the rejection of a society unable to satisfy expectations of upward social mobility and recognition of this educated middle-class. New religious consciousness might be a compensatory strategy "that enables downwardly mobile – or anomalous – sections of the new lower middle class to imagine that they could narrow the gap between the cultural capital that they possess (qualifications and training) and their social status in the bureaucratic institutions (healthcare, culture, education, etc.) where they are employed" (Hervieu-Léger, Champion 1986: 177).[16] Interestingly, studies of the 1960s social movements also

---

15   Strikingly, the "middle class" preponderance in Siddha Yoga was emphasised by interviewees defining themselves as "working class" and expressing a social gap in the London local Centre: "I didn't like the way the MCs (Master of Ceremony: a person leading meditation and chant in Siddha Yoga) were talking and maybe at times I thought they were too middle class, bourgeois, and I thought they were very stuffy. – What do you mean, "stuffy"? – Very conservative, very limited lifestyle, limited point of view, everything is just done in a certain way. You know someone who perhaps hasn't ever really let their hair down and votes Conservative, very set in their ways. I think there are people like that in Siddha Yoga".

16   My translation. This was also the way D. Hervieu-Léger and B. Hervieu analysed the 1970s neo-rural communities in France: D. Hervieu-Léger, B. Hervieu, 1983: 69-73.

described the expression of the struggle for power and status of a "new class" of knowledge workers", against an "old class" of business owners and executives" (while the latter own the means of production, the new middle class is defined by its organisational and skill assets; Kriesi, 1989: 1078-1116). Indeed, NRMs share with ecology, women's movements etc., a counter-cultural dissent and a concern for individual autonomy, here expressed in religious terms – a quest for emotion and personal experience along with a critique of religious institutions perceived as being oppressive. Pierre Bourdieu also analysed the "adolescent counter-culture" in terms of aspiration to a higher class. According to him, it expresses the new petite bourgeoisie's "refusal to be pinned down in a particular site in social space" although their practices constantly speak of classification in the mode of denial. Alluding to Transcendental Meditation, yoga, zen, martial arts and oriental medicine, alternative therapies and many others, Bourdieu analysed these counter-cultural practices as the expression of a "desperate effort to defy the gravity of the social field" (Bourdieu, 1989: 370).

Protestation tendencies inherited from the counter-culture persist today among neo-Hindu movements' disciples and probably the other NRMs that expanded during the 1960s. In Siddha Yoga and Sivananda Centres, this is evident in the first place by disciples' values and ethics, continually opposing "materialism" to "spirituality". Most of the disciples who were interviewed strongly rejected consumerism, career ambitions, mass production and standardisation encouraged by capitalism. Perceived as corrupt, illusory and a recipe for enslavement to social pressure, interviewees instead gave precedence to a quest for aesthetics, authenticity, freedom and self-realisation embraced in their religious choice. Their practice of meditation, chanting or yoga was indeed part of the constitution of the make up of a new way of life; it gave a concrete form to this quest, as well as their monist belief which expresses the urge for harmonious integration in the world. The urge to free oneself from social constraints and pressures was also expressed by typical socio-professional trajectories. Nearly two thirds of interviewed disciples of Siddha Yoga and Sivananda Centres chose at least once in their life to travel for a long period of time, or took up a new occupation in artistic activities, yoga or alternative therapies, or lived in the ashram community. In other words, they gave precedence to self-employed, vocational activities that were unstable or even unpaid in order to achieve independence and self-fulfilment, whereas they had often given up jobs which had brought them financial security. Here, the quest for the self not only influences religious options, but also socio-professional choices.

In the light of the relative deprivation approach that analysed the counterculture as a crisis of the middle bourgeoisie, these socio-professional changes of direction supported by "spiritual" values and alternative lifestyles might still be sociologically interpreted as the expression of downward mobility of a section of the educated middle classes – or as a fear of it. Interestingly, the sociology of employment and work has identified indicators of downward mobility with a devalorisation of one's occupation and with personal dedication to eclectic types of training and extra-professional projects, in contrasting to the professional identity they strongly reject. In short, they seek to realise an *identité pour soi* which would be true and authentic (Dubar, 2000: 243-257). Personal vocation and creativity, the desire for self-fulfilment and autonomy, as well as the rejection of social and professional constraints have been underscored among individuals caught up in downward social mobility, and more generally among those whose professional identity is less secure and permanent in highly differentiated societies. Accordingly, the quest for self-realisation among Siddha Yoga and Sivananda Centres disciples might be a response to downward mobility and social frustration. Nevertheless, it seems to me much more complex, if one takes into account their cultural capital as well as their previous occupations which were generally successful. It is therefore difficult to decide whether their purpose is to escape from (real or anticipated) downward mobility or, on the contrary, to deliberately choose instability and to nurture a "withdrawal from economic necessity" characteristically from the culture of the bourgeoisie (Bourdieu, 1989: 54), especially because they have the financial and cultural means to make this choice. In terms of protest, H. Kriesi's approach of New Social Movements might be more convincing. They would represent "one of the arenas of confrontation between two camps in the new middle class": the "technocrats" who have organizational assets, and the "specialists", especially those working in welfare and creative professions (Kriesi, 1989: 1085).[17] It is indeed the cultural and social specialists who are also predominant in many NRMs, including Siddha Yoga and Sivananda Centres, rejecting bureaucratic systems and defending their autonomy through alternative religious choices and alternative life-styles.

3.2 The preference for a practical and inner-worldly method of salvation

Although the counter-culture has been pivotal in the diffusion of neo-Hindu movements in the West, it can only partially explain their relative success in the third millennium among new generations of disciples who hadn't experienced the "road to India" of the 1960s and 1970s. Besides, the fifty year old disciples are no longer young adults trying to make their way in the socio-economic system. More importantly, despite the fact that NRMs had supported social protest by offering religious utopia, community life and alternative lifestyles, it seems obvious from the different neo-Hindu movements that I have studied that nowadays the protest dimension has been largely attenuated. The negative discourse about today's pervasive materialism, alienating bureaucratization and consumerism none-theless coexist with an indifference to social and political matters. Indeed, most of interviewed disciples see no point in mobilizing in unions, political parties, charities, demonstrations, or even new social

---

17   On the "opposition of interest between, on the one hand, the 'technocrats' in private enterprises *and* public bureaucracies who try to manage their organizations most efficiently and, on the other hand, the 'specialists' who try to defend their own and their clients' relative autonomy against the interventions of the "technostructure".

movements, with which they share the counter-cultural legacy. Yet they sometimes feel concerned for the environment (it is supported by their belief in immanence), nevertheless they primarily aim at individual fulfilment. Only personal growth is believed to be a significant part of individual, and hence collective, progress.

These radically individualistic religious expectations are satisfied by the practical methods provided by contemporary gurus. It is worth beginning by noting the fact that generally disciples have explored a wide range of heterodox paths regardless of ritual, doctrines and cultural background, from neo-Hindu teachings to Buddhism and Taoism, personal development, shamanism, alternative and holistic therapies, Chinese medicine and massage, reiki, martial arts... Thus their relation to Sivananda Centres and Siddha Yoga is not a permanent, total and exclusive commitment, but their teachings are selected, sometimes along with others, to contribute to a set of personal religious resources. What gurus presented as "practical religions" is indeed assessed for their applicability to one's own lifestyle (here it's not so much the disciples who adapt to the teachings) and their effectiveness. Siddha Yoga and Sivananda's teachings have been described to me as a "science of life", a "universal mechanics", a "spiritual technology"[18], and often as "tools". These metaphors are extremely revealing about instrumental, rationalized and individualized appropriation of religious teachings: the "user" chooses different means according to their effectiveness and adequacy for dealing with personal needs. The appropriation of these religious "tools" also makes the user autonomous, and enables him to take care of himself and be in charge of his/her "self-perfection". Indeed, several disciples from Sivananda Centres and Siddha Yoga think, or wish, they didn't need the group or the guru to use the teachings and would prefer to regard the teachings as resources to cultivate a perfection or development of themselves. This is more than an aspiration; it is also an

---

18   "How would you define *yoga*? – I think it's like a technology of spirituality, because it teaches you techniques of how to manage the mind and the body, to bring it into a state of harmony so that you can be a channel for peace and so on". Yoga student, London Sivananda Centre.

imperative, expressed by the recurrent reference to "working on one-self", which also implies that it is they who have to elaborate their identity and their personal trajectory themselves.

3.3 The socio-economic dimensions of self-perfection

Beyond this psychologization of religion, I believe the use of the practical methods of salvation offered by Siddha Yoga and Sivananda Centres, along with other personal growth methods and alternative therapies, might tell us a lot about the responsiveness to the social pressure to perform well that is pervasive nowadays in large sections of western societies. In his research, A. Ehrenberg claims that the "society of change" demands an individual defined in terms of trajectory, one who must be in permanent evolution. This type of society also accentuates social and psychic pressure on individuals (Ehrenberg, 1995: 126). Taking the example of post-psychoanalytic therapies developed in the United States in the 1960s, R. Castel also stressed the growing importance attached to human beings perceived as owners of a kind of capital (their "potential") that they have to manage in order benefit from it in terms of relational skills and social success (Castel, 1981: 170). From this point of view, the success of neo-Hinduism can thus be easily interpreted in terms of the popularity of practical salvation goods in the shape of "performance spirituality" (Hervieu-Léger, 2001: 97), which might satisfy a quest for self-perfection/social adequacy in a world expecting individuals to change permanently. The beneficial effects of practices such as yoga, chanting and meditation, have often been described by disciples as a feeling of harmonious integration in their environment, as well as the improvement of communication skills, hence relations with others. Self-perfection resulting from the practices and lifestyles offered by Siddha Yoga and Sivananda Centres' teachings is also said to reinforce one's capacity to cope with difficulties. Difficult childhood, family issues or problems at work are described as some sorts of tests that enable people to progress if they know how to accept them. Underlying self-perfection and acceptation, it is easy to detect the values of flexibility and adaptability that are expected from the "society of change", rather than social contestation and reform.

This increasing importance attributed to resilience and self-transformation has economic consequences, according to R. Castel, who in his writings underlined the normative aspect of the all-encompassing use of psychology in society. Analyzing the recent development of new American therapies, he cast light on the striking correspondences between the alleged free and self-fulfilled individual praised by post-psychoanalytic therapies, and the human model de-manded by post-industrial society. Because of the rapid obsolescence of techniques, workers are more and more defined not by their position and role, but by their aptitude to develop by themselves new skills, that is to say, their so-called potential (Castel, 1981: 190; 2001: 146, 151). What Castel named the "myth of auto-realization" (Ehrenberg, 1991: 173) resonates strongly with the salvation path praising "self-realisation" in neo-Hindu movements and many other contemporary religious movements and alternative therapies. It is, according to him, a form of social alienation, which is no longer im-posed explicitly through coercive social forces, but through the inter-nalisation of norms impelling individuals to find by themselves the tools of self-invention and perfection in order to become autonomous and polyvalent, to take initiatives, and to develop responsiveness, teamwork and communication skills, etc. This is encouraged, in the economic private sector, by a growing number of experts, whose di-verse methods seem to paradoxically associate utilitarianism with "mysticism" (Stone, 1982: 107-130, 127). Indeed, their aim is to increase efficiency in bureaucratic and capitalistic societies, while inviting participants to see in self-fulfiment, services to and communication with others as the ultimate end.

Because of their ambiguous in-between position in the organisation of work, educated middle-classes are expected to exhibit efficiency, responsibility, initiative, flexibility and a willingness to permanently update their skills (Le Goff, 2003)[19], hence probably to be particularly receptive to this encouragement to develop personal potential. In addition to this external encouragement of professional and personal growth, they have at their disposal financial resources and sometimes a more flexible timetable, which leave time for extra-professional projects and activities. More importantly, it is well worth remembering that this intermediary social stratum has emerged thanks to the democratisation of education which is characteristic of post-industrial societies. In other words, skills transferred by educational institutions have been essential to the rise of this stratum, especially because they are defined by their organisational and skill assets, not by owning production means. In this sense, it wouldn't be surprising if the educated middle-classes gave precedence to acquiring and developing skills that were highly appreciated in the professional sector. With the ongoing democratization of education and rising unemployment rates in western societies, it wouldn't be surprising if this became imperative in some ways. To return to the question of religious salvation goods, it seems that Siddha Yoga and Sivananda's use of the semantics of professional training underscores a socio-cultural affinity to this social group, which seeks to acquire new skills through "workshops", "training courses" and "intensives" allowing them to improve their professional performance. It is obviously not a tendency exclusive to these two neo-Hindu movements: J. Beckford previously cast light on an identical tendency among new religious and healing movements (NRHMs); he cast light on the strong affinity between the ideal of re-trainable and adaptable employee and "the ethos of many NRHMs, for they are agreed on the desirability of encouraging positive attitudes towards the idea of personal change and growth (Beckford, 1984: 259-272, 267).

---

19   See also Boltanski, L., Chiapello, E. (1999) *Le nouvel esprit du capitalisme*. Paris: Gallimard. Dupuy, F. (2005) *La fatigue des élites: le capitalisme et ses cadres*. Paris: éd. Du Seuil et de la république des idées.

4. Conclusion

This chapter attempted to give an account of the diffusion of neo-Hindu movements in the West with special reference to the salvation goods offered by gurus and expected by western disciples. The diffusion of neo-Hindu movements in the West has entailed adaptation to the host culture, part of which involves the presentation of universalistic exoteric religious teachings removed from their cultural background. They take the shape of a praxis that can bring self-realization to practitioners, presented as the ultimate awareness of the divine absolute, as well as self-fulfilment in the here and now. The inner-worldly orientations are also underscored by innovative ways of disseminating the teachings, through "workshops", "intensives", "holiday camps" and "retreats". These spiritual trainings aim to satisfy pragmatic disciples who often combine different religious and therapeutic tools, participating altogether in a highly individualized method of "self-perfection". In brief, the appropriation of neo-Hindu beliefs and practices can be understood in the wider context of the imperative of developing one's "potential", a social pressure which is particularly strong among the educated middle-classes because of their intermediary position in social structures. Although Siddha Yoga and Sivananda Centres disciples express the wish to get free from the social constraints imposed by a bureaucratic and rationalized society, they paradoxically reveal a high sensitivity to salvation goods which, in the end, can be used as tools for adapting to the very same society. Yet it is unclear whether Siddha Yoga and Sivananda Centres' disciples respond to potential downward mobility and try to escape the loss of their class position, or look for upward mobility and deliberately choose a "withdrawal from economic necessity". Nevertheless, middle classes are the most sensitive to the to anticipatory or retrospective socialisation, according to A. Touraine. Their members act less in accordance with their present situation than with the background to which they aspire to belong or with the one they came from and to which they would like to return.[20] And this is precisely what might underlie Siddha Yoga and Sivananda Centres' salvation goods: practical religious goods, disseminated in "workshops" and "courses" in order to satisfy a desire for personal growth. All these religious offers and demands seems to speak precisely of social mobility.

To be sure, recent social changes (on-going democratisation of education, increasing unemployment, growing precarity of the job market, diversification of family structure, etc.) have accentuated the heterogeneity of social positions and trajectories, which call in question the characterization, diversification and boundaries of middle classes in post-industrial societies. Although strikingly, the success of comparable movements in India as well as in many other countries has also been analysed in relation to the urban middle classes' quest for self-fulfilment (Warrier, 2003: 213-253)[21], we might also question the comparability of social groups defined as "middle classes" in different societies. This is why the arguments of this chapter need to be refined, discussed and assessed in the light of different case-studies in the sociology of religion. Above all, there would be also much to gain from making connections with other sociological fields, such as the sociology of New Social Movements, social classes, cultural practices and employment, in order to understand religious choices.

---

20 Touraine, A. (2005), "Classes moyennes", *Encyclopaedia Universalis,* (DVD-ROM), version 10.

21 M. Weber also described the capitalistic development encouraged by the English colonization of India, and the development of "guru demagogues" and Hindu "plebeian sects" targeting the developing burgher strata. (Weber, 1958: 323).

References

Beckford, J. A. (1984) "Holistic imagery and ethics in new religious and healing movements", *Social Compass*, n°31: 259-272.

Boltanski, L. and Chiapello, E. (1999) *Le nouvel esprit du capitalisme*. Paris: Gallimard.

Bourdieu, Pierre (1987), "Legitimation and structured interests" in Weber's sociology of religion, in S. Lash, S. Whimster (eds), *Max Weber, Rationality and modernity*. London: Allen & Unwin, pp. 119-136.

–. (1989) *Distinction: a social critique of the judgement of taste*. London: Routledge.

Burger, Maya (2006) "What Price Salvation? The Exchange of Salvation Goods between India and the West", *Social Compass*, n°53: 81-95.

Castel, R. (1981) *La Gestion des risques: de l'anti-psychiatrie à l'après-psychanalyse*. Paris: Éditions de Minuit.

–. (2001) *Propriété privée, propriété sociale, propriété de soi: entretiens sur la construction de l'individu moderne*. Paris: Fayard.

Douglas, R. et al. (1997) *Meditation Revolution*. New York: Agama Press.

Dubar, C. (2000) *La socialisation: construction des identités sociales et professionnelles*. Paris: A. Colin.

Dupuy, F. (2005) *La fatigue des élites: le capitalisme et ses cadres*. Paris: éd. Du Seuil et de la république des idées.

Ehrenberg, A. (1991) *Le culte de la performance*. Paris: Calman-Levy.

–. (1995) *L'individu incertain*. Paris: Calman-Levy.

Esnoul, A.-M. (1952) "La Bhakti", in L. Renou et J. Filliozat (eds), *L'Inde classique, manuel des études indiennes*, vol. I. Hanoi. Ecole française d'Extrême-Orient: Paris, pp. 661-667.

Hervieu-Léger, D. (2001) *La religion en miettes ou la question des sects*. Paris: Calmann-Levy.

Hervieu-Léger, D. and Champion, F. (1986) *Vers un nouveau christianisme?* Paris: Les éditions du Cerf.

Hervieu-Léger, D. and Hervieu, B. (1983) *Des Communautés pour les temps difficiles: néo-ruraux ou nouveaux moines.* Paris: le Centurion.

Kriesi, H. (1989) "New Social Movements and the New Class in the Netherlands", *The American Journal of Sociology*, n°84(5): 1078-1116.

Le Goff, J.-P. (2003) *La barbarie douce: la modernisation aveugle des entreprises et de l'école.* Paris: La découverte.

Muktananda (1981) *En compagnie d'un Siddha: Entretiens et conversations avec Swami Muktananda.* Paris: Guy Trédaniel, éditions de la Maisnie.

–. (1986) *Où allez-vous? Un guide pour le voyage spirituel.* Paris: G. Trédaniel.

–. (1990) *Le jeu de la conscience.* Paris: G. Trédaniel.

–. (1995) *Méditez.* Paris: Siddha Yoga, éd. Saraswati.

Prashad, V. (2000) *The Karma of Brown Folk.* Minneapolis, Londres: University of Minnesota Press.

Sivananda (1950) Preface of *How to become rich, by... Swami Sivananda.* Rishikesh: the Yoga Vedanta Forest University.

Stone, D. (1982) "Les Oncles d'Amérique", in D. Friedmann (ed.), *Thérapies de l'âme, l'inflation du psychologisme.* Paris: Autrement.

Vivekananda (1985) *The nationalistic and religious lectures of Swami Vivekananda.* Madras: Sri Ramakrishna Math.

Vishnu-Devananda (1995) *Le grand livre illustré du yoga.* Paris: Centre Sivananda de Yoga Vedanta.

Warrier, M. (2003) "Processes of secularization in contemporary India: Guru faith in the Mata Amritanandamayi Mission", *Modern Asian Studies*, n°37(1): 213-253.

Weber, Max (1958) *Religion of India.* New York: Free Press; London: Collier Macmillan.

Weber, Max (1996) *Sociologie des religions.* Paris: Gallimard.

Maya BURGER

What is the Price of Salvation? The Exchange of Salvation Goods between India and the West

1. Introduction

This article takes up Max Weber's terminology of "salvation goods" – along with the notion of the religious market, which is somehow inevitably connected to it – which has come into common terminological use lately[1], in order to discuss their validity in the field of the modern history of yoga.[2]

In Weber's view[3], religions offer something to their adherents worth striving for; he qualifies this "something" by the term "salvation goods" *(Heilsgut)*.[4] Wanting to explain social action *(soziales Handeln)*, he demonstrates that such actions are not performed at random, but are linked to values and to a search for meaning. Though Weber does not define religion, he tries to show that it is the main

---

1   See Stark and Bainbridge (1980) and Iannacone (1992). I am using "religious market" in the generally accepted sense of the term without explicit reference to the theories discussed by others in this volume. For a critical view, see the article by Steve Bruce in this issue.

2   I am entering this fascinating topic with the double limitation of being neither a sociologist nor an economist. I do hope, however, that the material presented and the many questions it has raised will contribute to the debate around the notion of religious market.

3   I am referring here mainly to Weber's chapter, "Die Wirtschaftsethik der Weltreligionen: Vergleichende religionssoziologische Versuche" (1920/1978: 237-275).

4   For an extensive treatment of the question, refer to the article by J. Stolz on this issue.

provider of meaning for human actions.[5] Hence salvation goods, as
aims *(Heilsziele)* proposed by religions and the means to reach it
(Heilsmittel), are factors enabling the explanation and understanding
of human actions and social constructions (for sociology), as well as
the construction of a comparative understanding of religions (at least
their written traditions) according to the underlying world-view they
express.[6] Social behavior – and moreover economic attitudes (or
ethics[7]) – are deeply impregnated by religious goals or salvation goods
inasmuch as these reveal various characteristics according to the
world-view they stem from. They can be actively sought or passively
received, individual or collective, contemplative or active; they are
bound to historical situations, to psychological needs as well as to
social stratification. Salvation goods are not only transcendental, but
also very much of this world *(habitus)*.[8]

Is it possible to apply the notion of salvation goods and of the religious market as a hermeneutical tool for looking at a specific
situation in the history of yoga, where yoga is taken as an example of
an aspect of a non-Western religion (Hinduism) in a situation of

5   According to Weber: "die aus der Art der Gottesvorstellung und des
    'Weltbildes' folgende rationale religiöse Heilspragmatik hat unter Umständen
    weittragende Folgen für die Gestaltung der praktischen Lebensführung
    gewonnen" (1920/1978: 259).

6   As Weber put it: "Ideen, beherrschen unmittelbar das Handeln der Menschen.
    Aber: die 'Weltbilder', welche durch 'Ideen' geschaffen wurden, haben sehr oft
    als Weichensteller die Bahnen bestimmt, in denen die Dynamik der Interessen
    das Handeln fortbewegte. Nach dem Weltbild richtete es sich ja: 'wovon' und
    'wozu' man erlöst sein wollte – und nicht zu vergessen – konnte" (1920/1978:
    252).

7   By the economic ethics *(Wirtschaftsethik)* of a religion, Weber understands
    religiously grounded motivations *(Antriebe)* for action.

8   As Weber put it: "Die untereinander verschiedenen Heilsgüter, welche die
    Religionen verhiessen und boten, sind für den empirischen Forscher keineswegs
    nur und nicht einmal vorzugweise als 'jenseitigs' zu verstehen" (1920/1978:
    249). Most salvation goods were worldly oriented: health, long life, wealth. It
    was only what Weber calls the religious virtuosi (ascetics, monks, etc.) who
    were seeking for other-worldly goods. But Weber says that even here these
    other-worldly goods were in fact this-worldly *habitus*.

global exchange and encounter? To put it plainly: does Weber's terminology help us to understand yoga as an export product on a world market? Additionally, does the metaphor (or is it more than a metaphor?) of a religious market yield fruitful insights into the understanding of the globalized situation of yoga today?

Having outlined Weber's perspective, even briefly, I shall now turn my attention to yoga and treat its recent history as a test case for the Weberian proposition linking "religious" salvation with market strategies.

The history of yoga is a long one. Yet, in the past 100 years, yoga has left its country of origin to conquer the world. In the context of reflecting on salvation goods and the religious market, we might put it this way: yoga has become a product on the world market, and, in more recent years, one of the most widespread techniques of relaxation and well-being.

This fact cannot but intrigue the historian of religions. What has happened to yoga in recent history that it should deserve such a fate? For centuries, yoga has been seen in India as a technique used by ascetics to make the body strong or even immortal and to gain, through renunciation, ultimate salvation.[9] As a philosophical system it allows its adepts to discover the true nature of things and/or the cessation of any connection with the cycle of existences and so finally to attain a state of salvation beyond any worldly connection.

However, during the 20th century, yoga has undergone a fascinating change. For the researcher, it has become a means of understanding and measuring the important mutations that have occurred in the modern history of Indian religious traditions, as well as a way of understanding new approaches and demands introduced into the field of contemporary spiritual inquiries worldwide. The encounter between India and the West[10], so closely linked in their history since

---

9   In Weber's terminology, yoga could be traditionally qualified as a contemplative, individual salvation product that isolates the yogi (a virtuoso) from society in search of the liberating goal.

10   W. Halbfass (1988) talks about the hermeneutical encounter situation between India and Europe obliging the researcher to study India and Europe

the mid-19th century, may well provide a good illustration with which
to test the conceptual validity of Weber's notion of salvation goods
and the usefulness and limits of interpreting through the notion of the
"religious market".

2. The yoga renaissance

A key figure in the renaissance of yoga in India and in the world is
Swami Vivekananda (1863-1902).[11] Swami Vivekananda's participation in the Parliament of Religions in Chicago in 1893 is a well-known
and much studied episode in the history of the encounter between
India and the West.[12]

   Swami Vivekananda travelled to the West without any money and
without having even been officially invited to the Parliament. A monk
of the Ramakrishna Mission, he had decided to raise funds for his
nation. He was convinced that he could *sell* something to the West.[13] It
might not necessarily be the idea of "market" that Vivekananda had in
mind, but he certainly wanted to exchange (Indian) spirituality for
(Western) material goods.[14] This comes neither from a Vedantic nor
from a yogic mentality, which implies that Vivekananda had other

---

   simultaneously in order to understand their respective colonial and postcolonial
   history.

11 The role of Vivekananda in the history of yoga has been studied by E. de
   Michelis (2004).

12 I am of course aware of the epistemological difficulties related to the use of
   constructed concepts such as Occident and Orient, East and West, however, we
   may recall that these "entities" have played an important role in the history of
   ideas.

13 Vivekananda's teacher and master, Ramakrishna, had a horror of money. Not
   only was it not something one should think about, Ramakrishna would not even
   touch it. Vivekananda certainly did not have Ramakrishna's aversion to money
   and he was very aware that money was needed for the Indian population.

14 *Complete Works of Swami Vivekananda*, vols 3 and 5.

sources and motivations. When and how did he start to consider spirituality a marketable commodity? He stayed in the West for over three years and according to the demands in vogue at that time, he introduced yoga as *the* Indian spiritual way, indeed, as the basis of all religions: a scientific path leading to supra-consciousness and the foundational technique – most accurately worked out in the Indian context – allowing one to live and experience what all religions preach as their goal.[15] It was during this time that he ordered the central text of yoga – the Yogasūtras of Patañjali – from his fellow monks in India. He translated and commented on them for Western audiences and propounded his views at the first yoga camp held in America. Swami Vivekananda travelled widely and frequently corresponded with Christian Scientists, Theosophists and members of cultic milieux, to name only the most important groups. His discourse can be understood only in light of his connection to these spiritual groups and his urgent need to defend the superiority of Vedanta over other religious views. He truly was a missionary.

We should not forget, however, that Swami Vivekananda was first and foremost a monk and that the only goal of yoga for him was salvation, liberation and spiritual freedom. Yoga is a way of renunciation, whether exercised in the world by detaching oneself from the fruits of one's acts *(karma yoga)*, or as a monk devoted exclusively to the search for liberation *(rāja yoga)*. Hence, in spite of the fact that he introduced yoga to the world and traded it as a spiritual necessity for a materialistic universe, his yoga was of a very different type from what it subsequently became.[16]

---

15   *Complete Works of Swami Vivekananda*, vol. I, "The science of Rāja-Yoga proposes to put before humanity a practical and scientifically worked out method of reaching this truth" (1974: 128); "Rāja-Yoga is the science of religion, the rationale of all worship, all prayers, forms, ceremonies and miracles" (1974: 165); "The yogi proposes to himself no less a task than to master the whole universe, to control the whole nature" (1974: 133).

16   For him, the only goal of yoga is *samādhi* that is "When the mind goes beyond the line of self-consciousness, it is called *samādhi* or superconsciousness" vol. I (1974: 180).

This transformation of yoga into a market product of well-being is an element of the encounter between India and the West that was ushered in by colonialism. It is far from irrelevant that the British, who conquered and ruled India, were a nation of traders. They introduced Indian goods (cotton, pepper and tea, to be sure, but also the knowledge of Sanskrit and of the literary and religious texts written in Sanskrit) to the world market. As a result, the East-West encounter is a complex one, operating on many levels. Seen in a larger context, "market" turns into something like a symbol for one aspect of what may be called the mechanics of encounter. Such mechanisms can be categorized thus: travel (as Vivekananda did); the giving of public lectures (to people who had to buy tickets, which Vivekananda did to earn a living during the first months after the Chicago meeting, though he cancelled the contract with his agent when he found out that he was being exploited; thus Vivekananda himself entered the market, as it were, as a product, not a trader); the writing of books; and, last but not least, something akin to what we might term a hermeneutics of encounter, where a situation of encounter becomes a subject of reflection in its own right. The latter is constituted by an analysis of the rhetoric of encounter undertaken through the study of the concepts at stake as they change through being translated and traded. Yoga is one such concept.[17]

On his return to India, the Swami was not acclaimed so much for having raised money for his mission, but rather as a national hero who had been able to offer the world a salvation product (in his vocabulary, spirituality) developed and produced in a downtrodden and dominated nation.

---

17   A. Choné (2003) has done some interesting work on yoga-related concepts, for example, those integrated by theosophy and anthroposophy.

3. The world market and pilgrimage

If Vivekananda gave the first impulse to the renaissance of yoga, a complex history of its reception was to follow (see Fuchs, 1990; Baier, 1998; Ceccomori, 2001; Alter, 2004; de Michelis, 2004; Strauss, 2005). My example will concentrate on the yogic tradition of one of the greatest masters of the 20th century, Tiruvanamalai Krishnamacharya (1888-1989), whose teaching has become the preferred approach for thousands of students around the world.[18]

Let us start in the late 1920s. T. Krishnamacharya introduced his yogic technique in the royal palace of Mysore, a provincial city of Southern India; here he established a new yogic tradition.[19] It is based on a strict knowledge of postures and can be qualified as a strenuous, forceful yogic path. But whereas colonialism and Vivekananda coincided in Weber's lifetime, the example we have chosen to focus on belongs to a period that Weber could only have imagined.

Krishnamacharya was not paid for teaching yoga, but his knowledge of yoga and his mastery of its practice were recognized as a qualification by a king who acted as his sponsor. The king's motivation was probably not pecuniary; rather, it was personal (he needed the therapeutic help of yoga) and probably political (he sent T. Krishnamacharya around India to hold yoga demonstrations).[20]

T. Krishnamacharya was born in 1888. His devotion to his study led to him being acknowledged as a pre-eminent scholar famed for his erudition in many traditional fields of Indian knowledge (grammar, philosophy, ayurveda). He had also studied the practical side of yoga and medicine during the seven years he spent with his master in the Himalayas. During his stay in Mysore, he cured the Maharaja Krishna

---

18 T. Krishnamacharya's life has been written by T. K. Desikachar (1998); another valuable source is Srivatsan's biography of Krishnamacharya (1997).

19 The history of the Mysore Palace tradition has been studied by N.E. Sjoman (1996).

20 He sent, for instance, B. K. S. Iyengar to Pune to demonstrate yoga. The latter founded his own yoga tradition in that city.

Rajendra Wodeyar and was subsequently appointed yoga master to the royal family and allowed to establish his own yoga centre. It was under the patronage of the royal court of Mysore that Krishnamacharya developed a yoga technique, known *aṣṭaṅga vinyāsa* yoga. *Vinyāsa* is the technique that characterizes his yoga of this period. In other periods, he emphasized different methods or styles of teaching. Though he claimed it was based on old texts and traditions, historical evidence clearly shows the integration of new methods into his yoga: elements of Western gymnastics as used for military training by the British Army, for example (Sjoman, 1996). During his time in Mysore, he trained some of the world's best-known yogis: B. K. S. Iyengar, Pattabhi Jois, as well as his own sons, T. K. V. Desikachar and Shribhasyam. Indra Devi was the first Western student and woman to receive yoga training from T. Krishnamacharya. She took yoga into the world, first to South-East Asia, then to her homeland in Russia, to the USA and finally to South America.[21] After Indian independence in 1947, T. Krishnamacharya left Mysore and went to live in Chennai with his family.[22] Tiruvanamalai Krishnamacharya died in 1989 at the age of 101.

But let us return to the so-called Mysore tradition.[23] The reception history of Krishnamacharya's yoga will be illustrated here through the example of his pupil, Patthabi Jois, who was his disciple for many years. Today, Jois claims to teach the true and unique tradition of T. Krishnamacharya of the Mysore period, while other disciples have

---

21   Indra Devi's example provides a very important mechanism of the spread of yoga. With most of the examples we have studied, it was through a personal encounter with a Western scholar or student that an Indian master would become known and his yoga spread. Indra Devi's activities as a yoga teacher started in the late 1930s.

22   There his yoga changed in many ways over the years, becoming far more adjusted to the individual needs of the people and the demands of a fast-changing society.

23   The material presented here stems from a three-year SNF research project: "Yoga between India and Switzerland: the history and hermeneutics of encounter".

changed it to adapt it to their own ways. Thus, he shares Krishnamacharya's aura by being the faithful heir to his tradition.

Pattabhi Jois was born in 1915 and learnt yoga from T. Krishnamacharya from the age of 12 years, after meeting the master by chance in his hometown of Hassan. He then moved to Mysore to learn Sanskrit and yoga. In 1937, with the help of the late Maharaja Krishna Rajendra Wodeyar, he was appointed to teach yoga at the Sanskrit college. He continued to do so right up to his retirement in 1973. It should be emphasized that for many years Patthabi Jois taught only Indians. There were no foreign students at Mysore University at that time. He taught yoga as philosophy (studying Sanskrit and teaching texts) as well as practice. Pattabhi Jois did not have a patron in the way T. Krishnamacharya did, unless one considers the Indian Government, who pays the salaries of university teachers, as the modern version of the kings of earlier times. It may be useful to remember that education is free in India and that training in yoga was therefore available free to students. A traditional *guru*, on the other hand, is not paid, though he may be served and he might receive a farewell gift once the training of a student has been completed.[24]

Pattabhi Jois had three children, and his grandson Sharat (his daughter's son), born in 1971 is presently co-director of the Asthanga Yoga Research Institute founded in the 1980s; without any doubt, this makes the institution a family affair.

The western career of Guruji (as he is called by his students) began with his meeting the Belgian André van Lysebeth, in 1967.[25] Van Lysebeth, like the earlier colonialists, was looking for something in India. It was not tea or pepper, but spirituality, recalling therein what the good Svami Vivekananda had promised to the West. One quotation may be sufficient here:

---

24 It is only recently that yoga in India has become a means to make money; traditionally yoga and money were not compatible.

25 Van Lysebeth has played an important role in constructing a European yoga; he encountered this style of yoga during his second trip to India and integrated it with his previous knowledge, based mostly on the yoga of Sivananda.

Je suis conscient d'avoir ainsi une occasion unique de voir en action des suc-
cesseurs des anciens yogis, dépositaires de la tradition et des techniques
millénaires auxquelles les occidentaux ont si rarement accès. Je me sens
transporté non pas seulement à des milliers de kilomètres de l'Occident, mais à
des milliers d'années en arrière (Van Lysebeth, 1965: 30).

Jois entered the export market in 1972, as a result of his having been
discovered by some American students, who took him to the USA in
1975. From there his type of yoga spread very quickly throughout the
United States, but also in France, Germany, Russia, Japan, Israel, New
Zealand, Australia, in short, around the world. Thus, Pattabhi Jois
entered the international yoga market and started to *sell* his yoga tradition.

Does it require a "system" to make your type of yoga recognizable
as a market product? Clearly, there is an advantage in possessing and
using a label and a name that identifies the product (comparable to a
trademark) Here the mechanics of the market may have combined
with the traditionalism of a man who never changed his yogic practice
and who was lucky that the term, *aṣṭaṅga vinyāsa* yoga, used by his
teacher Krishnamacharya (for the method of connecting positions
actively) was as yet "free" of copyright.[26]

The authority and fame of Pattabhi Jois's yoga come from his
claim to teach the true yoga of the Krishnamacharya heritage: the yoga
he learnt from him in 1927 and which constitutes a great tradition.
This tradition goes back ultimately to a certain Vamana Rishi, who
wrote the yoga *Korunta*, a text acquired by Krishnamacharya and
which was taught to Pattabhi Jois. However, the text itself has been
lost, adding to the mystery that surrounds Krishnamacharya's life and
the origins of his yogic technique.

T. Krishnamacharya was a Brahmin and belonged to the religious
tradition of the Vaiṣṇava, more specifically the *viśiṣāṭdvaita* tradition

---

26   I am well aware that the notion of *vinyāsa* is contested today, and students and
     teachers prefer to talk about *aṣṭaṅga* yoga only, which makes it the yoga *par
     excellence* by referring directly to the tradition of Patañjali who calls his yoga
     by this name. However, the particularity of the yoga of Krishnamacharya of that
     period and, in consequence, of Jois is *vinyāsa*.

of Rāmānuja. Though this is important in itself for the history of yoga, it is mentioned here only because Krishnamacharya himself claimed to belong to an ancient lineage of spiritual tradition. In a dream vision, a lost text of this tradition dating back to the 11th century was revealed to him. By virtue of this dream and revelation, Krishnamacharya became the embodiment of the very old and important yogic tradition of the sage Nāthamuni. Jois builds on this by claiming in turn to belong to the same ancient tradition, thus appropriating for his school a special aura of revelation and antiquity. Traditionalism of this type is conventional in India and partly constructs a teacher's authority. In the Indian context, to be Vaiṣṇava, no less than to be a Brahmin, are elements of this type of yoga, distinguishing it from other types. On the Indian market, these elements form part of the trademark. However, it is doubtful whether they are recognized as such by the Western market. By calling his yoga "Aṣṭaṅga", Jois links himself to the tradition of Patañjali, though neither the *āsanas* taught nor the techniques of *vinyāsa* are found in Patañjali. On the other hand, of the eight parts of Patañjali's yoga only two (*āsanas* and *prāṇayāma*, i.e. breathing control) are important in Jois's *aṣṭaṅga* yoga. Thus, the situation of encounter and the expansion of the market from India to worldwide changed the name of the trademark and the tradition primarily evoked by it.

In continuation of the textual tradition, Jois has written a small book called *Yogamālā*, which he first published in Kannada, the local language, in 1962. At that time there were no Westerners on the horizon and consequently yoga afforded no means to make money. It is only during his international career that the book was translated into English by his Western disciples and adapted slightly to a Western audience (Jois, 1999). In it, he describes his vision of yoga and gives tips on to how to practise the basic postures of his series.

In order to understand the problematics of this type of yoga as a salvation product in an open market, it is necessary to briefly characterize its techniques and goals. Jois's is *hatha* yoga at its purest. It is, as the name suggests, the yoga of force; as such, it is a mainly body-oriented yoga. Whereas certain types of yoga emphasize the role of the mind as being more important than the body for the path to salvation or spiritual freedom, Jois emphasizes control of the body as the absolute precondition for progress. When the body is under control, the control of the mind follows automatically. The *vinyāsa* indicates a postural yoga in movement that is accompanied by controlled breathing while doing the postures. The purpose of *vinyāsa* is the cleansing of the body. As Jois says, the combined action of breathing and posture "boils the blood".[27] Blood is dirty and causes disease. With the heat that is produced in doing this kind of forceful yoga, the blood is cleansed and becomes thin and circulates freely. Impurities are also removed along with the sweat provoked by its strenuous practice. In fact, so difficult and demanding are the postures, that sweating is truly a distinguishing feature of this yoga. It is through sweat that diseases and impurities leave the body. The idea is similar to an alchemical process:

> In the same way that gold is melted in a pot to remove its impurities by the virtue of the dirt rising to the surface as the gold boils, and the dirt then being removed, yoga boils the blood and brings all our toxins to the surface, which are removed through sweat.[28]

This method thus makes the body healthy, strong, and pure like gold. After purifying the body, the nervous system is purified, as well as the sense organs. The process is done on three levels: posture, breathing and the place where you look or concentrate while practicing. These cover the three levels of purification: body, nervous system and mind.

This yoga requires years of intense practice. Jois claims there are six series of postures. However, most of the students never get beyond the first two. His grandson, Sharat, is said now to have concluded the sixth series. The goal proposed by Jois seems almost out of reach. To this unreachable goal, we must add that Jois does not award diplomas that would allow foreigners to teach his yoga. Only very advanced students (above series 4) have received a teaching certificate from the

---

27   As quoted on the web page of the Ashtanga Yoga Research Institute, www.ayri.org/method.htlm, accessed 4 April 2005. I am also referring to the introductory pages of Jois's *Yogamālā*.

28   See previous note.

master.[29] This is in stark contrast with other yoga schools, some of which deliver teaching certificates after a six-week course, the case, for instance, of the Sivananda tradition. The product offered by Jois is not something one can buy and export. Jois likes to say that his yoga is only 1 percent theory and 99 percent practice.[30] Such practice indicates that it is not something which can be easily obtained. It is rather something that one has to appropriate by *doing* (not by having); in this sense Jois's yoga is not a market product, yet it could be qualified as a salvation good.

The historian of religions cannot but be puzzled by the situation presented by the yoga offered by Jois. How is it possible and why do students go for such a strenuous program, in many ways far too complicated and difficult for them to dream of ever reaching the proposed goal? There is no immediate benefit in the form of a piece of paper or diploma that would allow them to teach; there is hardly any chance of reaching the goal of the proposed program, series 6, given that very few bodies are physically capable of such effort and contortion. Hence, we are justified to inquire what is it that attracts so many foreigners (and the number is steadily increasing) to the yogic path offered by Jois? Is it the high price – as much in terms of the money required as of effort – that attracts the crowd? (Following the slogan that the more it costs, the better it must be.) Is it the attraction of a goal that can never be reached? Is it the physical effort, which pushes the practitioner invariably to the utmost limit of what the body can bear? Is it the psychological dimension of flagellating the body that is beneficial? Is it the alchemical transformation of a dirty body into the promised healthy, shining figure? Is it the fact that the practitioner is assimilated into an old and pure tradition, upheld by a gentle, graceful, modest master? Or is it belonging to a very select elite, whose identity is defined by the members being disciples of that master?

---

29   A student jokingly told me one day: "I have spent so much money, over $58,000 and so many years, but I don't even have a certificate!" Oral communication during field work in Mysore, 2003.

30   Personal interview with Jois in August 2005.

The emphasis shifts from applying the "market" as the herme-neutical tool to asking what defines a "product" in this specific market. Would Weber recognize a "promise" as such a product? Does or can a "product" bought by several people constitute a group? Are we arriving at a definition in which a "sect", or even a religion, can be characterized by its customer profile?

These (Weberian?) questions make us to turn our attention to the Ashtangis (as Jois's followers call themselves) as a social group. During their time in Mysore, the Ashtangis have evolved into a very organized and coherent group possessing a strong identity; this is re-inforced by their not being allowed to attend any other yoga classes during their work with Jois.[31] I should mention at this point that yoga has been influential in the city ever since T. Krishnamacharya's time. Many yoga schools are now established there, both for Indians and Westerners. Because of Jois's fame – and this has only increased with the presence of famous students such as Madonna – numerous foreigners have been attracted to the city. One consequence of this is that new yoga schools open up in the city every year; yoga thus con-stitutes a flourishing business. Yoga teaching for foreigners and yoga teaching for Indians are undertaken separately. The division is not only economic – foreigners pay far more than Indians – there is segregation on the level of practice too: Westerners are not taught the same things or in the same way as Indians. There are then two parallel markets in Mysore; and, with regard to the perspective of encounter, it is of considerable interest to inquire as to where and how, if at all, the two markets meet and interact. In fact, it is obvious that in Mysore they do not meet at all. This leads us to acknowledge that the *market* defines yoga as two *different* products, thus teaching us something about the typology of yoga and its history.

Ever since the creation of the Ashtanga Research Institute – now located in a new setting in an upper middle-class residential neighbourhood of the city – up to a hundred students attend its yoga classes daily. In an almost ceremonial routine, students take part in early morning sessions of the *āśrama* to complete the series they are

---

31   There is an inscription fee for the first month added to the general monthly fee.

currently learning, executing the same postures day in, day out, year after year. And year in, year out, students return to learn more and to live for a while under the guidance of the recognized master, turning their yogic practice into a ritual of self-transformation.

The Ashtangis have turned the city of Mysore into a place of pilgrimage for yoga. Observation of the historical development of yoga in the tradition of Krishnamacharya suggests the replacement of the market metaphor with one of pilgrimage (again as a hermeneutical device, and yet also as a historical fact, which is also the case exactly with the market and product analogy). With regard to yoga, the concept of pilgrimage may actually be more revealing as it has the advantage of including the many layers of the phenomenon.

The concept of the market places the emphasis on goods that are available, whereas with the metaphor of pilgrimage we come closer to describing the actual situation. When Jois travels (which he has been doing once a year), we can say that he himself is the exportable "product". But when the students come to Mysore as customers who travel to get something, they are not obtaining a product which they can hold in their hands. As previously mentioned, it is not possible to buy salvation – especially when even a teaching diploma is extremely difficult to obtain. We might say that what is being offered in this market is a transformation, or rather a practice of selftransformation (which would fit in well with Weber's idea of salvation goods, obtained in this world by living a state that prepares for salvation in the next). Following Alan Morinis's definition of pilgrimage as "a journey undertaken by a person in quest of a place or a state that he or she believes to embody a valued ideal" (1992: 4), we can well say that Mysore yoga is a pilgrimage. In its typology, we could see the Jois pilgrimage as initiatory, by which we mean a method of self-transformation; but it could also be seen as instrumental inasmuch as cure for disease may be a goal for some students. In many ways it is devotional in the sense that people are attracted to the master who represents the aspired goal of peace and radiant health.[32] The Indian

---

32 The categories of obligatory and wandering do not apply to this specific yoga pilgrimage.

concept *tīrtha* may also apply to the kind of journey we are witnessing here. *Tīrtha* means literally a passage, a ford, a way to cross a river, which is often understood as the place where we may change or transform ourselves, a location where one can gain access to another "more ideal cosmological realm, whether the movement be somatic and territorial or a change of another sort, semantically assimilated to movement: for example, approaching the state of consciousness of one's guru" (Morinis, 1992: 23). What is certain is that we are witnessing a pilgrimage of self-transformation. Yet even an anti-phenomenological perspective, one that views pilgrimage as an ongoing process of constructing discourses, can apply in this case.[33]

As with all institutionalized pilgrimages, this one can be proud of the elaborate infrastructures that guide students through their journey. The website is full of practical tips on how to reach the place, how to prepare, and how to attend to all the salvation goods on offer. The traveller will not only find practical information on the website, however. There are also personal testimonies of Ashtangis returned from their own pilgrimages and sharing their experiences with others. All this provides invaluable resource material for the researcher.[34] In Mysore, Ashtangis tend to stick together, eating out at the same restaurants, meeting at the same swimming pool, going to the same astrologer, getting a massage from the same Ayurvedic centre, attending the same painting classes – all goods that belong to the image or identity that the Ashtangis share.[35]

---

33   For example, Eade and Sallnow (1991: 1-27).

34   Many sites can be found under Mysore, yogasite.com or www.alanlittle.org/ yoga.links.html; www.alanlittle.org/yoga/MysorePics.html; www.alanlittle.org/ yoga/GurujiNY2000/GurujiNY2000/html

35   It is of course very difficult to draw an exact picture of the crowd surrounding Pattabhi Jois and the variety of people and motivations are numerous. However, it seems obvious that most of his disciples are Americans or from the Anglo-Saxon world, such as New Zealand, Australia. There seems to be a cleavage between European and American students of *aṣṭaṅga* yoga. The Europeans tend more often to join another *aṣṭaṅga* teacher in town, who seems to be more in tune with Europeans and their demands. Some have told us that they left Jois because of the American hegemony. Many students at the Institute are yoga teachers at home and come to Mysore regularly, but there are of course also

If the concept of pilgrimage seems to be appropriate to characterize the many dimensions of foreign yoga students, the picture has to be drawn differently from the point of view of the Indians. For those who profit from the Ashtangis' presence in the city, the marketable product is not yoga (the self-transformative process) so much as the yogis. From the point of view of Mysore's population, pilgrimage is a marketing strategy.

Let us briefly recall the comparative economics: for a Westerner, 150 Swiss francs for the rent of a three-roomed furnished apartment is cheap, whereas the equivalent 4500 rupees amounts to a respectable monthly salary for an Indian. In Mysore itself, Indians have found employment guiding the newcomers, providing them with housing and lodging, scooters and other goods and services. Around the area of the Yoga Institutes, Indians rent out their houses, build second and third storey buildings and let them to foreigners, who pay prices which could never be asked of Indian tenants. The city has changed over the years, gearing itself to making as much profit as possible from a flourishing market.[36]

To conclude, we have to admit that paying attention to the market and money as pragmatic realities is necessary. The Weberian terminology of salvation goods, together, on a more theoretical level, with the connected concept of the religious market, can constitute a useful tool for understanding Jois's yoga and raises questions that might otherwise be overlooked. However, if we return to the question in the title, "What is the Price of Salvation?", we realize that his typological approach does not do justice to the complexity of the situation. For instance, while the notion of cost is a function of the religious market, especially when connected to salvation, salvation for Jois has no price;

---

newcomers and simple students. As already mentioned, there are only a handful of certified yoga teachers round the world. All the others are just doing it without certification from the Research Institute.

36   The economic endeavour shown by the people of Mysore actually contradicts Weber's own view of Indian traditions as "marktfeindlich" and reminds us of the limitations of assimilating Indian traditions in general to the Brahmanic tradition.

it can be neither sold nor bought. He is, in this sense, a traditionalist.[37] What he "sells" is ritualized physical yoga training, the goal of which is something that he places beyond reach. Extracting money from people is a way of asking for renunciation. Jois does not sell salvation: in the Indian way of thinking *samādhi* has no price. The only thing he is selling is the path: you have to sweat for many years. In his view, his yoga teaching and earning money may well have a religious dimension. He invests, for instance, in building a temple in his home village, thus keeping up with his sectarian religious tradition. But what of his Western followers?

The Ashtangis pay for something that actually cannot be bought. We need criteria other than the market metaphor to understand why students follow a path that actually turns out, paradoxically, to be one of renunciation: what they pay is not what they get. And yet they do pay.

Weber was right in many ways, particularly because he has granted us the opportunity to pay attention to the economic side of salvation goods, be they transcendental or immanent. However, today's global market blurs the relevance that Weber's approach might still have. The encounter situation transforms salvation goods, related or produced by a religion, subjecting them to the impact of world-views that now stem from many different sources.[38] In the highly complex situation of encounter, the approach based on the notion of salvation goods may not provide the key to understanding the intricate layers of mixed world-views and culturally bound interpretations or misunderstandings.

---

37 Traditionally, yoga was defined as a path of renunciation *(vairāgya)*. The ecularization or esotericization of yoga has led to a view of it as an art of living. Jois has turned from a traditional teacher into a successful and expensive teacher.

38 In this short article, I have deliberately avoided addressing the methodological questions raised by the concept of globalization. On the topic of mixed culture, see the summary by Charles Stewart (1999); on the important concept of syncretism for the Comparative History of religions, see the recent reader by Leopold and Jensen (2004).

Approaching yoga from the angle of the religious market has allowed a perspective onto aspects that would have remained invisible had we not taken these parameters into account and particularly aspects pertaining to the differentiation of yoga's international and local markets: yoga as an export market – teachers traveling to take yoga abroad, students traveling to search for yoga in India; yoga as a trademark – tradition as a criteria of authority; yoga and religious affiliation; yoga and its salvation goods – well-being, salvation, transformation, books, diplomas; and yoga and its customer profiles – Indian and Western.

The religious market approach is not, however, entirely satisfying. There are patterns of behavior and attitudes that cannot be explained by such general models and these do not obey market logic (and which market?) in every respect. Hence, while the comparative history of religions may use this approach as a heuristic tool, along with others, it would, as its primary task, subordinate the Weber-inspired typological approach to thoroughly historical[39] and contextual investigations.

References

Alter, Joseph (2004) *Yoga in Modern India: The Body between Science and Philosophy*. Princeton, NJ: Princeton University Press.

Baier, Karl (1998) *Yoga auf dem Weg nach Westen: Beiträge zur Rezeptionsgeschichte*. Würzburg: Königshausen und Neumann.

---

39 According to von Stuckrad (2003: 911): "History, in this perspective, is an analytical term that does not explain anything in itself. It is located on a different level of argument. It is a metaterm needed for interpretation at the interface of past and present. It should not be mixed up with the 'facts' themselves – which would lead to essentialism – but, rather, should be regarded as a reminder that there are facts 'out there' that influence our positions or even determine our concepts."

Ceccomori, Silvia (2001) *Cent ans de yoga en France*. Paris: Editit.

Choné, Aurélie (2003) "La réception de l'Inde chez les ésotéristes occidentaux de la fin du XIXe siècle", in *Passeurs entre Inde et Europe*. Fédération nationale de Yoga, Ysé Tardan-Masquelier (éd.) *Revue française de Yoga*. No 27. Paris: édition Dervy, pp. 45-77.

De Michelis, Elizabeth (2004) *A History of Modern Yoga: Patañjali and Western Esotericism*. London: Continuum.

Desikachar, T. K. V (1998) *Health, Healing and Beyond: Yoga, and the Living Tradition of T. Krishnamacharya*. New York: Aperture.

Eade, J. and Sallnow, M. J. (1991) "Introduction", in *Contesting the Sacred: Anthropology of Christian Pilgrimage*. London: Routledge.

Fuchs, Christian (1990) *Yoga in Deutschland. Rezeption. Organisation. Typologie*. Stuttgart: Kohlhammer.

Halbfass, Wilhelm (1988) *India and Europe: An Essay in Understanding*. Albany: State University of New York Press.

Jois, Pattabhi (1999) *Yogamālā. The Seminal Treatise and Guide from the Living Master of Ashtanga Yoga*. New York: North Point Press.

Leopold, A. M. and Jensen, J. S., eds (2004) *Syncretism in Religion*: A Reader. London: Equinox.

Morinis, Alan (1992) "Introduction: The Territory of the Anthropology of Pilgrimage", in A. Morinis (ed.) *Sacred Journeys: The Anthropology of Pilgrimage*. Westport, CT: Greenwood Press, pp. 1-27.

Sjoman, Norman E. (1996) *The Yoga Tradition of the Mysore Palace*. New Delhi: Abhinav Publications.

Srivatsan, Mala (1997) *Srī Krishnamacharya. The Pūrnācārya*. Chennai: Krishnamacharya Yoga Mandiram.

Stewart, Charles (1999) "Syncretisism and Its Synonyms: Reflections on Cultural Mixture", *Diacritics* 29(3): 40-62.

Strauss, Sarah (2005) *Positioning Yoga: Balancing Acts across Cultures*. Oxford: Berg.

Swami Vivekananda (1974) *The Complete Works of Swami Vivekananda*, 14th edn. Calcutta: Advaita Ashrama.

van Lysebeth, André (1965) "Destination Rishikesh", *Yoga* 28: 30.

von Stuckrad, Kocku (2003) "Relative, Contingent, Determined: The Category 'History' and Its Methodological Dilemma", *Journal of the American Academy of Religion* 71(4): 905-912.

Weber, M. ([1920] 1978) "Vergleichende religionssoziologische Versuche", *Gesammelte Aufsätze zur Religionssoziologie*. Tübingen: J.C.B. Mohr.

Jean-François MAYER

Salvation Goods and the Religious Market in the Cultic Milieu

1. Introduction

During a visit to one of the first "esoteric fairs" in Zurich, at the end of the 1980s, an exhibitor expressed interest in our research on "alternative religiosity" in Switzerland. What particularly aroused her curiosity was to know whether a scientific enquiry could reveal to her which new themes and products might prove to have "great potential" for her commercial activities.

In a paper given in 1997 at the SISR[1] conference in Toulouse, Hildegard Van Hove explained that she had come to prefer, to the extensive use of the term "New Age", that of "spiritual market", referring to "independent and freely accessible initiatives constituting a 'supply' among which 'consumers' are free to make their choice". The very use of the word "market", she further noted, "highlights the disparity of the existing trends" – because diametrically contradictory ideas appear side-by-side (Van Hove, 1999). The metaphor of the "market of religions" sometimes provokes reactions. However, when a researcher approaches different manifestations of the *cultic milieu*, the notion often seems adequate. Indeed, to approach the *cultic milieu* results in leading the researcher to believe that the "religious market" is not merely a metaphor there but perhaps corresponds to reality. This situation turns out to be encouraged by a more general social attitude, which approaches many practices in terms of "consumption" and con-

---

1   Société Internationale de Sociologie des Religions.

siders the practitioner as a "consumer". This reality surpasses the subset that we will consider here, but puts it in adequacy to the contemporary environment and, as we will see further on, renders the boundaries of the *cultic milieu* uncertain. In this article, we will attempt to illustrate this functioning through a few examples chosen from the Swiss field, but equivalents of which it would be easy to find in other countries.

Perhaps more than the term "market", the adjective "religious" could be contested. Indeed, psychological experiences, the quest for well-being, and the search for a better quality of life motivate the practitioners just as much as do sacred doctrines or a connection with supra-human dimensions. The question nevertheless becomes more complicated when we observe that these motivations are frequently accompanied by a quest for meaning. Must any quest for meaning be automatically qualified as "religious"? At what point does it become so? We find ourselves in a gray area in a field with shifting boundaries: the terms para-religion or quasi-religion sometimes spring to mind. As Valérie Rocchi has well shown, "psycho-mystical belief is more complex than the simple alternative 'religion or therapy'", even if she notes a clear "predominance of therapeutic activity over religious activity" in the current context of these circles (Rocchi, 2003: 179).

Moreover, the very notion of *cultic milieu* is today the object of different uses. A work published under the direction of Jeff Kaplan and Heléne Lööw applies it to radical political groups, whether they arise from environmental activism or the far right (Kaplan et al., 2002). The authors foreground the *cultic milieu* as an expression of opposition to prevalent ideas and as a social environment, where theories and speculations often considered suspect by people who do not belong to the milieu can be discussed, debated, and reformulated. The only thing that unites the participants would be a "shared rejection of the paradigms, the orthodoxies, of their societies" (Kaplan et al., 2002: 4).

It was not in the broad sense that Colin Campbell – to whom we owe the development of the notion of *cultic milieu* – understood it in the beginning: he placed the *cultic milieu* at the point where "deviant science meets deviant religion" (Campbell, 1998: 123). Nevertheless, the extensive applications have their pertinence and may reinforce the usefulness of the concept of the *cultic milieu*. One of the characteristics of the latter is to integrate beliefs not strictly religious but claiming to break with *mainstream* approaches, which can also engage in interaction with political convictions. For example, the success of "conspiracy theories" in certain sectors of the *cultic milieu* creates bridges in this direction.

Nevertheless, we will use the concepts of cult and *cultic milieu* in their most current sense, which refers to the wider milieu to which the *cults* belong, giving them a basis of credibility and providing a potential reserve of audience members for the messages that they are disseminating. This milieu "continuously gives birth to new *cults*, absorbs the debris of those that are disappearing, and produces new generations of individuals with a propensity for *cults*"; although these cults are sometimes of a transient nature, the *cultic milieu* pre-exists them and will survive them. The vast majority of those who circulate in the *cultic milieu* will never adhere to a movement. The *cultic milieu* must be understood as a permanent phenomenon, and not one connected with a specific trend or particular historical context – which distinguishes it from neighboring concepts, such as the "mystico-esoteric network" developed by Françoise Champion, which belongs to a post-1970 period (Champion, 1990), thus representing rather *one* incarnation of the *cultic milieu*.

Referring to the tripartite typology of *cults* advanced by Stark and Bainbridge (Stark et al., 1985: 28-30), we will be interested *in audience cults* and *client cults*, that is, in situations which are those of a consumer or a client, while the third element of the typology, the *cult movement*, would represent a status of member. In an interesting field study on the *cultic milieu* in one region of the United States, Danny Jorgensen observes that, the more a group experiences a process of "sectarianization", the less the "esoteric community" (expression used to denote its field) is likely to consider the group as belonging to it (Jorgensen, 1992: 59). The *cults*, to a certain extent, need the *cultic milieu*, but are situated rather in its periphery, the requirement of attachment to a group contrasting with the multiplicity of successive or simultaneous experiences encouraged by the atmosphere of the cultic milieu, whose fairs and other events place many kinds of offers side by side.

Even if structured groups often attract in priority the attention of sociologists and the media, their adherents are relatively few, as the results of successive federal polls show in Switzerland (Bovay, 2004). On the other hand, the flourishing of literature and practices that convey spiritual elements outside dominant religious traditions represents a development that touches a not insignificant segment of the population, including among regular church-goers, and probably even more – even if no surveys exist that would permit confirming it – among those who call themselves "unaffiliated".

2. Mystery Park: scientific heterodoxy or new belief?

We will first consider a theme park: Mystery Park, built in the surroundings of Interlaken (central Switzerland) on the initiative of Erich von Däniken (born in 1935). A best-selling author translated into many languages, since the publication of his first book in 1968, Erich von Däniken maintains that throughout history (notably in the remote past relegated to the order of mythological periods) beings from outer space would have visited the Earth. These events would have left traces that archeology reveals and beliefs that transformed the extraterrestrials into gods. The extraterrestrials would also have genetically modified a cell taken from an already existing hominid and implanted it in a female hominid in order to give birth to a child endowed with intelligence: this would be the famous "missing link" of evolution.

Unlike the prophets ("contactees") of groups assembling believers in "flying saucers" around a particular message, Däniken does not appear as a messenger of the extraterrestrials entrusted with a mission.

Nevertheless, while Däniken does not establish a "flying saucer religion", neither does he belong to the line of "secular ufology" that is limited to investigating the enigma without claiming to produce a solution. Between these two poles defined by the Danish researcher Mikael Rothstein (Rothstein, 1999: 19-24), Däniken corresponds to a third term, which is situated precisely – and here we meet again the theory of the *cultic milieu* – at the intersection of religion and science. Däniken does not claim to possess a message of salvation, yet he supplies knowledge that constantly enters into the religious field. He states further that his work contributes to the transformation of human consciousness in the perspective of a New Age: "The new world brings a new religion, the new consciousness is a cosmic consciousness, a cosmic religion", he declares in an interview, adding that it is necessary to reject the divisions induced by religious systems (Schneider, 1990:8). He is aware of the implications that his theories have on the religious field. The Dänikenian discourse plays with religious references reinterpreted in the light of an approach that claims to be founded on facts alone. The New Age style music CD, "World of Mysteries", put on the market in 2005, concludes with a work entitled *Reditus Deorum* ("The Return of the Gods"), sung in Latin, which is also a way to refer to the sphere of the sacred. "Because one thing is certain," writes Erich von Däniken at the end of the brochure accompanying the recording, "these gods of ancient times have promised to return. They will keep their promise."

The remarkable book by Wictor Stoczkowski (1999) has shown that Däniken's work, a "strange theological concept" of gnostic type (Stoczkowski, 1999: 125, 133), was also the fruit of a lineage. Stoczkowski identifies the influence of science fiction literature, but the "Ancient Astronauts" theory also draws from the heritage of Madame Blavatsky (1831-1891) and theosophical literature: it is "a fact of tradition that belongs to the long-term" (Stoczkowski, 1999: 222). In addition, he notes, "the occultist subculture is constantly with us, always alive, changing, and creative in its way" (Stoczkowski, 1999: 281). Dänikenism is thus an integral part of the *cultic milieu*, even if Mystery Park does not claim to be either a center of esotericism or an amusement park in the usual sense of the term (Mystery Park Team, 2003: 7).

Mystery Park opened its doors in 2003. Through several "theme worlds", pavilions dedicated to different epochs and cultural zones, it dramatizes the theses of Erich von Däniken in an attractive and popular format, having recourse to modern techniques of multimedia presentations – to the point of seeing Erich von Däniken suddenly appear in the form of a hologram! Besides catering to the perennial fascination for the mysterious and being a place of entertainment in a tourist area (viable even on rainy days during vacations since visitors can remain in shelter and enjoy both the exhibits and the bucolic vista of the surrounding landscape), what does Mystery Park have to offer? It offers knowledge and an explanation of the world. This explanation is not constraining; the answers are suggested in the form of questions, avoiding direct statements and apparently leaving visitors the freedom to decide, even if all the information they receive is going in one direction. This explanation of the world is global, even if only a smaller circle of the convinced will accept it whole. In addition, a visit to Mystery Park appears on its own site as a sort of initiatory experience that does not identify itself:

> The enigmas shown in Mystery Park and the mysteries coming from ancient civilizations and from science and research are not part of the esoteric world. This 'mystical' world, where people have to 'believe', has nothing to do with the world of 'mysteries', of real enigmas.
> The themes of Mystery Park represent true verifiable facts. These relate to existing archeological discoveries, ancient writings and mythologies that can be studied in libraries, rituals of different cultures documented by ethnologists, and discoveries based on technology and the natural sciences.
> Here, people do not have to BELIEVE anything, as is so often the case in esotericism. On the contrary, individuals may come to their own conclusions or find new interpretations and solutions through their own thought processes.[2]

---

2   www.mysterypark.ch/index.html?node=116&pageid=56& [accessed 12 April 2005; no longer accessible, June 2006]

Mystery Park does not confine itself to whispering to its visitors that our ancestors probably received visits from space messengers. A visit to the bookstore permits one to observe the presence of an assortment of not only books by Erich von Däniken, but also major titles appearing in most of the so-called "esoteric" bookstores in German-speaking Switzerland. The enchanted scientism that challenges traditional beliefs accommodates itself perfectly to the themes favored by the trends of alternative religiosity.

One of the best-sellers of the Mystery Park bookstore, to believe its website, is an *Erich von Däniken Enzyklopädie* (Dopatka, 2004). More than 450 pages long (including almost forty pages of dense bibliography), this encyclopedia gives hundreds of entries about different cultures and world mythologies, but also about people: next to a few well-known names are mentions of figures found in the movement of the controversial knowledge promoted by Erich von Däniken and his *Ancient Astronaut Society* (founded in 1973). This builds a set of references specific to this universe, enabling those who locate themselves in it to accede to an apparently coherent corpus.

Mystery Park represents a subversion of Christianity and other religions as radical as a museum of atheism would be; all the traditions are there the objects of a euhemeristic interpretation, suggesting the intervention of extraterrestrials through different civilizations and reinterpreting religious heritages in this sense. However, while a Soviet-style museum of atheism would get a chilly reception in central Switzerland, Mystery Park – despite the criticisms emitted here and there on the lack of scientific foundations of the enterprise – benefits from the support and the promotion of institutions as diverse as Swisscom (principal Swiss telecommunications company), the Federal Railways, Fujitsu, Sony, Swatch, and Coca-Cola. This poses furthermore the question of knowing to what extent the *cultic milieu*, having arrived at this stage of respectability, still stands in the status of opposition to the paradigms and orthodoxies of a society supposed to define it. The opposition certainly still remains in relationship to the Churches or to the scientific world, but arguments like those of Däniken enjoy a high rate of acceptance in popular culture (which would not be the case if they appeared as a specific religious message). At first glance, one could hesitate to place Mystery Park within the context of the *cultic milieu*: upon closer inspection, does it not rather show how – through one of its multiple facets – the *cultic milieu* has come to a sort of institutionalization that blurs its boundaries? More than to a development of the *cultic milieu*, this appears related to the loss of ascendancy of traditional religions on the collective imagination.

If reputed and "established" businesses do not hesitate to grant support to Mystery Park, it is certainly not because their board of directors adhere to the Dänikenian discourse, but because this type of patronage is advantageous in a strategy of advertising and commerce. While Däniken certainly dreams of the possibilities of disseminating his ideas that Mystery Park provides, the latter at the same time is deliberately set within the context of leisure (choice of a tourist site) and the development of theme parks. Entrance to Mystery Park costs 48 Swiss francs for the purchase of a full rate ticket. The Mystery Park internet site enables one to purchase not only books or videos, but also shares: a certificate for 100 shares costs a little over 2,200 francs.

The functioning of the *cultic milieu* thus comes to meet market logic, and not just on a small scale, but marshalling the same resources as any commercial firm, including partnerships with reputed names. This cooperation is established on a non-ideological basis, even if the plan that lies behind the theme park has the promotion of certain theses as an objective. The initiatives of the *cultic milieu* are adapted to market logic with flexibility in a secularized environment, better than could religions with monopolistic ambitions.

3. Fairs, salons and practitioners of the *cultic milieu*

As for the "esoteric fair" mentioned at the beginning of this article, it provides an excellent example of the functioning of this "spiritual market" defined by Hildegard Van Hove (1999). In twenty years of existence, the very name of this event has evolved, probably in part so as better to adapt to the new "market" realities. The *Esoterische Messe* is today called *Lebenskraft* ("life force"), "fair for esotericism, consciousness and health", thus amalgamating several themes with "great potential". The successive editions of the fair reveal a massive presence of everything that is supposed to help visitors to live better and feel better about themselves: whether this is a matter of techniques or machines, all aim to satisfy this aspiration. However, this includes a little extra: health goes together with "consciousness", indeed with "esotericism" and everything that it implies of secret knowledge. Discussions with some of its exhibitors quickly unveil the spiritual background of what could sometimes appear to be practices based on technology: for example, the working of a particular machine having therapeutic values was revealed to its creator during the course of group meditation sessions, and so on.

Those who go through this "market" in search of attractive offers are aspiring to salvation goods that surpass earthly happiness, even if the latter is a not insignificant component of it. As in traditional religious offers, immanent and transcendent goods cannot be distinguished: the well-being provided by different techniques is frequently associated with an expectation of inner development and spiritual awakening. Unlike traditional religious offers, however, the functioning of the *cultic milieu* is largely subject to market laws: with the exception of stands representing religious movements that are present simply to spread a message and are not counting on covering their expenses, the majority of exhibitors at the same time have a commercial goal. These people make a living or hope to do so from the practice they are providing. This fact distinguishes them clearly from religious movements, in which some of the most prominent members can exercise their activity as unpaid volunteers. In two years of research on workshops or seminars providing different types of personal development experiences, Hartmut Zinser pointed out that he never met anyone unemployed (Zinser, 1988) – and with good reason, since everything necessarily has to be purchased.

Over the years, the "esoteric fair" has seen a proliferation of practitioners giving "life counseling" (which includes palmists, card readers and counselors by *channelling*): according to the stand, fees for a thirty-minute session (generally including a recording, so the client can take the cassette home) vary from 60 to 100 Swiss francs.

Similarly, new "niches" for new products appear; thus, during the 2001 edition, five or six stands offered – among other things – little pills (each one manufactured differently) supposed to counter the negative effects of radiation from mobile or cell phones. The simultaneity of these initiatives demonstrates the existence of channels of communication by which new supplies for new experiences are constantly broadcast. The technological developments of our societies thus afford as many opportunities to develop new markets: this does not mean renouncing new technologies, but rather having recourse to protective or purificatory practices for protection from their supposed noxious effects. This is accomplished by the method of techniques presented as "scientific", which are simultaneously as many commercial products. Technological innovations enable the creation of "derived products" on the market of the *cultic milieu*, which is all the easier as this milieu is found to be in osmosis with them and does not adopt the separatism of certain sects.

The *cultic milieu* shows itself open to the constant rearrangement of ideas and practices on an individualized basis, even if the backdrop remains the same. The encouragement of non-exclusive experimentation contributes to the syncretism of the practices. An already old investigation of the "new body practices" has noted, "If each is focused on a type of practice, none of those in which I took part is 'pure', all include exercises and practices borrowed from other ones" (Perrin, 1985:99). The tendency is not reversed, on the contrary, in a milieu where the exclusive is disliked and where the criterion is to validate "what is good for you". The multiplicity of techniques must satisfy both curiosity and the appetite for novelty. Let us not forget that betting on several of them at once gives practitioners more possibilities to ensure sufficient revenue for themselves: syncretism is therefore also stimulated by very material factors.

Every year, the magazine *Recto-Verseau* publishes a *Guide du Mieux-Être en Suisse romande*. The practitioners are categorized according to the techniques employed, which are grouped into broad categories ("Symbolic Approaches", "Personal Development", "Naturopathies", "Psychotherapies", "Body Techniques", "Touch Techniques"). In attending to the names of the practitioners, one soon observes that the same names frequently appear behind several practices. Thus, the Holopsonic Institute[3] established in Lausanne, offers, in addition to its "third generation psychophonotherapy", several "options" ("the therapeutics given in each case is suggested on the basis of reading the pulse for its specificity, frequency, and duration"): chromotherapy, color-energy, geobiology, oil and vitamin therapy, etc. Again in the canton of Vaud, Keola[4] – an effort behind which one of the many practitioners comes from the Osho movement – offers conjointly Reiki, aura-soma, crystals and mandalas, family constellations, astro-constellations, meditation, Hawaiian shamanism, and more. The examples could be multiplied infinitely, just as the possibilities to rearrange, recompose and recast the techniques are infinite.

4. "Custom-made rituals" – the market beyond the *cultic milieu*

A certain number of practices respond to expectations and needs that seem to manifest in a framework exceeding the cultic milieu. The *Recto-Verseau* directory includes in its 2005 edition the entry "Celebrancy of Life Events", where the company Gesrituels[5] appears, founded by Philippe H., a pastor who had been unemployed for two

---

3   www.holopsonic.com
4   www.keola.com
5   www.geslider.ch (this website no longer exists)

years. Philippe H. began by noticing a need for rituals in modern Western societies to mark the major life stages, even if this need is today dissociated increasingly often from the will to belong to a religious community. The observation in itself is noteworthy, since it implies that rituals are no longer necessarily associated with insertion in a stable community, but in a group constituted according to the desires of the individual and capable of being recomposed at will from one ritual to another. In the same way, these rituals will be adapted to individual development instead of providing a fixed framework.

The ritual counselors thus supply "custom-made rituals", by constructing "a ceremony that really corresponds to one's personal aspirations" and by abstaining from "promoting or passing on any religious message" (Herzoc, 2005). Philippe H. declares that he wants to respond to a need, while conserving his beliefs and remaining "ready to take up a Protestant ministry again", but at the same time observing that "Christian culture has no more meaning" for many of his fellow citizens (*La Côte*, 12 January 2005). This observation is indissociable from that of the existence of a market: in the beginning, the ritual counselor was faced with the need to find a professional activity. He explained to a television journalist:

> A custom-made ritual is a little like a made-to-measure suit: there is a basic structure, a basic pattern, cut to the size of the client, with variations that the client will request.
>
> Rites of passage are no longer experienced in the same way as they were forty years ago (...) in this context, I believe that there is a market in French-speaking Switzerland, as elsewhere in Europe.[6]

Is it nevertheless pertinent to associate this example with the *cultic milieu*? Yes, insofar as such an approach corresponds to a break with the traditional models for the accomplishment of rituals. In addition, the fact that the author of this initiative contributes an article about it to *Recto-Verseau* and appears in the directory published by this peri-

---

6   ARC telecast, "Les nouveaux rituels", *Télévision Suisse Romande*, 5 February 2005.

odical, shows that the audience of the *cultic milieu*, without exclusively comprising the clientele of ritual counsellors, represents a promisingly rich source of it. The new ritual specialists may not all directly belong to the *cultic milieu*, but their approach at least shows affinities with the latter, starting with a syncretism of references. The case of Gesrituals is not isolated: Netzwerk Rituale has already existed for years in German-speaking Switzerland ("Ritual Network", www.ritualnetz.ch), which assembles several "ritual providers". There is also Fachschule für Rituale ("Specialized School for Rituals", www.schule-fuer-rituale.ch), whose three-year training program results in a diploma in Ritual Celebrancy. Reading the biographies of some of its facilitators makes them appear like people who gained qualifications through a quasi-initiatory experience:

> During a three-month stay in a cave in Crete and after that in a simple country house, she researched and experimented with different elements such as music, singing and ritual, meditating and working with the body.

From Mystery Park to ritual celebrants, one cannot prevent oneself from thinking that the themes and practices of the *cultic milieu* are spreading beyond the limits of this milieu, and – to remain in the context of our analysis – are acquiring new shares in the "market of salvation goods".

5. Conclusion: Fusion of metaphor and reality

The logic of the market encourages the syncretism of practices and beliefs. Does this logic cause it? Everything depends here on the definition that we assign to the "market". If we understand it in the strict sense, in a strictly commercial dimension, at the most commercial logic has the function of an adjuvant. On the other hand, if we understand the market in a wider sense, that of the search for salvation goods, the logic of the "religious market" seems indeed to represent an encouragement of this syncretism. The functioning of the market rejects monopolies. It demands a multiplicity of beliefs and practices, chosen according to the inclinations of each "client". The latter is free to refuse, indeed even to criticize other practices, but while accepting the principle that "everyone chooses what is good for him". On this basis, there is no reason to confine each practice to its field; combinations and rearrangements are perfectly acceptable.

Weber stressed that, far from relating "to the 'beyond' exclusively or even primarily", salvation goods relate first to this world (Weber, 1996: 345-346). From this viewpoint, the approaches that we observe in the *cultic milieu* have nothing strange about them: the salvation goods that are supplied there provide an improved quality of life and open a transformation of consciousness.

Unlike religions, the *cultic milieu* does not expect an exclusive and enduring commitment from its participants: no one, observed Danny Jorgensen in his research on the "esoteric community", "wanted to define the qualifications for membership, especially if it meant excluding other people, their beliefs and their groups" (Jorgensen, 1992: 61). The creation of barriers is not expressed as an expectation of obedience to rules, prohibitions, a particular lifestyle or personal commitments, in other words, anything that enables a religion to create distinctions between those who belong to it and those who do not (Iannaconne, 1992: 127). The obtaining of salvation goods has another price, which often corresponds, in the *cultic milieu*, to costs in the strictest sense of the term: the ability to pay for a seminar, a consultation, or a tool enabling one to obtain the desired benefits. The payment in money here represents the toll to gain access to the salvation goods. Although one can, of course, maintain convictions characteristic of the *cultic milieu* without spending any money or practice meditation for free, for example, the fact of not paying will limit one's access to a limited range of salvation goods.

The expression "religious market" goes beyond its commercial and economic aspects. It is generally applied to the contemporary religious situation as a metaphor to express the multiplicity of beliefs and practices in alternative religiosity, where each person becomes free to make a selection on a broadly individualized basis. Choices are individual and – with the exception of a few rigid groups – belonging requires, increasingly less, unconditional and total dogmatic adhesion. The professionals of the *cultic milieu* can, of course, reason in terms of the market and know that they have to develop adequate strategies in order to gain market shares that will provide them with a living. By nature, they are equipped to respond to this logic. There is thus a conjunction of the metaphor and the concrete reality of a market, with its laws of supply and demand.*

UPDATE - Due to financial difficulties, Mystery Park (see part 2 of this article) was closed in 2007. Its future at this point is uncertain.

References

Bovay, Claude (2004) *Le Paysage religieux en Suisse*, Neuchâtel: Office Fédéral de la Statistique.

Campbell, Colin (1972) "The Cult, the Cultic Milieu and Secularization", in *A Sociological Yearbook of Religion in Britain – 5*. London: SCM Press, pp. 119-136 (reprinted in Kaplan et al., 2002, pp. 12-25).

–. (1998) "Cult", in W. H. Swatos, *Encyclopedia of Religion and Society*. Walnut Creek (California): Alta Mira Press, pp. 122-123.

Champion, Françoise (1990) "La nébuleuse mystique-ésotérique. Orientations psychoreligieuses des courants ésotériques et mystiques contemporains", in F. Champion and D. Hervieu-Léger, *De l'Émotion en religion. Renouveaux et traditions*. Paris: Centurion, pp. 17-69.

---

*   Translated by Christine Rhone

Dopatka, Ulrich (2004) *Die grosse Erich von Däniken Enzyklopädie. Die phantastische Perspektive der Menschheit.* Oberhofen am Thunersee: Zytglogge.

Herzoc, Philippe (2005) "Cérémonies, rituels et méditation", *Recto-Verseau*, 158 (April) : 41-43.

Iannaccone, Laurence R. (1992) "Religious Markets and the Economics of Religion", *Social Compass*, 39:1 (March): 123-131.

Jorgensen, Danny L. (1992) *The Esoteric Scene, Cultic Milieu, and Occult Tarot.* New York-London: Garland.

Kaplan, Jeffrey and Lööw, Heléne (2002) *The Cultic Milieu: Oppositional Subcultures in an Age of Globalization.* Walnut Creek (California): Alta Mira Press.

Mystery Park Team (2003) *Der Weg zum Mystery Park.* s.l. (Interlaken): Mystery Park.

Perrin, Eliane (1985) *Cultes du corps. Enquête sur les nouvelles pratiques corporelles.* Lausanne: Ed. Pierre-Marcel Favre.

Rocchi, Valérie (2003) "Des nouvelles formes du religieux? Entre quête de bien-être et logique protestataire: le cas des groupes post-Nouvel Âge en France", *Social Compass* 50:2 (June) : 175-189.

Rothstein, Mikael (1999) *I culti dei dischi volanti.* Leumann (Torino): Editrice Elledici.

Schneider, Adolf and Inge (1990) *Interviews im Zeichen der Zeit.* Thun: Jupiter-Verlag.

Stark, Rodney, and Bainbridge, William Sims (1985) *The Future of Religion: Secularization, Revival, and Cult Formation.* Berkeley: University of California Press.

Stoczkowski, Wictor (1999) *Des hommes, des dieux et des extraterrestres. Ethnologie d'une croyance moderne.* Paris: Flammarion.

Van Hove, Hildegard (1999) "L'émergence d'un 'marché spirituel'", *Social Compass*, 46:2 (June), pp. 161-172.

Weber, Max (1996) *Sociologie des religions* (texts selected and translated by Jean-Pierre Grossein). Paris: Gallimard.

Zinser, Hartmut (1988) "Ekstase und Entfremdung. Zur Analyse neuerer ekstatischer Kultveranstaltungen", in H. Zinser,

Religionswissenschaft: eine Einführung. Berlin: Dietrich Reimer Verlag, pp. 275-284.

Index

Contributors

VERONIQUE ALTGLAS holds an ESRC fellowship at the faculty of Social and Political Sciences, University of Cambridge. She has a PhD from the Ecole Pratique des Hautes Etudes (Paris). Her research areas are the globalisation of religion, transformations of religiosity in modern societies, and the cross-national comparison of the responses to religious diversity. She has conducted research on the diffusion of neo-Hindu movements in the West, especially in France and Britain, as well as on anti-semitism in France. Recent publications include: *Le nouvel hindouisme occidental* (Paris, 2005). ADDRESS: Véronique Altglas, Faculty of Social and Political Sciences, University of Cambridge, Free School Lane, Cambridge CB2 3RQ. United Kingdom. [email: va242@cam.ac.uk]

JEAN-PIERRE BASTIAN is Professor of Sociology of Religion at the University Marc Bloch in Strasbourg and Director of research at the Institut des Hautes Etudes de l'Amérique latine, Paris III. Among his publications are: *Le protestantisme en Amérique latine, une approche socio-historique* (Geneva, 1994); *La mutacion religiosa de América Latina* (Mexico, 1997 and 2003); *Europe latine-Amérique latine, la modernité religieuse en perspective comparée* (Paris, 2001, Mexico, 2004). ADDRESS: Centre de Sociologie des Religions et d'Ethique Sociale, 9 place de l'Université, 67084 Strasbourg Cedex, France. [email: bastian@umb.u-strasbg.fr]

PIERRE-YVES BRANDT is Professor of Psychology of Religion at the University of Lausanne and Dean of the Faculty of Theology and Religious Studies. His interests include children's representations of God, psychological construction of religious identity and religious coping among patients with schizophrenia. Among his publications are: *L'identité de Jésus et l'identité de son disciple* (Fribourg, 2002);

Fonctions psychologiques du religieux, with Claude-Alexandre Fournier (Genève, 2007). ADDRESS: Décanat Théologie, Bâtiment Anthropole, Quartier Unil-Dorigny, CH – 1015 Lausanne, Switzerland. [email: pierre-yves.brandt@unil.ch]

STEVE BRUCE is Professor of Sociology and Head of the School of Social Science at the University of Aberdeen. He previously taught at The Queen's University of Belfast from 1978 to 1991. He is the author of 21 books on the sociology of religion, religion and politics, and terrorism. His publications include: *God save Ulster: the religion and politics of Paisleyism* (Oxford, 1986); *Religion in the Modern World: from cathedrals to cults* (Oxford, 1996); *God is Dead: Secularization in the West* (Blackwell, 2002); and *Politics and Religion* (Polity, 2003). ADDRESS: School of Social Science, University of Aberdeen, Aberdeen AB24 3QY, United Kingdom. [email: s.bruce@abdn.ac.uk]

MAYA BURGER has studied anthropology, indology and history of religions in Switzerland, India and the USA. She is presently Professor of Comparative History of Religions at the University of Lausanne. Her fields of interest are medieval and modern Indian traditions, the history of yoga, religions and encounter, religions and gender and comparative methodology. On this subject she has recently co-edited a volume on *Comparer les comparatismes. Perspectives sur l'histoire et les sciences des religions* (Paris, Milan, 2006). ADDRESS: Département interfacultaire d'histoire et de sciences des religions, Anthropole, Université de Lausanne, 1015. Lausanne-Dorigny, Switzerland. [email: maya.burger@unil.ch]

SILVIA MANCINI is Professor of Comparative History of Religions at the University of Lausanne where she teaches Epistemology of the Study of Religions, and Marginalized and Transversal Religious Traditions. Over the last years, most of her works have focussed on the Comparative History of Religions, and on Altered States of Consciousness explored through an interdisciplinary approach.

Among her publications are: *Da Lévy-Bruhl all'antropologia cognitiva – Lineamenti di una teoria della mentalità primitiva* (Bari, 1989); *Le Concezioni del lavoro fra mito e storia nella cultura antillana* (Rome, 1991); Postface à *Le monde magique* d'Ernesto De Martino (Paris, 1999); (Editor): *La Fabrication du psychisme. Pratiques rituelles au carrefour des sciences humaines et des sciences de la vie* (Paris, 2006). ADDRESS: Département interfacultaire d'histoire et de sciences des religions, Anthropole, Université de Lausanne, 1015, Lausanne-Dorigny, Switzerland.
[email: silvia.mancini@unil.ch]

JEAN-FRANCOIS MAYER obtained his doctorate in History at the University of Lyon in 1984. He is the author of a dozen books and numerous articles in different languages on new religious movements and other contemporary religious developments (bibliography: www.mayer.info). From 1998 to 2007, he was a lecturer in Religious Studies at the University of Fribourg (Switzerland). In 2002 he launched the website Religioscope (www.religion.info). He is also the contributing editor of the newsletter *Religion Watch* (New York). Among other works, he has published: *Les Nouvelles Voies spirituelles. Enquête sur la religiosité parallèle en Suisse* (Lausanne, 1993); and he co-edited *La naissance des nouvelles religions* (Genève, 2004). ADDRESS: P.O. Box 83, 1705 Fribourg, Switzerland.
[email: jean-francois.mayer@unifr.ch]

PETER-ULRICH MERZ-BENZ is Professor of Sociology, as well as Director of the "Forum 'Philosophie der Geistes- und Sozialwissenschaften'" in the Department of Philosophy, at the University of Zurich. His interests include sociological theory and the history of sociological theory, methodology of the social sciences, sociology of culture and sociology of religion. Recent publications include: *Macht und Herrschaft. Zur Revision zweier soziologischer Grundbegriffe* (Wiesbaden, 2007, reader, edited together with Peter Gostmann); and *Max Weber und Heinrich Rickert. Die erkenntniskritischen Grundlagen der verstehenden Soziologie*

(Würzburg, 1990; second edition forthcoming). ADDRESS: University of Zurich, Institute of Sociology, Andreasstrasse 15, CH-8050 Zurich, Switzerland. [email: merz-benz@soziologie.unizh.ch]

ENZO PACE is Professor of Sociology and Sociology of Religion at the University of Padova. He is a member of the Interdepartmental Centre for the Intercultural Studies and of the Interdepartmental Centre for Research on Human Rights of Padova University, and President of the International Society for the Sociology of Religion. He was Directeur d'Etude invité (1996 and 2000) at the EHESS in Paris. His main research field in the sociology of religion is secularization, new religious movements and sects, the younger generation, values and religion and Catholicism in Italy. More recently he has become interested in the sociology of Islam. He published: *Sociologia dell'islam* (Carocci, 2004, translated into Portuguese, Petropolis: Vozes, 2005). ADDRESS: Department of Sociology, University of Padova, Via Cesarotti 10, Padova, Italy. [email: vincenzo.pace@unipd.it]

TERRY REY (Ph.D. Temple University) is Associate Professor of Religion at Temple University, and was formerly Associate Professor of African and Caribbean Religions at Florida International University and Professor of the Sociology of Religion at Haiti's State University. He is the author of *Our Lady of Class Struggle: The Cult of the Virgin Mary in Haiti* (1999) and of *Bourdieu on Religion: Imposing Faith and Legitimacy* (2007, forthcoming). He is currently researching the relationship between religion and violence in the Congo. ADDRESS: Temple University, Department of Religion, 629 Anderson Hall, Philadelphia, PA 19122, USA. [email: trey@temple.edu]

FRANZ SCHULTHEIS is Professor at the University of St. Gallen. He is president of the Pierre Bourdieu Foundation (Geneva) and a member of the Swiss Research Council and member of the edition board of Actes de la Recherche en Sciences Sociales (Paris). He was Professor invité at the Institut d'etudes politiques, at Paris V., EHESS, Université de Strasbourg et de Louvain. His main research fields are sociology of lower classes, poverty, inequality and welfare in comparative perspectives. Recent publication: *Pierre Bourdieus Wege in die Soziologie,* Konstanz, UVK, 2007. ADDRESS: Franz Schultheis, Soziologisches Seminar SfS-HSG, Universität St. Gallen, Tigerbergstr 2, 9000 St. Gallen, Switzerland. [email: franz.schultheis@unisq.ch]

JÖRG STOLZ is Professor of the Sociology of Religion at the University of Lausanne and Director of the Observatory of Religions in Switzerland (ORS). His interests include quantitative and mixed methods studies, secularization theory and rational choice models. He has recently co-edited the book: *Eine Schweiz – viele Religionen. Risiken und Chancen des Zusammenlebens* (Bielefeld, 2007). ADDRESS: Observatoire des Religions en Suisse, Bâtiment Provence, CH–1015 Lausanne, Switzerland. [email: joerg.stolz@unil.ch]

Malcolm Brown

After the Market

Economics, Moral Agreement and the Churches' Mission

Oxford, Bern, Berlin, Bruxelles, Frankfurt am Main, New York, Wien, 2004. 321 pp.
Religions and Discourse. Vol. 23
Edited by James M. M. Francis
ISBN 978-3-03910-154-2 / US-ISBN 978-0-8204-6964-5 pb.
sFr. 82.– / €* 56.50 / €** 58.10 / € 52.80 / £ 37.– / US-$ 62.95

* includes VAT – valid for Germany   ** includes VAT – valid for Austria

How are the churches to say anything useful about the market economy which is so dominant in everybody's life today? Too often, Christian responses have failed to take the moral arguments for markets seriously enough. The market's assertions of liberal individualism and the impossibility of agreement about distributional justice undermine much Christian comment and church practice.

Old divisions within Christian ethics offer little help. Liberal theologies share so many foundations with the market that their critique has been muted or incoherent. Yet communitarian theologies, currently in the ascendancy, show little interest in economics and are not alert to the central dilemmas which markets seek to address.

The book critiques much of the churches' recent work on economic issues and proposes a renewed theological seriousness for mission in the economy, where the Christian faith might contribute authentically to moral agreement in a plural age.

Contents: The Churches' Engagement with the Economy in Britain since the Second World War – A Framework Drawn from McIntyre – Markets, Morals and Communities – The Liberal Tradition in Social Theology – Communitarian and Confessional Approaches to Social Theology – Reviewing Liberal and Communitarian Theologies – Dialogic Traditionalism: An Emerging Theological Model – Reconsidering Practice – Reconstructing the Churches' Engagement with the Economy.

«I commend this book because it is an important offering to the debate on what constitutes public theology and offers practitioners a model that roots practical action in a theology that can speak across disciplines.» (Terry Drummond, IMAgenda)

PETER LANG
Bern · Berlin · Bruxelles · Frankfurt am Main · New York · Oxford · Wien